*The Valley's Legends and Legacies II*

# THE VALLEY'S
# Legends & Legacies II

*by Catherine Morison Rehart*

*To Carole & Dave — Join!*
*Best wishes again!*
*Cathy Rehart*
*8/10/99*

**Word Dancer Press**

Clovis, California

Published by
Quill Driver Books/Word Dancer Press, Inc.
8386 N. Madsen
Clovis, CA 93611
209-322-5917
800-497-4909

Word Dancer Press books may be purchased for educational, fund-raising, business or promotional use. Please contact Special Markets, Quill Driver Books/Word Dancer Press,
Inc. at the above address or phone number.

**ISBN 1-884995-15-2**

Rehart, Catherine Morison, 1940-
    The valley's legends & legacies II/ by Catherine Morison Rehart.
        p.          cm.
    Scripts of the KMJ radio program, The valley's legends & legacies.
    ISBN 1-884995-12-8 (pbk.)
    1. Fresno County (Calif.)--History--Anecdotes.        2. Fresno County
(Calif.)--Biography--Anecdotes. 3. San Joaquin Valley (Calif.)-
-History--Anecdotes. 4. San Joaquin Valley (Calif.)--Biography-
-Anecdotes.                       I. Valley's legends and legacies (radio program)
II. Title.
F868.F8R44          1997
979.4'82--dc21

                                                        CIP

*First printing November 1997*

Front cover photo: *Grill Room of the Hughes Hotel c. 1895.*
*Fresno County Free Library*
Back cover photos: center; *Mariposa Street c. 1899, courtesy Joan Emerson,* clock-
wise from top; *see pages: 167,152, 13, 23, 293.*

Dedicated to

Laura Amanda, Myra Amanda, Lanthie Augusta,
Eugenie Loverne, Minnie Marsalete, Cleo,
Catherine Loverne, Mary, Georgia,
Catherine Evelyn, Anne Marie, & Courtney Anne

seven generations of women in the Stevens Family who
each had a role to play in our city of Fresno

to

Alan Amend
inspirational teacher and friend


and


to the memory of

Lewella Swift Forkner
beloved friend

# Contents

Foreword ........................................................................... xv

Preface ............................................................................ xvi
Acknowledgments ............................................................. xvii

### The Valley's Legends and Legacies II

The Legacy of "Pop" Laval ................................................... 1
The Editor & the Wild Hogs ................................................. 3
Churches, Canals & Cattle .................................................. 4
The Day the Temple Altar Was Saved ................................... 5
Courts & Courthouses ........................................................ 6
Movies and a Canny Scot .................................................... 8
The Architect and the Pit Bull ............................................ 10
Fresno Station .................................................................. 11
Baseball Heroes ................................................................ 12
The Street Named for an English Jurist ............................... 14
Blackmail & Murder in 1890 ............................................... 15
A Football Hero ................................................................ 16
The People's Railroad ........................................................ 18
Those Crazy Flying Machines ............................................. 19
Seventy-six Trombones ...................................................... 20
Historians & Pioneers ........................................................ 21
Festivals, Fetes & Raisins .................................................. 22
Earthquake Relief ............................................................. 24
Racquets & Whalebones ..................................................... 25
One-Handed Engineer & Dam Builder ................................. 26
A Special Friendship ......................................................... 27
The Jones Mill .................................................................. 28
The Kearney-Rowell "Josh" Dilemma ................................... 29
A German Beer Garden for Fresno ...................................... 31
The Father of Reedley ....................................................... 32
Big Hats & Bucking Broncos .............................................. 33
Preparing "Typewriters" ..................................................... 34

# Contents

Shipps, Trains, Wagons and Sheep ........................................ 36
The House on Fulton Street ..................................................... 37
History on Bulldog Lane .......................................................... 38
Sigma Nu on the Move ............................................................ 39
Of Knotholes & Courthouses .................................................. 41
The P Street Neighborhood...................................................... 42
Service above Self ................................................................... 43
Fresno's Hollywood "Hunk" ................................................... 44
Hot Salads & History .............................................................. 45
The Magical Grape .................................................................. 46
Fresno's Ragtime Rhythms ..................................................... 48
Tributes on a Spring Afternoon .............................................. 49
"The Grove" .............................................................................. 51
A Photographer for the Sierra ................................................ 52
A Log Cabin in the Woods ...................................................... 53
"Fresno" ................................................................................... 54
"Raisin Cane" .......................................................................... 55
Premiere Parties & Produce.................................................... 56
Yosemite's Enchanted Christmas ........................................... 57
The Big Fig Garden Flood ....................................................... 58
A Scrolled Cornice Bracket .................................................... 60
The Romain Home .................................................................... 61
A Newspaper & a Museum ...................................................... 63
Fresno's Ivy League Streets .................................................... 64
Fresno's First Airmail Service ................................................ 65
Taking Culture Seriously ........................................................ 66
The Short Home ....................................................................... 67
Kings River Switch .................................................................. 69
The Great Camp Pinedale Offensive ...................................... 70
An Old-Fashioned Pharmacy .................................................. 71
A 20th Century Fur Trapper .................................................... 73
The Valley's Swedish Village .................................................. 75
Raisins, Raisins & More Raisins ............................................ 76
Fashions & Foibles .................................................................. 77

# Contents

The Village in the Fig Gardens ........................................ 78
The Sample Sanitarium ........................................ 80
The Home of Clovis Cole ........................................ 81
The Fresno Adventist Academy ........................................ 82
Cameras & Coffee ........................................ 83
Fresno's Special Legacy ........................................ 85
The Champion & the Courts ........................................ 86
The Champ Wins Again ........................................ 87
The Messenger of the Gods ........................................ 89
A Close Shave ........................................ 90
DeVaux & Dempsey ........................................ 91
A Farm House in the Tower District ........................................ 92
Rolinda, Robbers & Rails ........................................ 94
Religion & Circuit Riders ........................................ 95
A Man Named Erclas ........................................ 96
Coalinga's Vanished School ........................................ 98
A Fair "Scandal" ........................................ 99
The Jensen Ranch ........................................ 100
Fresno's Prominent Silos ........................................ 101
A Royal Policy ........................................ 103
The Evinger Home ........................................ 104
James' Tale ........................................ 105
Fresno's Greene House ........................................ 106
A Honeymoon Cottage in Kearney Park ........................................ 107
The Giffen Estate ........................................ 108
Pans, Picks & Persistence ........................................ 109
Indians and Indentures ........................................ 111
Fresno's Japanese Bank ........................................ 112
The Streets of Laton ........................................ 113
Christmas at Kearney ........................................ 114
Elections in Early California ........................................ 115
The Rabbit Drive ........................................ 116
Beans & Burros ........................................ 118
A Friday Evening in Fowler ........................................ 119

# Contents

A Valley Called Wonder ........................................................ 120
Duncan's Vision .................................................................... 121
The Robinson Home .............................................................. 123
Those Irreverent Humbugs ................................................... 124
A Beauty Named Dagmar ..................................................... 125
A Twist of Fate ..................................................................... 127
Mayor of Broadway .............................................................. 128
The Hanger Home ................................................................. 130
Shakespeare & a Hot Stove ................................................. 131
Producers Dairy ................................................................... 132
A Fishy Prank ....................................................................... 133
A Sheep Man Named Kennedy ............................................. 134
Horses & Horseless Carriages ............................................. 135
The Spencer Home ............................................................... 136
The "Painted Dog" ............................................................... 137
The Home of Mr. Main .......................................................... 138
The Cobb Home .................................................................... 139
The Honorable Elisha Cotton Winchell .................................. 141
The Forces for Righteousness ............................................. 143
Justice in Fine Gold Gulch ................................................... 144
Stop, Go & Move On ............................................................. 145
The Knapp Cabin .................................................................. 146
A Tale of Two Trees ............................................................. 147
A Caveman Named David ..................................................... 148
A Ghostly Steamship ........................................................... 149
Camel's Thorn ...................................................................... 150
The Stoner Mansion ............................................................. 151
Tiburcio Vasquez .................................................................. 153
Budgets & Cents .................................................................. 155
The Hansen Home ................................................................ 156
The Sharer Home ................................................................. 157
The Oleander Social Scene .................................................. 158
The "Grapevine" ................................................................... 159
The Owen Home ................................................................... 160

# Contents

The Rooster Crows at Midnight .............................................. 161

Checkerboards & Courthouse Park .......................................... 162

Speedometers & Red Faces ................................................... 163

Mr. Dillion's War ................................................................. 164

Happy Birthday, Fresno County Free Library! ......................... 165

Ninetta Sunderland Huston .................................................. 166

Problems with Nudists ......................................................... 168

If I Were Mayor... ............................................................... 169

Josephine Ruth Gibson ........................................................ 170

Henderson's Experimental Gardens ....................................... 171

A Weighty Subject ............................................................... 172

The Great Emancipator ........................................................ 173

The Raisin—The Profitable Mistake ....................................... 174

The Corset Lady Cometh ...................................................... 176

The Kutner Home ................................................................ 177

The Gregory Home .............................................................. 178

The Alta 2 .......................................................................... 179

The Storm's Eye .................................................................. 180

A Clubhouse on Calaveras .................................................... 181

The Dance of Love .............................................................. 182

Life in Jail in 1888 ............................................................... 183

The Lady Editor .................................................................. 184

Pioneer Graves ................................................................... 185

Long Skirts & Leering Eyes .................................................. 186

The Sierra Poet ................................................................... 187

A Triple Celebration ............................................................ 188

An Unidentified Prospector ................................................... 189

Roeding Place ..................................................................... 190

A Tract Home on West Griffith .............................................. 192

The Maracci Home ............................................................... 193

A Man & His Museum ........................................................... 194

The Puppet Lady ................................................................. 195

A Ship Named McClatchy ..................................................... 196

Mr. Blanding's Dream House ................................................. 197

# Contents

The Home of Dr. Burks ....................................................... 198
The Carriage Painter .......................................................... 199
A. A. Rowell ....................................................................... 200
Space Ships in July ............................................................ 201
The Most Beautiful Baby ................................................... 202
A Society Debut .................................................................. 203
A Lyon & a Goat ................................................................. 204
Beating the Heat ................................................................. 205
The High Cost of Living ...................................................... 206
Building Safety ................................................................... 207
A Tree for a Horse .............................................................. 208
The Projectoscope .............................................................. 209
Colonel James N. Olney ...................................................... 210
Memories of Marching through Georgia .............................. 211
Coates & Traver, Architects ............................................... 212
Akira Yokomi ..................................................................... 213
The Ponderous Inkstand ..................................................... 214
Melons in August ............................................................... 215
Opening Night at the Barton ............................................... 216
A Dog & a Quack ................................................................ 218
Father of Raisin Day ........................................................... 219
The Courthouse—The Inside Scoop ..................................... 221
The Storekeeper & the Chicken ........................................... 223
The Fabulous Fascinator ..................................................... 225
An Opening Night to Remember .......................................... 226
Stages & Trains & Mail ....................................................... 227
Fresno's Flag ...................................................................... 228
Religion & the Mill Ditch ..................................................... 229
Eighty Flying Fingers .......................................................... 230
A Hidden Treasure .............................................................. 231
The Courthouse Elevator ..................................................... 233
Bibliocosmos ...................................................................... 234
The Central School ............................................................. 235
The Fresno Bubbler ............................................................ 237

# Contents

Picking Daisies ............................................................ 238

Love by Wire .............................................................. 240

The Petrified Woman .................................................. 241

A Photo Flash ............................................................. 242

To Dance or Not to Dance .......................................... 243

The Chicago Stump ..................................................... 244

The Donner Rescue ..................................................... 245

Scholarship & Service ................................................ 247

A Visit from the General ............................................. 249

Heaton School ............................................................ 251

The Skunk in the Cloakroom ....................................... 253

Fire on the Fourth ...................................................... 255

Mr. West Coast Relays ................................................ 256

Men & Women & Marriage .......................................... 258

Mr. Shaver & His Lake ................................................ 259

July 4, 1874 ................................................................ 261

A Ferry across the River ............................................. 263

Pages from a Pioneer's Memory .................................. 265

A Lawyer Named Grady .............................................. 266

A Man Named Shaw .................................................... 267

Livery Stables & Democracy ....................................... 268

Centerville & Canals ................................................... 269

John C. Hoxie ............................................................. 270

The Sad Tale of Traver ................................................ 271

John W. Humphreys .................................................... 272

The Traver Calaboose .................................................. 273

Lone Star ................................................................... 275

A Parkway for the River .............................................. 276

The Lewis S. Eaton Trail ............................................. 277

A House with a View ................................................... 279

The Man Who Lives on Missouri Hill ........................... 281

James Smith & Smith's Ferry ...................................... 283

Sunnyside ................................................................... 284

"Yank" Hazelton ......................................................... 286

# Contents

Can the Canal Builder and the Rancher Be Friends? ............ 288
The Dispute Continues .................................................................. 290
A Taste of Northern Italy ............................................................ 292
The Burris Family ......................................................................... 293
The Brooks-Foster Wagon ........................................................... 294
A Museum in a Park ..................................................................... 296
Centennial Farms .......................................................................... 297
Happy Jack & The Hangman's Knot ......................................... 298
Judge Samuel A. Holmes ............................................................ 299
Mr. Historic Preservation ............................................................ 301
Fancher Creek Nurseries ............................................................. 303
Dedication of a Courthouse ........................................................ 305
The Ultimate French Dip Sandwich .......................................... 307
Northfield's Great Lady ................................................................ 309
The Fresno Plaque ........................................................................ 311

Notes ............................................................................................... 313
Bibliography .................................................................................. 325
Index ............................................................................................... 333

About the Author .......................................................................... 348

# *Foreword*

I have been privileged to travel throughout many countries of the world. Although I have seen wondrous sights, few compare in beauty or variety to the San Joaquin Valley.

We are also the gateway for people from all over the world who wish to experience the majestic beauty of Yosemite and Sequoia-Kings Canyon national parks.

The abundance of rivers, lakes and streams nestled in our magnificent mountains, rolling foothills and fertile farm land make us the heart of the nation's agricultural industry and a vision to behold.

In this valley there are quaint towns with proud heritage and large bustling cities both of whose success is based largely on the bounty of our crops.

Too many times we make the mistake of not looking at our history for the guidance to shape our future. As citizens of the great Central Valley, it is imperative that we do not take our past for granted. A community without a sense of its history is a community without a soul.

The rich, diverse heritage of our area has given us many beautiful historic buildings. Many have been lost because we have not cared enough to get involved in seeing that they were preserved. Each time a building is torn down, we lose a piece of history; each time a building is saved, we enrich the beauty and substance of our community.

As a former educator and businessman and now a servant of the public, I feel a deep responsibility to improve the lives of all Fresno County residents. I know my decisions will affect many families well into the future.

I feel pride and thankfulness for this Valley. I like living here and love the people. Thank you Cathy Rehart for making our past come alive.

—Stan Oken
Chairman, Fresno County Board of Supervisors

# Preface

Fresno holds a very special place in my heart. In 1873, my great-great uncles, A. T. and Clark A. Stevens, journeyed here from Michigan. They bought property on L Street and a large corner lot at Fresno and L streets where they had their place of business, the Black Hawk Stables. Seven generations of my family have lived here continuously since that time. We each have watched this city grow from the perspective of our respective generations. We have participated in the life of the community in each stage of its growth. We have lived, loved, and sojourned here. Fresno is part of us and we are part of Fresno. It is our place.

During the years I was growing up, my grandmother lived with us. She shared her stories of life in Fresno and her love for this city. It was her legacy to me.

In order to understand our city and our valley, we need to know its history. We need to know about the people and events that shaped our valley and then we can see the roles we can play to continue to improve our community. School children, especially, need to study local history to learn an appreciation for their community. This will make them better citizens. If this book can help facilitate the study of local history, nothing would please me more.

It is a privilege to have the opportunity to write about one's place and to share one's thoughts with one's community. These scripts are, in a sense, love letters to the one constant in my life—my city, my county, my home.

—Cathy Rehart

# Acknowledgments

A work such as this cannot be accomplished without the help of many people. My gratitude to the following cannot be overstated.

My sincere thanks to Steve Brown of Image Group Marketing Communications, Inc. and to the Laval family for allowing me to use photos from the Laval collections. A special thank-you to Steve, who spent several days tirelessly searching for photos to complement specific scripts. His efforts have greatly enhanced this book.

Special thanks to John Kallenberg, Fresno County librarian, for his support; Linda Sitterding, Fresno County history librarian, for her patience, assistance, invaluable brainstorming sessions, and for making photos from the library's archives available to me; William Secrest, Jr., Fresno County History Room, for his assistance; Doug Hansen, the *Fresno Bee*, for our frequent chats sharing ideas and information; Marjorie Arnold, Nancy Ramirez and Mabel Wilson at the *Fresno Bee* library for allowing me access to their files; and John Panter and Robert Ellis, two archivists of the Fresno Historical Society, for allowing me to peruse special collections, diaries, books, and for granting me unlimited access to the Ben Walker collection.

I wish to thank Mary Graham for reading many of the scripts prior to submission to KMJ. My sincere gratitude to Bobbye Sisk Temple for editing this work and for her most helpful suggestions and unfailing friendship.

It has been a pleasure to meet so many people connected to local businesses and organizations. The information they have provided has been invaluable, and I am most grateful. Their contributions are listed in the bibliography of this work.

I wish to thank all those who granted me personal interviews. Their rich knowledge and stories have added substance and interest to this work. They are acknowledged in the endnotes and bibliography.

Several close friends have provided invaluable help in this project. Robert M. Wash not only made his extensive clipping files available to me, but also offered ideas for scripts and edited them for accuracy. In short, he generously shared his vast knowledge of the history of Fresno County. William Secrest, Sr. also opened his files to me and provided photos for this book as well as for the first volume. John Edward Powell, architectural historian, has graciously shared his knowledge of historical buildings and has provided invaluable information from his files. I am deeply grateful.

Several friends have provided photographs from their personal collections for this book. They are credited in the cut lines for the photos. Their generous offerings have added a personal flavor to the book and have added to our visual community history. My deepest thanks to them.

I want to thank the staff at KMJ for conceiving the idea for this project, for making it happen, and for their unfailing kindness and support to me. Special thanks to the general manager of KMJ Radio, Al Smith, for making the scripts come alive; to John Broeske, program director, for his excellent ideas and production expertise; and to Rich Withers for his creative handling of the production elements in the studio.

Special thanks also to Alan S. Wertheimer, Robert Koligian, Jr., and Dr. John Zelezny, whose friendship and wise counsel are deeply appreciated.

On a personal level, I want to thank my cousin, Mary Helen McKay, who never failed to offer accurate information, marvelous story ideas and encouragement; and my unbounded gratitude to my children, Bill, Anne, and Kate, who have been unfailing supporters of this project.

Most of all I am grateful to all the KMJ listeners. Your calls have meant a great deal to me. Al Smith forwarded your letters to me so that I would know what stories you would like to hear. I have tried to follow up on your ideas whenever possible. I have saved all your letters and, if I have not yet written on the subjects that you requested, I may do so in the future.

—CMR

*The Valley's Legends and Legacies II*

For many of us who call Fresno home, the images that come to mind when we think of the early years of our city exist, in large part, because of the camera and discerning eye of Claude C. "Pop" Laval, a man who has become a Fresno legend.

Laval was born in New York City on November 8, 1882. His family later moved to Braddock, Pennsylvania, where he worked as an architect and civil engineer. A friend who had an eight-by-ten-inch box camera which he could not make work sold it to Laval for five dollars. Fascinated, Laval used the camera on many of his construction jobs. Before long, he left the construction business behind and began a career in commercial photography.

In 1911, he moved to Fresno, joining his mother and sisters, who had already settled here. After a short stint working as a handyman for Dr. Rowell, he started taking commercial photographs once again—this time in the area from Stockton to Bakersfield—a career that would last for fifty-five years.

When one thinks of "Pop" Laval, one has to think of "firsts." As recalled by his son, Claude C. Laval, Jr., and his grandson, Jerome D. Laval, he brought the first movie camera into the valley; flying over Fresno in a balloon, he took the first aerial pictures of the city; and, "he had the first panoramic camera in this area and the first smokeless flashlight apparatus."

He took pictures of mountains, crops, businesses, streetcars, presidents, and ordinary people. Perhaps it is the street scenes, evoking the hustle and bustle of the life of the city as it grew over the years, that are most memorable. Glancing at these, one sees the fashions of each period, notes the transition from horse-drawn vehicles to cars, and looks, perhaps longingly, at the historic buildings that no longer grace our city.

For almost ten years, "Pop" Laval wrote a column for the *Fresno Guide* which shared his reminiscences and feelings for the valley with his readers. After his death in 1966, his grandson, Jerome D. Laval, compiled several books of his grandfather's photographs. A 1996 calendar titled *Valley Times Remembered* presents a selection of these photos.

The history of a community is recorded in the written word. But it is through photographs that it comes alive. "Pop" Laval's photographs have provided a true living history for the Fresno community, a priceless legacy for us all.

There was a time when the town of Millerton was over-run with packs of wild hogs. Hideous beasts, they had heads like alligators with long snouts, and their backs were as sharp as a saw. Every night they came down from the hills looking for food. They broke into kitchens and cellars. Anywhere they could find entry was fair game. The only way to get rid of them was to kill them, but their hides were so tough that how to dispatch them posed a problem.

One night the wild hogs made a terrible mistake. They broke into the office of the local newspaper, the *Millerton Times*, wreaking havoc mainly because they were frustrated at finding no food.

The following morning the editor of the paper, Samuel J. Garrison, arrived to find the results of their visit. He was outraged. He swore he would get revenge.

There was a hog breeder in town named Seymour who wanted to rid the town of these wild animals so his tame hogs would no longer be threatened by them. Editor Garrison decided that there was no better person to get rid of these beasts. He hired Seymour to shoot them.

The next evening Seymour and Garrison hid outside, waiting for the hogs to appear. Sure enough, the pack came right on time. They broke a cellar door open and went inside. Garrison, with a long pole in hand, chased the hogs out of the cellar. Seymour, using two revolvers, shot twelve of the hogs as they ran by. Garrison and Seymour were delighted with their night's work until they realized that instead of killing the wild hogs, they had killed twelve of Seymour's tame ones.

As A. Y. Easterby and Moses Church continued to build canals, bringing water to turn parched valley land into productive farm land, a problem arose. Yank Hazelton and other Kings River cattlemen did not want their grazing lands taken over by farmers. Not content to merely ask Church to leave, Hazelton threatened him and plotted several assassination attempts against him, all of which failed.

Church stood strong in the face of all of this, even during the last direct attempt, in which he was badly beaten, suffering severe bruises of the jaw and nose. This peaceful, God-fearing man finally began carrying a gun for safety. Church's high moral standards had become well-known throughout the county, but his ideals led to a misunderstanding among the members of one particular household in Millerton.

In 1874, Mr. Daley wanted to leave Millerton for Fresno. Mrs. Daley refused to follow, stating that, like Millerton, Fresno was a God-forsaken town that did not have even one church. Mr. Daley assured her that, indeed, there were many churches—one on every corner. After much discussion, Mrs. Daley finally agreed to move to Fresno.

After they were settled, she realized that her husband was wrong. In a fury of anger she chided him for not telling the truth. "I've walked all over Fresno," she said, "and not a single church exists."

"Oh," Mr. Daley replied, "you meant buildings. I was referring to Moses Church and all his relatives!"

# The Day the Temple Altar Was Saved

In February, 1885, twelve buildings in Fresno's Chinatown caught fire. At first, the structure which housed the Chinese Temple altar seemed safe because it was separated from the other buildings in the area.

Then the wind began to change and, thus, the direction of the fire. All the faithful fled the temple, except for the high priest. He came outside and positioned himself at a point fifty feet in front of the building to fight the fire demon alone. His thin body began to sway sinuously, his arms waved above his head, his long, braided queue began to swing wildly back and forth, and the incantations which escaped from his mouth grew louder and louder. Soon a crowd began to gather—to watch and to wait.

No effort was made by those watching to halt the fire—the high priest was alone in his battle with the evil demon. The fire slowed its advance on the temple building. Flames began to lick at the roof. As the fire billowed suddenly upward, the high priest's arms waved higher. His chanting increased. The roof fell in, the walls collapsed, and the fire burned itself out; but, miraculously, the temple altar sat unharmed. The high priest was victorious. Those who watched could hardly believe what they had seen.

The site for Fresno's first courthouse was chosen in this manner. In 1874, the Central Pacific Railroad offered Fresno's city fathers land for county offices—four city blocks at Fresno and O streets.

The city's commercial center was clustered around H Street and the railroad. To reach this area from the proposed government center, it would be necessary to walk through tumbleweeds and thickets of lupine. The city fathers refused the offer.

A new site was proposed at Mariposa and L streets. This was accepted and plans for a courthouse began to develop. Before the courthouse was built, however, a temporary office was set up. The recorder, tax collector, county clerk, sheriff, treasurer and surveyor all had a space in the small building.

The California Bridge & Building Company of Oakland won the courthouse contract in May of 1874 and construction began on the new building in October of that year. The cornerstone was laid on October 8. By the time the building was finished, 800,000 bricks had been used in its construction.

In August of 1875, the new courthouse was formally accepted by the county. Over the years it was added to and embellished—once it even had a copper dome, the substructure of which later caught fire and melted the dome. As the years went by, it became a much-loved symbol of Fresno County. It had been said it would "stand for a thousand years," but in 1966, it was razed to make room for a new, more modern building.

Looking at the modern building, it's tempting to think back to the time before either courthouse was built. At that time court was held above Shannon & Hughes Store and Saloon. The office of the district attorney was a small room at Len Farrar's Magnolia Saloon.

1. Old court house. 1884.

A view of the Fresno County Courthouse in 1884. A copper dome was added in 1895. On the night of July 29, 1895, the roof caught fire and the dome melted. The building was rebuilt and was the focal point of the community until 1966 when it was demolished.

*Fresno County Free Library*

A site on Fulton, just north of Fresno Street, was chosen for Fresno's first movie house. The Kinema Theater, built in 1913, not only was Fresno's first movie theater, but also one of the first on the West Coast. Moviegoers could reserve overstuffed chairs in the loge section, and in the summer a cooling system using tons of ice assured first-class comfort. A built-in organ provided mood music for the silent films of an educational or comic nature. On occasion, between films, live acts would be presented on stage.

In 1914, a flood kept famous Scot singer and comedian Harry Lauder from traveling to a booking in Los Angeles. Seizing this opportunity, the manager of the Kinema invited Lauder to perform on its stage. The *Fresno Morning Republican* stopped its presses and inserted Lauder's picture into the paper. Lines of fans circled the block trying to get tickets for his performance.

That night, Lauder played to a packed, sold-out house. It was so crowded that some of the audience had to sit on the stage. It was one of the biggest nights the Kinema was ever to experience. Because Lauder was on a farewell tour, the crowd thought they would never see him again. However, canny Scot that he was, Lauder made several "farewell tours" and returned to Fresno a number of times. And, of course, he always played to a packed house.

Scottish comedian, singer and song writer, Sir Harry Lauder, brought his Kilty Band to Fresno several times during the early 1900s.
*The Image Group from the Laval Historical Collection.*

# The Architect and the Pit Bull

The architect of Fresno's 1907 city hall was a talented man. His list of important architectural achievements included the F. K. Prescott mansion, the United Presbyterian Church, the O. J. Woodward residence and the Grand Central Hotel. In later years he would design the Mason Building and the Mattei Building, both of which still form part of Fresno's skyline. However, in his private life, he was almost as colorful as Mayor Parker Lyon, the man who hired him to design a building to house the city departments.

Being enamored of fast motorcars, he purchased a fifty-horse-power National, a car which was a real speed demon. His speeding tickets soon grew into quite a collection.

An avid sportsman, he spent a lot of time hunting and fishing, but his favorite hobby was training his prize pit bull terrier, Pat. Pat's astounding tricks made newspaper copy all over the country. One of Pat's tricks involved grabbing one hind leg in his mouth and hopping to his master. A similar trick involving Pat's tail was notable also. However, the finest performance was Pat's feat of memory regarding cards. A pack of cards was spread on the floor and, when asked to bring the four aces, followed by two kings, Pat would hesitate for a moment and then bring the cards to his master in the order in which they were called.

Not content with teaching only one dog, architect Eugene Mathewson trained trick dogs for other notable Californians as well, including J. D. Spreckles, who was largely responsible for the regeneration of the city of San Diego after the end of the real estate boom of 1887, thus making a name for himself as the trainer of dogs for the elite as well as the designer of their buildings.

Home is a word of varied meanings—a structure or a location, the place of one's family or the place of one's birth. Fresno's birthplace is located at a site which is marked by the Southern Pacific Depot. Built in 1889, the depot is the oldest commercial building in Fresno. The structure, in its long history, has borne witness to the pageant of the life of this city.

As long as passenger service was available, the depot was the scene of leave-taking and returning. Young people who were college-bound, soldiers leaving to meet their regiments in wartime, families returning from holidays and, always in the air, there was a sense of excitement, anticipation, joy, or heart-wrenching sadness. The old depot has seen all this.

Late one Christmas Eve afternoon, in the time of the Vietnam War, the author was waiting outside the depot for her family to arrive. The train pulled into the station. As the train door opened, a young Army private jumped out, duffel bag in hand, and stood firmly on Fresno soil. His face scanned the skyline, he dropped his bag and threw his arms outward as if to embrace the city he loved. "Home," he whispered, "I'm really home!" He picked up his bag and rushed out among the people of his home town. The old depot stood silently by.

Today, after a careful renovation project, the depot has a new life as an office building. Once again, it bears the name Fresno Station with pride and dignity. For those who call Fresno home, the depot holds a special place in our hearts.

Perhaps it is the long hot summers or the good water, or maybe it's just the enthusiastic nature of its citizens, but Fresno has produced an impressive number of major league baseball players.

Frank Chance, who moved to Fresno in 1877 as a year-old infant, was Fresno's first and probably finest contribution to major league baseball. After playing for the Fresno Tigers, he joined the Chicago Cubs in 1898 and became part of the legendary double-play combination—Tinkers to Evers to Chance. From 1905 until 1912, he managed the team and was a player as well. He led the Cubs to two world championships and four league pennants. His name is enshrined in the Baseball Hall of Fame.

Fresnan Monte Pearson became a pitcher for the New York Yankees. He pitched four winning games in four successive World Series. Dutch Leonard, Lefty Jones, Ted Wills, Jr., Len Tucker, Jim Maloney, Dick Ellsworth, Dick Selma, Pat Corrales, Darryl Patterson and Wade Blasingame also were outstanding in the major leagues. Fresno High graduate Tom Seaver won the Cy Young award three times for his skill as a pitcher.

Not only did Fresno produce these fine ballplayers, but it played host to other baseball legends as well. November of 1920 saw Ty Cobb playing an exhibition game for a city playgrounds benefit. In 1927, Babe Ruth and Lou Gehrig, New York Yankees teammates, led opposing teams in an exhibition match. Gehrig's team won 13 to 3. Babe Ruth returned in 1931 for another exhibition game. In 1935, Joe DiMaggio trained in Fresno with the Seals at Chance Field, located at Ventura and Cedar avenues.

Over the last hundred years, Fresnans have cheered from the bleachers or yelled at their radio or television sets, rooting for their hometown heroes. Baseball fever is certainly a part of Fresno's history.

The arrival of someone famous was something to look forward to, especially when they were kings such as Babe Ruth. Ruth (third from left) made a trip throughout the United States accompanied by Lou Gehrig (left) and was met in Fresno by Father John J. Crowley. *The Image Group from the Laval Historical Collection.*

# The Street Named for an English Jurist

In 1888, J. P. Vincent and A. M. Drew began mapping land adjacent to and northeast of the old city lines of Fresno. They called this parcel the Altamont Addition. Because this new area did not have direct access to a connecting road into the city, they had to buy a parcel that would give a right-of-way to Stanislaus Street.

By the time the plot map was ready to be filed with the Fresno County recorder's office, several lots had been purchased on the main road of the addition. This new road, which, over the next hundred years, would grow from a county road to a tree-lined street to a major commercial arterial, had as its first residents a number of attorneys. As a joke, someone said to Mr. Drew that this street should be called Blackstone in honor of Sir William Blackstone, the famous English jurist. Mr. Drew immediately wrote the name on the map. And that is how Blackstone Avenue got its name.

For many years, as you have driven on this major street, your vision has been assaulted by signs of all shapes and sizes which seem to fill every empty space. This, in combination with heavy traffic and buildings of nondescript styles lined endlessly along its edges, does not bring to mind beauty in any shape or form.

However, thanks to Tree Fresno, who put together the winning combination of an environmental enhancement and mitigation program grant from the State of California, donations from business owners on Blackstone Avenue, and donations from the community, the center islands have been planted with trees and shrubs, recalling the days when this was a lovely tree-lined street of fine residences, home to many of Fresno's leading attorneys.

# Blackmail & Murder in 1890

The year 1887 saw the arrival of a handsome couple from the east, Mr. and Mrs. John Dewey Fiske. Their decision to settle in Fresno was made during a stopover on their return from a two-year honeymoon tour of the world. Within hours of their decision, Mr. Fiske purchased business property, including the Fresno Opera House on I Street (now Broadway) and an impressive home on M Street. Well-launched in the multiple careers of lawyer, capitalist and theatrical manager, he was prepared to become an influential member of the community.

However, word of his dark past and difficult personality began to surface. His law career in Massachusetts had been characterized by malpractice and malfeasance in office, which had led to his disbarment. It also became a matter of public knowledge that two bitter divorces had preceded his present marriage.

Anxious to acquire the rights to a car-coupling patent, he offered inventor Joseph Stillman an insufficient amount of money for the patent. When Stillman refused, Fiske threatened to tell Stillman's wife that Stillman had had a liaison with Fiske's French maid. The story was untrue, but Stillman became enraged and began to stalk Fiske. Several arguments ensued. The more Fiske threatened, the more frightened and angry Stillman became. Finally, on a hot July evening in 1890, Fiske met Stillman near the entrance to the Grand Central Hotel on J Street (now Fulton Street). Stillman slapped Fiske, who began beating his assailant with a cane. Stillman drew his gun. Fiske turned to run. Three shots rang out. Fiske lay dead on the sidewalk.

Fulton G. Berry helped carry Fiske's body to Burke & Monroe's drugstore where Dr. W. T. Maupin pronounced him dead. Cries of "Hang him!" could be heard in the streets.

The next day hundreds of Fresnans, including many women, crowded the morgue where the body of thirty-three-year-old, handsome John Fiske lay in state for public viewing. Stillman was tried for murder and sentenced to life in prison. Although the city was now officially five years old, the specter of the Wild West continued to haunt Fresno.

Stevens Bancroft, all-American tackle for the Golden Bears, in the 1928 Big Game that traditionally pitted University of California at Berkeley against Stanford University, intercepted a pass and ran seventy-five yards to score the first touchdown.

The Blue and Gold. *Associated Students of the University of California. 1929. Author's collection.*

Fresno has had its share of football heroes, but probably none more colorful than Stevens Bancroft. Grandson of one of Fresno's earliest pioneers, Clark Stevens, Bancroft inherited his family's intelligence, stubbornness, independence and pride. With a pioneer spirit worthy of his forebears, Bancroft stirred up excitement everywhere he went.

In his four years at Fresno High School, he was the star tackle of the football team. He graduated from high school in 1924 and entered the University of California at Berkeley, where he continued his athletic career. He was made captain of the football team and was named an all-American tackle for the Golden Bears. Observers at the time said that to watch Bancroft intercept a pass and run for a touchdown was to witness a wild pioneer spirit in action.

Saturday after Saturday, he'd win the game for Cal and then adjourn to Red's Beanery, a local hangout, where he'd stir up another kind of entertainment, which usually lasted until dawn or until the police arrived. Bancroft was blessed with a winning personality; it was said that even the Berkeley police liked him. He attracted people wherever he went. He often said that he had enough dinner invitations to last the rest of his life.

The "Galloping Goose," his stripped-down Ford, made many trips from Cal to his grandparents' home in Pacific Grove where

In the 1928 football game that the University of California Golden Bears played against the Trojans of University of Southern California, Stevens Bancroft makes a flying tackle. The Blue and Gold. *Associated Students of the University of California. 1929. Author's collection.*

they had moved when his grandfather retired. At the wheel would be Bancroft, clad only in a pair of jeans.

After college, Pan American Airlines hired him and trained him to fly their new China Clipper. His sense of adventure drew him to the challenge and, over the years, he became one of Pan Am's top pilots. His years of flying were highlighted by several parachute jumps to safety, including a bailout over the Amazon jungle.

Fishing with his good friend Ernest Hemingway in the Florida Keys, he caught a marlin which he had stuffed and mounted. He then presented it to his grandmother, Clara Stevens, who hung it over her bed in her home on Seventeenth Street in Pacific Grove, California.

In 1937, Bancroft married movie actress Mae Clarke, but the union lasted only three years.

At the time of his death in 1961, Bancroft was adored by the women in his family, but his male relatives looked on him with dislike liberally laced with envy.

It is said that Miss Clarke, until her death, kept a photo on her bureau of her handsome Fresno pilot in his captain's uniform.

Since the founding of Fresno in 1872, the Central Pacific Railroad had held a monopoly on the goods that were shipped out of the San Joaquin Valley. Fresno was well known as a railroad center, but, by 1890, resentment against the Central Pacific had grown into hatred. The railroad company was commonly known as the "octopus," whose tentacles seemed to reach out to strangle the valley's industry, agriculture and commerce as prices to ship goods continually rose.

Several rival railroad lines were proposed, but the cost to secure a right-of-way was very high and the proposals were dropped. In 1891, an organization named the Traffic Association of California was formed in San Francisco. Its purpose was to secure rate adjustments so that San Francisco could become a distribution point for the valley's goods. To achieve this goal, another railroad line had to be built through the valley. Claus Spreckels, the sugar baron, and other capitalists purchased subscriptions for the new line which was incorporated as the San Francisco and San Joaquin Valley Railway.

The reaction to this move was enthusiastic. Newspapers supported the venture and citizens were urged to become subscribers. The thrust of the editorials was that it was one's patriotic duty to support this new venture. Construction of "The People's Railroad" began in Stockton on July 22, 1895. The line reached Fresno on October 2, 1896. The first train to travel the new route was called the "Emancipator." When it reached Fresno it was greeted with bands, speeches and fireworks.

The *Fresno Morning Republican* hailed the new line, saying it was ushering in a new era of development and prosperity. Today, the "People's Railroad" is called the Santa Fe Railway. Its depot at Tulare and Santa Fe avenues stands as a symbol of the growth of Fresno and of the initiative of its people.

The weekend of February 4, 5, and 6 of 1910 was one of feverish excitement for the residents of Fresno County. An event of tremendous magnitude was being held at the county fairground. Sponsored by the chamber of commerce, this event led Fresno merchants to declare a holiday and to close their stores. Special trains bringing valley residents to Fresno were added to the Southern Pacific and Santa Fe railroad schedules. The weatherman kept a watchful eye on climatic conditions and, finally, predicted good weather for the weekend.

At the fairground, concessionaires selling all kinds of food and souvenirs began setting up their stands early. As people poured into the fairground on the first day, it began to look as though thousands would attend. Indeed, the weekend attendance totaled thirty-five thousand people, half the population of Fresno County at that time. No one went away disappointed.

On that momentous weekend, record crowds saw Charles K. Hamilton and Charles F. Willard soar through the air in their biplanes in the first air show ever held in Fresno County. For most Fresnans, this was the first time they had the opportunity to see men actually fly in those marvelous newfangled machines called airplanes.

Music has been of great importance to Fresnans. Fresno's early churches had organized musical groups. The opening of the Barton Opera House led to the need for an orchestra to accompany theatrical productions. In 1890, Fresno's first band, the Fresno City Park Band, was organized by D. C. Smith. Other bands followed, including the Raisin City Band, the Wienerwurst Band, the Fresno Military Band, the National Guard Band and the Fresno Municipal Band. Fresno's summer climate of hot days and balmy evenings made Sunday evening band concerts in Courthouse Park a memorable part of life in turn-of-the-century Fresno.

In the 1920s, '30s and '40s, Sunday afternoon concerts at the Lisenby Memorial Bandstand in Roeding Park became important events to savor. Marching bands, dance bands and jazz bands all became an important part of musical life in Fresno. The Rainbow Ballroom on Broadway became the most popular arena for local dance bands for many years.

Today, the Fresno Municipal Band continues to be a part of the cultural life in Fresno. If you are fortunate enough to attend one of its concerts at Fresno's Woodward Park on a warm summer evening, you may also enjoy a starlit sky overhead, feel a light evening breeze and hear crickets creating their own music when the band ceases to play. At such a time, remember that you are savoring one of Fresno's cherished traditions—one that has lasted for over a hundred years.

On March 22, 1919, more than sixty people interested in the preservation of the history of Fresno County gathered at city hall. Among their number was the head of the history department at Fresno State Normal School, the Fresno County librarian, one of the earliest residents of Fresno County, a newspaperman, a writer, a professor and many Fresno pioneers. The first order of business was the adoption of a constitution and a set of by-laws. The latter document outlined the purposes of the new organization. To collect, compile and preserve the written records of Fresno County was a major goal. Another aim was to collect photographs and to receive and hold in trust artifacts relating to the county's history.

Meetings were held once a month. Members presented papers on local history and then deposited them in the archives that this new group hadestablished. The object was to record as much history as possible while many of the pioneer settlers were still alive.

The organization continued to grow and to collect. In 1947, it became a state-recognized non-profit corporation. Now, more than seventy years later, this group administers two site museums. The archives, begun by the first members, now holds thousands of photographs, maps, oral histories, local government records, biography and reference indexes, and written records that document the history of Fresno County from the 1850s to the present. The artifact collection consists of period clothing, textiles, furniture, silver, musical instruments, toys, agricultural implements, furniture from the 1874 Fresno County Courthouse and regional Indian baskets.

Today, with a membership of more than one thousand people, the Fresno City and County Historical Society, with its unique resources, is able to interpret our community's past through exhibits, publications, slide presentations and outreach programs to the schools. It serves as a regional history reference and study center. The goals of the founders have been accomplished and will continue to serve as a guide for the society's leadership as Fresno's history continues to unfold in the next century.

# Festivals, Fetes & Raisins

Since raisin prices were low in 1909 and sales were declining, growers decided something had to be done to make raisins nationally known and desired. An idea suggested by former Fresnan James Harsburgh was taken under consideration. After some discussion, it was decided to accept his idea of a springtime festival honoring the raisin. A parade with floats and marching bands was the first part of the celebration. Following it was an automobile race which later became known as the Raisin Day Classic.

Each year the festival grew in scope and prominence. Eventually, floats were brought from all parts of California. People followed them, coming to Fresno to be a part of the celebration. The Raisin Queen, chosen from the most beautiful girls in the San Joaquin Valley, reigned over all the festivities.

After 1920, Hollywood sent some of its best-known stars to rule as Raisin Day King. Tom Mix, Monte Blue, Lew Cody, and William Russell were so honored, Tom Mix holding the title twice.

During festival month, the nation's leading hotels, railroads, and steamship lines featured raisin dishes on their menus and advertised the festival that was to take place in Fresno. The celebration had, indeed, gained national stature.

The last festival was held in 1932. By that time, the Raisin Day Festival had not only helped make the raisin nationally known, but it had put Fresno on the map as well.

James J. Rolph Jr., enjoyed one of the pleasures of being Governor of California during the 1931 Raisin Day parade when he kissed the hand of Queen Aileen Higgings of Modesto. *The Image Group from the Laval Historical Collection.*

# Earthquake Relief

On April 18, 1906, the citizens of Fresno rallied to help the people of San Francisco, who had suffered a devastating earthquake. Women began to cook food and bake bread which they took to the relief headquarters. A committee was set up to arrange a mass meeting to discuss and organize the most effective way Fresnans could help. The committee visited local businesses, asking them to close during the meeting which was scheduled for two o'clock. Only one business owner declined.

At the appointed hour, the Barton Opera House began to fill with people. By the time everyone had arrived, the crowd was estimated at one thousand. Frank Short, chairman of the meeting, gave an eloquent speech. "San Francisco is our town," he said. "We look to San Francisco for everything. We have friends and families there. It is impossible to exaggerate the magnitude and importance of the situation. It is imperative that we help." He urged the sending of supplies, but stressed that money would be the greatest help. After he spoke, the call for donations was given. They came so fast the secretary had a hard time writing them down quickly enough.

Louis Kutner of Kutner & Goldstein made the first donation of $500. The same amount was pledged by almost all the other department stores. The fraternal lodges followed and then individuals began to contribute. When all the money was counted, the donations totaled $35,000. The Chinese community, with its donation of $10,000, made the largest single contribution. It was handled through their own committee.

When San Franciscans were in trouble, Fresnans responded nobly and generously. It was a proud moment in the city's history.

Today, women's tennis is a very popular sport. The young and not so young woman of the late 1990s may not only belong to a tennis club, but also may be spotted in the supermarket in her tennis togs after a competitive morning game. Have you ever wondered what women's tennis was like a hundred years ago?

Fresno's first tennis club was organized on June 18, 1891, at the office of Dr. W. T. Maupin. It was a private club, located at Tulare and N streets, and boasted three tennis courts. Women were invited to play, but the apparel of the day made it difficult to have a very vigorous game. Instead, the woman of 1891 would just lob the ball across the net in a graceful, feminine fashion and then relax over a cup of tea.

Just how much of a handicap the fashion of the time proved to be can be seen in the following quote from an article which appeared in the *Central Californian* in 1891 and was reprinted in the *Fresno Bee* on October 27, 1935. "If you are going to wear stays…stay off the team's field. You don't want to be inside a whalebone fence with steel gateposts when you are trying for a good delivery and when the size of your waist will be of no consequence as compared to the style of your playing. Put on a plain round skirt full enough to allow you to take a sizable stride. It should not quite reach the instep. Get a flannelette shirtwaist with a pocket, a cap with a visor and regulation rubber-soled shoes. Having arrayed yourself in this garb straightway forget you have it on, else you won't play decently."

In spite of ladies' fashions, tennis increased in popularity. When the woman tennis player of today is tempted to wax nostalgic about the "good old days," it is a sure bet she would not dream of trading her trendy togs for sensible long skirts and flannel shirtwaists.

The year 1880 saw the arrival in Fresno of a twenty-year-old man. His first job was in a sawmill where he lost his left hand in an accident. Forced to find a new career, he enrolled in an engineering school in San Francisco. He graduated in 1883 as a civil engineer. Four years later, he was named Fresno's city engineer and was responsible for surveying and laying out Fresno's first sewer system.

In 1896, he became the engineer for the Fresno Canal and Irrigation Company and for the owners of Laguna De Tache, a large land grant comprising over sixty thousand acres of land. In his work for these companies, he designed extensive irrigation systems.

Of all his many engineering projects, the one for which he is most remembered is the planning of Pine Flat Dam on the Kings River. When the project was completed, he was given the keys that turned on the switch at the dedication service.

His large home, which he built in 1915, still stands on Kearney Boulevard.

At the time of his death in 1950, he was the last surviving signer of the original petition to incorporate the city of Fresno in 1885.

Today, a school and an avenue bear his name and stand as lasting tributes to his accomplishments. Who was this engineer extraordinaire? His name was Ingvart Teilman.

In the early 1850s, a Chinese blacksmith named Ah Kitt arrived in America in search of adventure. Gold had been discovered and fortune seekers were flocking to California. Ah Kitt's travels took him to the small town of Millerton on the San Joaquin River where miners panned for gold. He opened a blacksmith shop near the river bank where he could water his horses. Here he met Jefferson Shannon, a hog raiser and a blacksmith, who also brought his livestock there for water.

Although neither man spoke much of the other's language, a friendship sprang up between them. In time, they bought McCray's Stable, thus forming the first Caucasian-Chinese partnership in central California.

In 1867, Ah Kitt's first son was born. He named him Jefferson Shannon Kitt after his close friend. By 1883, both families decided to move to Fresno. They came together and opened a blacksmith shop on Merced Street between H and I streets (now Broadway). The Kitts were one of the first families to settle in what came to be known as Chinatown. The friendship between the Kitt and Shannon families was to last for more than four generations.

In the late 1890s, John Tuck settled in Fresno and married Ah Kitt's daughter, Becky. John became the official Chinese interpreter for the municipal, superior, and federal courts. He was given the sobriquet "Mayor of Chinatown." Today, Ah Kitt's grandson, Frank Tuck, is affectionately known by the same title. He provides a direct link from modern Fresno to our county's beginnings in the little town of Millerton.

# The Jones Mill

In 1877, long before it was called Fulton Street, J Street was a dirt road. The few buildings that faced the road were simple wood-framed structures. Some of them had been rebuilt with wood brought from Millerton. On the corner of J and Tulare streets stood the office of the *Expositor* newspaper. Next door, on the J Street side, Calvin Jones built a boarding house which would later be known as the Jones Hotel. Just north of this hotel Jones constructed a rather oddly shaped building that looked more like an enclosure to those viewing it from the street.

Passersby were quickly aware that loud, unusual noises emanated from within this odd place. When entering the structure, the source of the noise was clearly evident. A boiler, an engine and a set of millstones were crushing barley for stock feed. After a short while the mill was improved so it could grind wheat as well. When the mill stones got too smooth, Jones and his helper would roughen the stones using a special tool.

Jones' wife kept a herd of cows in a corral behind the mill. Every morning and evening she milked them and hired boys to deliver the milk to her customers. Often the cows would be let out of the corral and driven out to graze on open land a few blocks away.

By the mid-1880s, Moses Church's Champion Mill had become tough competition and Calvin Jones sold his property and moved his family out of town.

Today, the Mason Building on the Fulton Mall marks the site of Fresno's first flour mill and the Jones Hotel.

J oshing" was a new word, coined in the latter part of the nineteenth century. It referred to the habit of some newspaper editorial writers of poking fun at well-known people. It was a tool that the editor of the *Fresno Morning Republican*, Chester Harvey Rowell, used to great advantage. Not everyone found humor in it. One of those who did not was the aloof raisin baron of the Fruit Vale Estate, M. Theo Kearney.

In 1898, Kearney was hard at work organizing the first raisin growers association. Rowell supported the association and gave it free publicity. Then he found that Kearney had secretly voted himself and his associates large salaries. Rowell threatened to print the amounts in his paper. Kearney forbade him to do this, saying that the growers were not smart enough to understand these things. Rowell said that unless Kearney made the amounts public, he would. Kearney gave in.

Then a reporter for the *Republican*, writing an article on a lawsuit between Kearney and a raisin grower, said that "Michael" Kearney was "escorted" to court. Kearney was furious. He told Rowell his name was Martin and he had not been escorted, he had gone to court freely. The newspaper printed a retraction and began the article, "M. Theo (not Michael) Kearney." This made Kearney even more irate. He resigned as president of the raisin association and said he would not hold the office again until certain newspapers stopped their vulgar habit of joshing.

Rowell was warned about feuding with Kearney, who was the most powerful man in the community, but he wrote an editorial anyway, chiding Kearney for deserting the association over such a petty thing. Kearney quietly reassumed his office.

One day, a man named Colonel Trevelyan, who claimed to be the last survivor of the famous "Six Hundred" at the charge of Balaklava, visited Rowell's office. He urged Rowell to meet face to face with Kearney to work out their differences. Rowell said that he knew Kearney would not visit him and he was sure that Kearney would not let him in his office. Trevelyan said he would arrange a meeting.

On the appointed evening, Rowell was ushered into Kearney's

presence. Kearney immediately voiced his strong opinion against joshing. "There is only one person in the world who refused to be joshed," Rowell said, "and his name is Kaiser Wilhelm." Kearney, who socialized with the German aristocracy on his yearly travels, banged his fist on the table and roared, "That's a josh and I'll not stand for it." They never spoke to each other again.

In 1880, a young German immigrant arrived in New York, full of ambition and determined to make his way to San Francisco because he had a letter of introduction to John Weiland, owner of Weiland's brewery in that city. However, he did not have much money and could not afford the necessary train fare. To solve his problem, he worked his way across country from town to town doing odd jobs.

After arriving in San Francisco, he met with Mr. Weiland and was hired to manage the Weiland distributorship in Fresno. The year was 1881 and this young man was rather amazed to find himself in a wide-open city like Fresno. The saloons, which existed on every corner, were of the type that made respectable people wince. Seeing them gave him an idea. Why not open a place where families could come for lunch and refreshments? A German type beer garden would offer Fresno's citizens something more respectable.

He opened his new establishment at the corner of Fresno and Fulton streets. It was called the New Palm Garden and had a side entrance on Fresno Street. This allowed easy access to the Barton Opera House directly across the street, making it convenient for theatergoers. The New Palm Garden was a great success and was a meeting place for Fresnans for over thirty years until it was forced to close when Prohibition laws went into effect in 1920.

Edward Schwarz made his dream of a German beer hall a reality. Like so many others, he had played an important role in the development of Fresno.

Gold fever was a contagion that brought thousands of people west. Thomas Law Reed's father was one of the men who came to the gold fields of California. His family received two letters from him before he disappeared, a probable victim of the rough frontiersmen who surrounded his mining claim.

Thomas Law Reed and his two older brothers fought in the Civil War. Reed suffered a shoulder wound in the battle of Shiloh. In 1883, Reed married Amantha Ann Smith. After running a cheese factory in Michigan, they moved to California, settling in Yolo County.

In 1884, Reed was offered an opportunity to farm in Fresno County. He moved his family to Smith's Ferry on the Kings River. James Smith built a hotel at the site for travelers who would require food and lodging. It was here that the Reed family lived while their home was being built on the wheat farm and vineyard that Reed had planted.

As more people came into the area, Reed donated a portion of his property for a schoolhouse. He acquired more and more farming property and became known as one of the major wheat growers in California.

A site for a new town was surveyed in 1888. Reed sold the first lots. He also served as the first president of the chamber of commerce for this new and growing community.

He suffered financial losses when the wheat market declined, but then made a fortune in oil in Bakersfield and paid off all his debts.

Thomas Law Reed, a kind and generous gentleman, honest in all his dealings, was known as the "Father of Reedley." The citizens of that community can be proud of the man who gave his name to their city.

Springtime in Clovis means more than enjoying the wild flowers that blanket the foothills near the city. It is a time of year when townsfolk begin to await, with eager anticipation, a unique festival that not only provides fun and thrills for the locals, but for visitors who come from other parts of the county as well. As the long-awaited weekend approaches, banners appear on street lamps and in store windows.

This event began in 1914 as a community picnic sponsored by the Women's Club to raise money for their building fund. It was held on a vacant lot on Pollasky Avenue between Fourth and Fifth streets. Food was plentiful. Games and races of all kinds provided fun for everyone. A few local boys even tried to ride a mule in a makeshift corral. It was such a success that each year more attractions were added, including a horse show, a parade, calf roping and steer wrestling.

In 1935, an association was incorporated to promote and plan this annual event. By this time, two days were required to fit in all the activities.

Today a stadium that accommodates 10,000 people is the setting for competitions. Ushered in by Big Hat Day and a colorful parade, the Clovis Rodeo provides its community with a sense of identity and pride. And, those valley residents who attend know full well they are going to experience a weekend of down-home fun for the whole family.

# Preparing "Typewriters"

On September 1, 1891, an important event in the history of Fresno took place. Advertisements in the *Fresno Expositor* heralded the formation of an institution that would teach students the finer points of business and commerce. Since this new school would be open to both men and women, the ads also were aimed at assuring the men of Fresno that women were not going to be trained to take over their jobs.

Mr. W. C. Ramsey, the owner, had successfully operated a similar school in Modesto. Using the same format, the Fresno institution would train students for positions as secretaries and bookkeepers in local businesses. A new machine designed to make business letters look more professional was available for the students. It was called a typewriter. The women who were being trained to use this new machine for secretarial duties were called "typewriters."

The new school opened with eighty students. It was located in the Edgerly Block on the corner of J (now Fulton) and Tulare streets in the heart of Fresno's business district. In 1996, this school celebrated 105 years of service to the business community of the San Joaquin Valley. Since its opening, more than sixty thousand people have trained within its doors and found employment in over one thousand businesses. Known first as Fresno Business College, then Chestnutwood Business College, later Heald Business College and, today, Central California Commercial College or 4C's Business College, the school continues to fulfill an important role in the Central Valley.

Today, computers are replacing the typewriters, but the person who operates these machines is still an important ingredient for a successful business. And, it is this person that this institution has trained so effectively for more than a hundred years.

Several Heald's students were trying the two hand technique while working with their adding machines April 18, 1919. *The Image Group from the Laval Historical Collection.*

# Shipps, Trains, Wagons and Sheep

For the families of our pioneers, the path to Fresno County was not always an easy one. Each family who settled in the central San Joaquin Valley showed tremendous determination and courage. One large group left Mississippi soon after the Civil War, journeying to New York by train and then to Panama by steamer. The Isthmus had to be crossed by train and then another steamer took the party to San Francisco. One member of the group, a two-year-old named George, lost a hat in the Atlantic Ocean and then proceeded to lose another hat in the Pacific.

The group settled near Vacaville in Solano County and found work on ranches in the area. Two of the men decided to explore California and began a trip that took them as far south as Los Angeles. On their way back to Vacaville, they came through Centerville and Millerton. On their return, they told the others that they had decided to move to the San Joaquin Valley. Everyone agreed on this plan.

They purchased a one-year supply of food and bought sheep with their remaining funds. Loading all their goods on wagons, they headed south. When they reached Jones Ferry, where Friant is today, the sheep were herded across the San Joaquin River a few at a time. The party continued south and settled at Big Dry Creek.

It was in this manner that David Cowan Sample and the families of Major Thomas Nelson and William Walter Shipp came to Fresno County. They lived in an adobe house on the Blasingame Ranch until they could bring lumber down Tollhouse Road to build homes.

David Cowan Sample later married Sally Cole, a daughter of William T. Cole. They became the parents of eleven children. Today, the descendants of these dauntless pioneers still live in Fresno County.

Shortly after the turn of the century, a developer named John Forthcamp began to sell lots in the area just north of Divisadero Avenue that would become known as the North Park district.

A gentleman in his sixties who, although a native of Tennessee, had spent most of his life raising cattle in Texas, purchased six lots which ran north from the corner of Franklin and Forthcamp (now Fulton Street) streets. He decided to build a home on the four lots closest to the corner. He hired prominent local architect A. C. Swartz to design a Queen Anne style wood frame house. It had many interesting architectural features, including a multi-gabled roof with two round cupolas at the northeast and southeast corners. The house was completed in 1911 and the owner and his family, including his wife, four daughters and three sons, moved in.

Having acquired land in the Sanger area, this gentleman had dreams of becoming a citrus grower. However, his wife's death in 1912 put an end to his plans. Instead, he retired to his large house where he lived with his spinster daughter, Ida, until his death in 1925. Ida continued to live there until her death in 1960.

The house, which had become a Fresno landmark, had been used as a boarding house and had housed the offices of a nonprofit organization until the mid-1980s. As it sat in the right-of-way of the proposed Freeway 180 Gap Project, the house became the focus of preservation efforts. It was feared that, like so many historic valley buildings, the beautiful home of John William Proffitt would fall under the wrecker's ball. But, happily, that was not to be. The Proffitt Home was to survive to create its own legacy in Fresno history.

# History on Bulldog Lane

In 1987, five historic homes in the right-of-way of proposed Freeway 180 were offered for sale by the city of Fresno for one dollar each. Bids for these homes had to be submitted to the city. Prospective owners had to meet stringent requirements, including owning the property on which the structure would be placed and being able to afford the costs of moving and restoration.

One of the homes, the 1911 Proffitt Home, was awarded to the Zeta Kappa Chapter of Sigma Nu fraternity. In a twist of irony, a historic home from Fulton Street, which in the 1940s and 1950s had seen many of its older homes being used for sorority houses, was going to move to the corner of Bulldog Lane and Millbrook Avenue near California State University, Fresno. It also was heartening to many people that, in an era which was seeing the demolition of many historic structures, a group of young men was making a real commitment to the preservation of one of Fresno's finest historic buildings.

After getting the city's approval, the fraternity had to win consent from the other houses on fraternity row. In his letter to the other houses, Sigma Nu president Sheldon Solo stated that bringing this historic house to fraternity row would bring a sense of nostalgia to the area and would strengthen and enhance the Greek system. It was the consensus of the other houses that the Proffitt Home would make a fine addition to the row.

After many months of planning, a ground-breaking ceremony was held on May 1, 1988. The process of moving the house had begun.

After many months of preparation, the expensive and difficult process of moving the nearly eighty-year-old, three-story, 5,000-square-foot Proffitt Home to Sigma Nu's lot on Bulldog Lane had begun.

Late in April 1989, the house on Fulton Street was removed from its foundation. The top of the house was detached and the remainder of the house was cut in half vertically. The two largest pieces were loaded onto flatbed moving trucks.

On Saturday evening, May 6, a crowd began to gather on Fulton Street. Sigma Nu brothers, their friends and local preservationists all cheered as the first truck moved over the curb and onto Fulton Street. By 11:00 p.m., the two major portions of the house were at the intersection of Belmont Avenue and Fulton Street. The process took much longer than anticipated because the light standards at each corner had to be raised.

The trucks bearing the house made their way slowly to Echo Avenue, then turned south to Divisadero Street and moved along that avenue, turning south on R Street. As the house made its way along R, it moved through one of Fresno's first exclusive residential neighborhoods. Much of this neighborhood has been torn down, but the Proffitt Home was going to survive and was on its way to a new beginning in northeast Fresno.

At the corner where the Meux Home Museum stands, the old house made a left turn onto Tulare Street and headed east. Traversing the freeway proved difficult, but the median islands were crossed over and the trucks with their burden continued east. From here the route wound circuitously north to Shaw Avenue. Shaw proved exciting. By this time it was mid-morning on Sunday and traffic stopped at the sight of two trucks carrying portions of the huge Victorian house emblazoned with banners reading "Sigma Nu on the Move" rolling by.

As the trucks turned north on Cedar Avenue and then onto Bulldog Lane, the excitement increased. Sigma Nus gathered in the street. When the house began its progress down Bulldog Lane, the brothers formed a parade, walking ahead of their house, leading it home. The brothers sang, the trucks blew their horns and the onlookers, many of whom had followed the progress of this project for two years, applauded. In the words of Brian Marion, the Sigma Nu brother who had initiated the project, "It's a dream come true." For all who watched, it was an unforgettable day in Fresno's history.

During the demolition of the Fresno County Courthouse in the spring of 1966, one of the mysteries was the location of the cornerstone. No clues were available, but the small group of people searching for it noticed a small indentation at the southeast corner of the building a few feet above the ground. It took a jackhammer to penetrate the brick surrounding a large granite block lodged there. After a great deal of time spent hammering at the granite, it gave way and fell out onto the ground, revealing a copper box inside. As might have been expected, the box contained many newspapers, documents and coins relating to the year 1874 when the courthouse was built. But there was also one unpredictable item secreted away for those ninety-two years.

As planned, the box and its contents were placed in the care of the Fresno County Free Library.

Today, the box and all its contents are still in the library's vault, including a time-worn knothole that remains a mystery to those who oversee the vault. What significance could it have? Should this eight- by five-inch relic be treasured? Is it worthy of storage with the time-honored courthouse box?

Could it, perhaps, be the knothole from the green bush from whence Fresno was named? Could it be a knothole from the tree to which Jedediah Strong Smith tied his horse? Perchance John C. Fremont looked into this knothole and called to his sidekick, Kit Carson, to come and take a look at this superb example of treedom? Perhaps the Dalton brothers stashed their booty in this particular knothole or, maybe, Three-fingered Jack suggested to his partner in crime, Joaquin Murrietta, that the tree from which this knothole came would be the perfect meeting place for their gang.

All this speculation is well and good. But for the staff at the library, the puzzle of the knothole remains. They are afraid to throw it out. It might have a tale to tell, or was it all a part of midsummer madness in Fresno? The best of times and the worst of seasons? We may never know.

Entering downtown from Freeway 41, the new, futuristic Fresno City Hall catches the eye. Located on its two-block site on P Street between Fresno and Tulare streets, it faces the state and federal buildings across the street. For many years, the site of this new building stood vacant. What, one might wonder, was here before?

From the later 1890s until the mid-1950s this was a peaceful, middle class neighborhood. Modest frame houses interspersed with a few larger ornate Victorian structures lined P Street. Green lawns, picket fences and trees at the curb marked this as a typical turn-of-the-century neighborhood. Front porches provided a center for social life as neighbors gathered there on summer evenings. Five-cent cones from Jean's establishment on Tulare Street were piled high with delicious homemade ice cream that made a hot summer evening seem cooler.

The Webster family, who owned Webster's Drug Store at Van Ness Avenue and Mariposa Streets, lived at the corner of P and Fresno streets. Three Fresno High School student body presidents, Francis Newton, Dudley Harkleroad and Tadema White, grew up here. The Felix Lochers' son, Charles, went to Hollywood, changed his name to Jon Hall and had roles in the Charlie Chan movies. Later, he married actress Frances Langford. Another family, Dr. and Mrs. W. P. Miller, played a major role in enhancing the cultural atmosphere of Fresno. Emma Miller was a lecturer at Fresno State College for many years and gave literary presentations to local clubs. The Emma Miller Study Club was formed and named for her.

Since early in this century, the residents of P Street felt that someday Fresno's city hall would be built on their street. Even though it was not part of any master plan, they knew instinctively that to place it there would provide the logical anchor for the courthouse at the western end of the civic center. They were right, and today the people who grew up on this two-block area of P Street and their descendants are proud that their neighborhood dream has become a reality.

On December 13, 1915, twenty-three men sat down to-gether at the Hotel Fresno to discuss forming a new sort of organization. The new group would bring together business and professional men to volunteer their time in service to their community. This ideal of service as a basis of worthy enterprise had been brought to Fresno by Franklin Wright, newly arrived here, who had experienced this new idea in a club he belonged to in Oakland. The twenty-three men enthusiastically endorsed the formation of just such a club in Fresno.

The first president of the new group was H. E. Wilkerson. He oversaw the writing of the club's constitution and the addition of thirty-nine new members. During his term, the group took on its first civic project—the selection of olive trees which would border Highway 99 between the city of Fresno and Herndon Avenue.

From this rather humble beginning the group made grand strides forward. It led in the organization of a Boy Scouts of America Council, financed trips to summer camp for needy boys, endorsed a statewide effort to establish a society for crippled children, provided financing to initiate Christmas Tree Lane and gave grants to the YMCA, the YWCA, the Community Chest and the Salvation Army. Over the years the club has continued to improve the facilities at the Boy Scout Camp at Shaver Lake, including the construction of new buildings. In 1954, under the leadership of president Leon Peters, Playland at Roeding Park was built.

As the years progressed, the Fresno club sponsored the formation of other clubs in Fresno and throughout the valley. The community service aspects were expanded to include not only funding projects at Valley Children's Hospital, but also funding programs which dealt with vocational guidance and the formation of a dental lab at the Salvation Army headquarters.

For more than eighty years, the members of Rotary have made enormous contributions to the community of Fresno. The existence of this organization and the dedication of its members, which exemplifies the club's motto, "Service Above Self," has made Fresno a much better place in which to live.

The summer of 1947 found Fresnans all agog over the latest Hollywood heartthrob, Jon Hall. His first starring role was in the movie *Hurricane* starring Dorothy Lamour. This movie featured what was billed as one of the most expensive kissing scenes ever filmed. The scene, in which he and Miss Lamour shared the spotlight, was shot underwater in a glass tank and reputedly cost $8,000. The movie also starred C. Aubrey Smith and Mary Astor. Other films in which the actor had roles included *Charlie Chan in Shanghai* and *Mind Your Own Business*.

Soon after *Hurricane* was released, Hall eloped with actress Frances Langford. The wedding was followed by a honeymoon cruise to Tahiti in a fifty-two-foot ketch. A month later the couple married again because, in his nervousness, the bridegroom had put New York as his birthplace on the marriage license, instead of his real place of birth.

After the United States entered World War II, Hall reported for active duty in the Coast Guard Auxiliary. An experienced navigator, Hall served on two ships used for government service.

Two years later, in 1944, Hall was involved in a Hollywood ruckus at the home of band leader Tommy Dorsey. Allegedly, Dorsey knocked him down. Hall hit his head on a flowerpot. Eventually, the case was dismissed.

All this was of interest to the people of Fresno, for Jon Hall, who began his career as an understudy for Robert Taylor, was in reality Charles Locher, a native of Fresno, who had lived with his family on P Street, the site of Fresno's new city hall.

Eleven-year-old Manuel Estrada left Sonoma, Mexico, with his uncle and settled in Visalia. He later married Louisa Forquera, whose stepfather had originated the western saddle. Travelers came from miles away to buy saddles and also to enjoy the family's delicious food. In 1907, the Estradas decided to open a restaurant in Visalia. As the years went by, their daughters each established a restaurant in cities throughout California, bringing the total of Estrada eateries to seven.

The Fresno restaurant was started in 1917 by Cruz Estrada Dillard. First located on O Street, then on Van Ness Avenue and Inyo Street, the restaurant moved to its present location in a lovely old home at 380 North Blackstone Avenue in 1926. The family lived upstairs.

The food at Estrada's reflects a cuisine that was adapted to please the palates of the early settlers of the valley. The sauces and macaroni reflect the influence of the Italians who wanted less spicy food. The result is called a Spanish or early California cuisine. Cruz created a mouthwatering tostada compuesta that is unique to Estrada's and brings customers flocking to its tables.

Cruz's son Ralph, who served as a machine gunner on Iwo Jima during World War II, and other family members still operate the restaurant, maintaining the high standards that have been a family tradition for eighty years. Everything is made by hand. Once a week the family and staff gather in the kitchen to tackle the job of making tamales. Each step of the process is done as it was in 1917. The careful preparation is evident in the delicious result.

In 1986, during the presidential campaign, Congressman Chip Pashayan surprised the family by bringing his friend, George Bush, for dinner. The future president ordered a marguerita and guacamole dip. This was followed by a tostada compuesta, cheese enchilada, chile rellano, and ice cream. A handwritten note to Ralph expressed Bush's enjoyment of the meal and was accompanied by a golf shirt and a set of golf balls. How delightful to know that Cruz Estrada's scrumptious tostadas, long a cherished Fresno tradition, also have been savored by the president of the United States! It's the sort of knowledge that makes Fresnans smile with pride.

# The Magical Grape

E very September something magical happens in the vineyards of the central San Joaquin Valley. For those who have
the opportunity to drive through farm land on a regular basis, the
cycle of the seasons is very evident. The bare grapevines of winter
are pruned and stand out as stark silhouettes against the cold sky,
shadowy figures looming up eerily in the tule fog. As spring approaches green buds appear on the vines and turn into long
branches with luxuriant leaves that shade the newly forming clus-
ters of grapes. As the season progresses into summer the grapes
grow larger and hang heavily on the vines.

As harvest season approaches, the vineyards become a hub of
activity. Many of the grapes are picked and sent to market for
valley tables. Others are sent to wineries and become delicious
wines and brandies. For the grapes that remain, another purpose is
in store. They must stay on the vine until their optimum sugar
content is reached in late August or early September. Bundles of
paper trays begin to arrive. First, they are stacked at the end of
each vineyard row and are then spread evenly between the rows
next to the vines. The golden grapes are picked and spread evenly
on the trays to dry in the sun. By the seventh day, the tops of the
grapes have turned a dark color. The trays are then turned so the
bottom side of the grapes face the warm Valley sun. Then the trays
are rolled and turned over half way in a process called the "Biola
flip." By now, the grapes have become raisins and as they cure in
the tray, the moisture will even out between the juicier raisins
and the ones that are drier. The rolls of trays are picked up and the
raisins are dumped into bins. Next, they are placed in the raisin
shaker so all the sand is released. Then it's off to the packing house
and the supermarket shelves.

Raisins have become an important part of the commerce of
Fresno and the Central Valley. For those who live here, the mystery and magic of the process still exists as the golden grapes quietly soak up the September sun and turn into a delicacy enjoyed
all over the world.

Wooden grapetrays, used to dry grapes since the middle
1800s, have mostly been replaced by disposable paper trays.
*The Image Group from the Laval Historical Collection.*

# Fresno's Ragtime Rhythms

In 1885, in the town of Visalia, a future ragtime composer was born. As a small boy he moved to Fresno with his family. His mother was a talented musician who augmented the family income by teaching piano. His father was Fresno's first court reporter. The young boy inherited his mother's musical talents, but, as was the custom of the time, he followed in his father's profession and became a court reporter. He was hired by the firm of Gearhart, Baldwin & Price, a company that dealt with civil court cases.

Although he was considered an excellent court reporter, this young man was not entirely satisfied with his career. A gifted pianist, he began to compose music. About this time, he met J. Wesley Tilton, a musician who led the Fresno Military Band, which later became known as Tilton's Band. Between 1907 and 1914, the two men collaborated as song writers and publishers. The first musical arrangement they attempted was a song by Charles A. Pryor titled, "Oh, Ain't It Fun to Jolly in the Moonlight." Among their written hits were "That Society Rag" and the "Zig-Zag Rag." Their unique brand of sophisticated ragtime was popular locally and throughout the country.

Fresno's young ragtime composer was an inventor as well. His flat-leaf shorthand book and portable keyless lock were patented in 1928 and 1931.

A man of many talents, James W. Gearhart wrote his last songs in a residence in the 1200 block of North Van Ness Avenue in Fresno's Tower District. Today his toe-tapping music is still played by ragtime bands.

Dr. Chester Rowell rests on his front porch on K (Van Ness Avenue) near Tulare Street. The others in the picture are not identified. Dr. Rowell started the Fresno Morning Republican Newspaper and served three times as state senator. In 1912 he was elected mayor of Fresno.
*The Image Group from the Laval Historical Collection*

The history of all great cities contains moments when all the populace comes together to rejoice, give thanks or to mourn. On May 23, 1912, the citizens of Fresno united in grief when learning of the death of their mayor and friend, Dr. Chester Rowell. This man, who had played a great role in guiding the destiny of the frontier town of Fresno from 1874 until his death, was more than a political figure. As a physician, he had treated his patients, rich and poor alike, regardless of ability to pay. His good deeds were legendary.

At the news of his death, flags were placed at half mast. Many buildings were draped in black. Black crepe shrouded his city hall office. Two services were planned for Sunday, May 26. A private family service was held at 11:00 a.m. at the First Unitarian Church where later in the day thousands filed past his casket as he lay in state surrounded by bowers of floral tributes.

A public memorial service was scheduled at 2:00 p.m. in Courthouse Park. Here, at the heart of the city he loved so well, thousands of Fresnans stood beneath the huge shade trees in the shadow of the old courthouse, bowed their heads and paid their final respects. Many tears were shed as each person dealt with his own personal memories of the great man.

The Fresno Symphony Orchestra opened the service by playing Chopin's "Funeral March." The Reverend Clayton of the First Unitarian Church offered the opening prayer. Many eulogies followed, including a tribute from Benjamin Ide Wheeler, president of the University of California. Veterans of the Grand Army of the Republic arrived together to honor one of their own who had fought in the Union Army during the Civil War. Of the tributes offered on that spring afternoon in 1912, none was more significant than the shared grief of those in attendance, rich and poor, of many cultures and religions, gathering to show their love and respect. Perhaps a part of the resolution of the Chinese Merchants Association said it best: "...the death of one so broad and liberal in his treatment of his fellow men is a calamity to be deplored by all...."

Today, a seated figure cast in bronze is at the southeast corner of Courthouse Park. Designed by Armenian sculptor Haig Patigian and bearing the inscription, "Good Physician, Good Friend, Good Citizen," this memorial to Dr. Rowell will remind future Fresnans of this good man who left a rich legacy to his community.

# "The Grove"

The heat of an early Fresno summer was intense and un-yielding. The lack of large shade trees in the early days of the city made even a brief escape impossible. Ice, lemonade and whiskey helped and, after electricity became available, fans provided the some comfort.

For many families, the coastal communities beckoned. Pacific Grove, located on the Monterey Peninsula, was one of the most popular. "The Grove" was begun as a Methodist campground. It was a strict religious settlement with blue laws, many of which are still in place. But it was set along the most beautiful coastline in California and was cool and foggy in the summer. For Fresnans, it was the perfect getaway from the valley heat.

In the 1880s and '90s, the trip was arduous, lasting two or three days. Travelers left Fresno and journeyed by stagecoach to Pacheco Pass. The stage road over the pass was a hair-raising experience, and when the travelers arrived at Bell's Station a sigh of relief could be heard. A large hotel offered lodging, food and a respite from the jostling of the stage. The rest of the trip was easier. In Pacific Grove, rooms could be rented at the Centrella Hotel. Rooms also were available over Tuttle's Drugstore for one dollar a week.

By the 1910s, Pacific Grove was firmly fixed as the summer get-away for Fresnans. By then travel was easier. The family car had replaced the stagecoach. Packed to the hilt, the car would head out over the old stage roads of the west side. Stops to patch tires, traverse streams and cook meals along the way slowed down the trip, but if you left at three in the morning, you could reach Pacific Grove after dark that evening. Now the trip to "The Grove" takes just two and one-half hours.

As the heat of a Fresno summer soars, the descendants of those hardy Fresno pioneers still flock to this special place for a walk beside the sea to take a whiff of fragrant salt air and to let the mysterious bone-chilling fog envelope them just as it did their forbears. Some traditions are definitely meant to be cherished and savored.

The haunting beauty of Yosemite National Park, readily available to inhabitants of the Central Valley, is one of the special treasures that we share with visitors and speak of with pride.

But there are many who know of Yosemite's grandeur only through the photographs of a man who was born in San Francisco in 1902. During the 1906 earthquake his nose was broken by a falling brick. As a young man he studied music hoping to become a concert pianist. At the age of fourteen he visited Yosemite for the first time. Using a Number One Brownie box camera, he took his first photograph. The result fascinated him and he eventually studied with a photofinisher in San Francisco.

Until 1930, music and photography were equal interests for him. A year later he, Edward Weston and other photographers founded group f/64, dedicated to exploring the potentials of pure photography and named for the smallest available lens aperture.

In 1936, he had his first one-man show in New York. By this time he was an established West Coast photographer. His first photograph to win national fame was a view of Half Dome taken in 1927. As his career developed, he became a member of the board of directors of the Sierra Club, a position he held from 1934 to 1970. By 1974, he was considered the foremost photographer in the United States. His clean, crisp images of grand landscapes shared the beauty of our Sierra with those who could not travel to see them. He received numerous awards including the Medal of Freedom in 1980.

His special talents as a teacher were appreciated by over 5,000 students who attended his workshops over the years. Although he never lived here, members of his immediate family settled here, and the Fresno community claimed him as one of its own. His ability to capture and immortalize the beauty of Yosemite touched the hearts of Fresnans.

Who was this man? None other than Ansel Adams, the world's foremost nature photographer.

# A Log Cabin in the Woods

Visitors to Kings Canyon National Park have the unique opportunity to view the first building erected within Grant Grove. In the 1870s, this majestic and beautiful area, which contains the Giant Sequoias, was the property of Israel Gamlin, who had taken a squatter's claim to the area.

In the shadow of the tree that is today a memorial to General Grant, Israel Gamlin built a log cabin. The year was 1872. His cabin was rather primitive, containing only one room with a dirt floor. The first layer of logs rested directly on the ground. They were held together by corner notches, as were the succeeding layers. Each log was seven inches thick and one foot three inches high.

Before building the cabin, Israel and his brother, Thomas, found shelter in the Fallen Monarch log. Visitors can still see the evidence of their residency by looking at the burnt hole near the south side entrance. This was the exit point for their fire chimney. The log also was used to house overnight guests, thus becoming the first hotel in the district. It was also the first restaurant; here meals were cooked for visitors who came in search of the big trees.

Several years after the Gamlin brothers moved into the log cabin, the federal government began to survey the land. Finding that it contained so much natural beauty, Grant Grove was made a national park in 1890. Israel Gamlin gave up his claims to Grant Grove in return for timber lands elsewhere.

In 1892, the log cabin became a storage shed for the cavalry troops who guarded the park. It was dismantled and moved two-thirds of a mile southeast of its original location. Between 1902 and 1915, it was the home of L. L. Davis, the first civilian park ranger for the General Grant National Park. In 1932, a group of volunteers dismantled the cabin log by log and reassembled it at its original site.

Today, the restored Gamlin Cabin sits, once again, in the shadow of the magnificent General Grant Tree, the nation's official Christmas Tree. Listed on the National Register of Historic Places, it stands as a reminder of the early history of the Sierra and of the hardy pioneers who braved untraversed terrain to discover the hidden beauty of our mountain areas.

Raisins have long been a profitable commodity in the Central Valley, but leave it to Hollywood to make them rip-roaring good fun as well. In the mid-1980s, prime-time soap operas like *Dallas* and *Dynasty* won high ratings with viewers. Miniseries such as *The Thorn Birds* and *The Winds of War* also were tremendously popular. None of these programs was intentionally humorous, although there are some viewers who would probably disagree.

Producer Barry Kemp had been looking for an idea to spoof these programs. Reading one evening that Fresno had been listed at the bottom of a survey of desirable cities in which to live, Kemp had an inspired idea. Why not use Fresno and its number one crop, raisins, as the basis for a creative, satirical miniseries? The more he thought about it, the more perfect it seemed.

The story would center on two powerful families, the Canes and the Kensingtons, who were fighting for control of the raisin cartel. As the script began to take shape, it was decided that no laugh track would be used. In the manner of a true parody, it would be played deadpan and very seriously.

Trips to Fresno to scout out locations were made, including a trip to the home of California's first raisin baron, M. Theo Kearney. The producers decided not to use Kearney Mansion for exterior shots, but Kearney Boulevard would be used at the end of the program.

As all of Fresno held its breath, July of 1986 loomed on the horizon. It was then that the stars would arrive and filming would begin. The question that was asked by all was, "Will Fresno be able to laugh at '*Fresno*'?" Only time would tell.

July 15, 1986, the day the location shots would begin filming for the comedic *Fresno* miniseries, finally arrived. The Water Tower had been scrubbed and Kearney Boulevard had been spruced up. Fresnans were ready for the Hollywood invasion.

On that hot Fresno Monday morning, large vans that would be used as dressing rooms were parked east of the Memorial Auditorium. Fresnans crowded along Fresno Street. As actress Carol Burnett, who played matriarch Charlotte Kensington, emerged from her van to do her first scene, fans asked her to do her Tarzan yell. She gave forth with her trademark ape call that seem to carry to the highest reaches of the Water Tower across the street. The excitement had begun.

The zany plot of the show pitted two feuding raisin families, the Kensingtons and the Canes, against each other for control of the raisin cartel. Dabney Coleman played Tyler Cane, Charlotte's nemesis. Charles Grodin, who portrayed Cane Kensington, Charlotte's power-hungry son, described his character to Fresno fans that day as a sort of J. R. Ewing of *Dallas* fame.

As the day progressed and the heat soared to 102 degrees, fans watched as two thugs and Anthony Heald, playing Kevin Kensington, chased Cane around the top of the Water Tower. Catching Cane, Kevin tried to choke his brother, then the two thugs tried unsuccessfully to throw Cane over the railing.

The next day filming took place west of town. The two thugs took Cane for a ride, looking for a place to dump him. They ended up at the Quist Dairy at Polk and Church Avenues.

Shooting wrapped up. The actors and crew flew back to Hollywood. Fresnans were left to ponder a CBS news release which described the satirical miniseries as a sweeping saga of greed, lust and dried grapes in Fresno, "Raisin Capital of the World." They also were left with the memory of footage on the nightly news showing Mayor Dale Doig presenting Burnett, Grodin and producer Barry Kemp with a silver platter of raisins. Yes, indeed, Fresno has a sense of humor.

"The power, the passion, the produce"—the miniseries *Fresno* burst onto the TV screen the night of Sunday, November 16, 1986. A gala premiere party was held to celebrate this media event. For $125 each, 206 Fresnans were "Golden Raisins" for a day. This entitled them to attend a cocktail party at the Metropolitan Museum, dine at the Centre Plaza Holiday Inn, enjoy dessert at the Saroyan Theater, view the opening segment of *Fresno* and be whisked to and from the event by limousine. Premiere parties were held all over Fresno.

A particularly lavish one was hosted in Washington, D.C. by valley Congressman Tony Coelho. With over three hundred people in attendance wearing "Fresno" T-shirts, Coelho's party was one of the largest. As his guests feasted on California cuisine, they laughed uproariously at the show and joined Fresnans in giving the miniseries a "thumbs-up."

As the week progressed and the TV story unfolded each night, the laughing continued. After the final segment, which included Mayor Dale Doig dressed as the King of Siam at a Raisin Ball, Fresnans were relieved. The miniseries was a rich parody of nighttime soaps *Dallas* and *Dynasty* and left Fresno's image intact, or possibly, enhanced. After being the butt of jokes for so long, Fresnans got the last laugh. For one week in November of 1986, the entire country tuned in to *Fresno*. The name of our city was on everyone's tongue. As the miniseries drew to a close, the whole country saw Charlotte Kensington climb into the back of her station wagon and announce in her best Scarlett O'Hara voice that "Tomorrow is another day." As the scene ends, her chauffeur drives her down Kearney Boulevard and into history.

As Anthony Heald, the actor who played Kevin Kensington, said, "It takes a city with a personality to take a ribbing." As the country found out, Fresno has a great personality.

# Yosemite's Enchanted Christmas

Each Christmas season a sense of enchantment envelops Yosemite Valley. The stately evergreen pines are shrouded in white and the Merced River slows to a trickle that flows among snow-covered rocks. The valley is filled with silence. As the traveler drives along the slippery road, the majesty of his surroundings fills him with awe.

The Ahwahnee Hotel, his destination, is soon reached. On entering its doors he is transported to a Christmas celebration that, for most, exists only in the imagination, in that realm of wistful yearning for the gaiety, pomp, and rich texture of another era.

As evening comes, the halls of the Ahwahnee resound with trumpets as heralds summon guests to dinner. The huge doors of the dining room are opened and the guests enter Bracebridge Hall, the medieval preserve of Squire Bracebridge. Elizabethan-costumed hostesses greet the guests, who are escorted to their tables. As the heralds sound their trumpets once again, the Squire and his party proceed through the dining hall to the high table, where they will preside over festivities which will last for several hours. Choral music, a minstrel and the comic pranks of the Lord of Misrule set the tone for the evening's festivities. The Squire's Housekeeper leads a procession of lackeys, each carrying dishes for the Squire's approval. As each successive course is presented, the hall rings with the sounds of English carols. The fish, peacock pie, boar's head, flaming plum pudding and wassail bowl are borne in great state as they make their ceremonial appearance. Lastly, the Housekeeper presents branches of holly, symbols of Christ's Crown of Thorns, to the Squire. As the chorus sings "Deck the Halls," the Squire and his entourage leave the hall.

The mystical spell that the Bracebridge Dinner weaves for all its guests is the result of a desire to create a pageant at the Awhahnee that would become a tradition. In 1927, the year the hotel opened, a unique event was created using the Christmas portion of the *Sketch Book* by Washington Irving that has become a California legend. Those who are fortunate enough to attend carry with them memories of Christmas past that will never be forgotten.

# The Big Fig Garden Flood

Fresno, located at the convergence of three creeks, has seen many floods. One of the worst occurred in 1884 when flood waters rose to such a point that citizens had to use boats to travel to and from work.

Fifty-four years later, in March of 1938, the new development of Fig Garden, today called Old Fig Garden, came under siege. From February 28 to the third of March, heavy rains pelted Fresno, setting a rainfall record of over four inches for those dates. All of this water plus the runoff from a melting heavy winter snowpack caused the north bank of the Herndon Canal to become weak and to overflow. Most of the water extended north from Dakota Avenue to Indianapolis Avenue and westward to Palm Avenue and the Santa Fe railroad tracks. Hardest hit was the Lansing Way and Van Ness Boulevard area where water reached a depth of six feet. Adobe homes melted away. The residents of two-story homes fled the onrushing waters to the second floor of their homes and there awaited rescue.

Deputy sheriffs, Red Cross workers, American Legion members and other volunteers manned every available rowboat to rescue stranded homeowners. Some people were found standing on tables and beds in their homes, frantically awaiting help.

In 1948, Big Dry Creek Dam was completed. This structure was an effort to control the water from Big Dry Creek which flowed into the Herndon Canal. However, the city was still at risk from smaller streams such as Dog Creek and Red Bank Creek, which flowed into the canals that brought water through Fresno. Finally, in 1993, the Red Bank Fancher Creek Flood Control Project was completed. In this project, which was a joint effort of the Fresno Metropolitan Flood Control District and the U. S. Army Corps of Engineers, five major dams and reservoirs were constructed. At last, 109 years after the Big Fresno Flood of 1884 and 55 years after the Fig Garden Flood of 1938, Fresnans can enjoy the rain without worrying about possibly having to use rowboats to navigate through town.

A southerly view shows Van Ness Boulevard and the surrounding area under water the week of February 2, 1938. *The Image Group from the Laval Historical Collection.*

# A Scrolled Cornice Bracket

In the not-so-far distant past, downtown Fresno was a beautiful city filled with Victorian and Queen Anne buildings interspersed with stately Classic Revival multistoried structures dating to the early years of this century. It was a feast for the eyes and bustled with activity. It was the commercial and business center for the Central Valley.

Today, many of the turn-of-the-century buildings have fallen victim to the wrecker's ball and, in many cases, have not been replaced with another structure. As one traverses downtown Fresno and views the many parking lots and empty spaces, does one ever wonder what happens to historic buildings when they are torn down? Are their intriguing architectural components lost forever or do they end up on the mantelpiece of someone who cared enough to save them?

One particular building on T Street, called the Osborn residence, was torn down in 1983, but for a brief period of time lived on in another dimension. When the building was demolished, a local architectural historian and artist visited the site and salvaged a scrolled cornice bracket that had graced the facade of this once-important historic home. The bracket reposed in his rose garden collecting moss for almost a decade.

In November of 1991, it became the inspiration for a heroic-sized mural on the south wall of the Fresno Art Museum. Using bold, primary colors, the artist John Edward Powell, assisted by artist Mallory Moad, painted two juxtaposed views of the bracket that serve to eulogize the demise of the structure.

For at least one historic building that is lost to Fresno, a piece of it lived on for a short span of time, until August of 1992 when the building was repainted. In the meantime, the mural served as a reminder to the community that when a historic building is torn down, it cannot be replaced. As our architectural heritage is lost, the beauty and substance of our city is diminished.

As one leaves downtown Fresno and drives north on Van Ness Avenue, one leaves the business district behind and enters a neighborhood that was once residential. Few homes remain, but tucked beneath the trees on the northwest corner of San Joaquin Street and Van Ness Avenue stands an impressive structure that was once the home of Frank Romain, one of the pioneer agricultural developers in the Fresno area.

Born in Toronto, Canada, in 1861, Romain came to Riverside, California, after graduating from business college. He went to work for the Griffith-Skelly Company and soon was in charge of the entire plant.

He was sent to Fresno in the 1880s to establish a packing plant for his company in the "Raisina Vineyard" of the Central California Colony. It was probably the first operation of its kind in the Fresno area. In 1916, the Griffin-Skelly Company merged with four other companies to create the California Packing Corporation. This new company operated about one hundred canneries and packing plants in California and had assets of over sixteen million dollars. Romain was named manager of sixteen of these plants.

The importance of the role he played in the development of the packing industry of the Central Valley cannot be overstated. When he died in 1928, all of the valley packing plants closed at noon the next day as a sign of respect.

After his death, the home that he had built in 1904 was sold to the Sullivan, Burns and Blair Funeral Home. One of the partners, Hugh Burns, served in the California State Legislature for forty years.

The building was later sold to William Whitehurst, who also operated a funeral home within its walls. A prominent community leader, Whitehurst served as co-chairman for numerous political campaigns and was appointed by Governor Edmund Brown to the State Highway Commission. Whitehurst's son, Daniel, continued the family tradition of political involvement by becoming the youngest person ever elected to the Fresno City Council and by being elected mayor at age twenty-eight. At that time, he was the youngest elected mayor of a large American city.

Today, the Romain Home is listed on the National Register of Historic Places. Its significance lies not only in its link to the early agribusiness of Fresno County, but also in the rich legacy of public service that its succession of owners have left to this community.

On the northwest corner of Van Ness Avenue and Calaveras Street stands a structure which has had a happier
renaissance than have many historic buildings. Built in 1922 in a
modified palazzo style by Sacramento architect Leonard F. Starks,
it was designed to house the *Fresno Bee* newspaper operations. The
*Bee* was the newest branch of the Sacramento-based James
McClatchy Publishing Company. For the first ten years of its existence, the *Fresno Bee* had to compete with the *Fresno Morning Republican*, which had served the pioneer community of Fresno so
well. By 1932, the *Bee* had absorbed the *Republican* and had attained the role of the leading newspaper in the area.

As the circulation and press operations grew and new technology was introduced, the building underwent a number of al-
terations. In 1936, an important addition to the building was a
studio for Fresno's first radio station, KMJ. The architectural firm
of Franklin and Kump designed this facility.

Over fifty years after the structure was completed, the *Fresno
Bee* moved to a new, more modern facility on E Street in west
Fresno. The old building now stood empty and vulnerable.

At the same time, community efforts were underway to find
a site for a much needed museum. Generous donations from the
McClatchy family and the formation of a committee of community leaders to explore the development of the *Bee* building as a
museum site provided a beginning. As community support grew,
the museum project got underway. The result was a rehabilita-
tion project that converted the former newspaper site into the
Fresno Metropolitan Museum. Today, the building is listed on the
National Register of Historic Places and is a source of pride for the
community.

# Fresno's Ivy League Streets

As you travel north through the Tower District of Fresno, you may notice that many of the east/west streets are named for universities. When Fresno State Normal School was established in 1913, it was located one-half mile north of the city limits on what was then called an "extension" of Van Ness Avenue. The street that ran in front of the Administration Building was named University Avenue. One street that ran perpendicular to it was named College Avenue. When you stood in the middle of this street, you looked straight ahead to the front door of the Administration Building.

As residential neighborhoods developed around the school, which in 1921 became known as Fresno State Teachers College, many of the streets were named for eastern universities. The names Yale, Cambridge, Vassar, Harvard, Brown, Princeton, and Cornell all helped give the area an academic flavor. The area was popular among the faculty, many of whom purchased homes there.

When you travel north on Van Ness Avenue and make the sweeping curve onto Maroa Avenue, take note of the tree-lined streets of the surrounding neighborhoods. These add to the eastern feeling of the area. This, along with the Ivy League street names, is a reminder of the time when this Fresno neighborhood centered around Fresno State College.

From the 1920s well into the 1950s, the residents of the area walked to the college for live theatrical performances, lectures and concerts. The college was the cultural hub of the community.

Today, many of the original Fresno State buildings have been torn down. As of this writing, the library, with its original ceiling murals, is still in use. However, the Old Administration Building stands vacant. Once the center of campus life, this outstanding example of Spanish Renaissance architecture is in danger of demolition. Many of those trying to save the building attended school within its walls. For them, saving the building means saving the memories of an important part of their lives. If it is torn down, only the library and the Ivy League street names will remain to remind people of the brick buildings with the ivy covered walls that made up the original Fresno State College.

In the years before Senator Wilbur F. Chandler made his field available to the city for use as an airport, the San Joaquin Valley Aeronautical Association developed a map of a proposed airfield. It would be located on a 360-acre parcel on Barstow Avenue just west of Highway 99. The need for such a facility, where planes carrying airmail and parcels could land, certainly existed, but funds were in short supply for such a project.

However, area fliers made their concerns known in the local newspaper. The two existing fields, Mullins Field due west of Roeding Park and another near Blackstone and Barstow avenues, were so dangerous, they said, that their airplanes were being wrecked, to say nothing of the potential threat of personal danger when using these facilities. Mullins Field was so hazardous it was called Crematory Field.

In the light of this distressing situation, the Fresno County Chamber of Commerce launched a campaign to raise funds to make improvements to the Barstow property so that it could become a proper airfield. Roy Woodward chaired the fund-raising committee. Their goal of $5,000 was soon reached, a lease on the property was obtained, and the necessary improvements were made.

On September 15, 1926, the first flight arrived at the Barstow field, now renamed Maddox Airport. What excitement there was as city and county officials, businessmen and other interested onlookers witnessed the first landing of a plane carrying airmail from the north! Among the mail was a parcel addressed to Radin & Kamp containing garments that were needed for a sale that evening. Thus was Fresno's airmail service launched. Passenger service was available from Maddox Field as well.

When one longs for the "good old days" it is important to remember that they were often a mixed blessing. Although the airmail rate was a very reasonable ten cents an ounce, an air trip to Los Angeles or San Francisco took about two hours.

B ecause of its geographic location, halfway between San Francisco and Los Angeles, Fresno has always been a logical overnight stopping place for touring companies and concert artists. Its fine opera houses, Grady's and the Barton, provided a luxurious arena for performances which were enjoyed by Fresnans of the 1880s and 1890s. But what about the young people in the community? Did they appreciate the cultural arts as well?

In the mid-1890s, a three-story building was erected at the corner of Mariposa and O streets. Its rather imposing facade was capped by a large sign just under the eaves stating that this was the Central California Conservatory of Music. It was established to provide the young people of Fresno with an opportunity to enhance their character through the study of music. Within its walls, the sounds of piano, voice and numerous instruments could be heard.

The director of the conservatory was Professor Paul Fast, who had received his musical training in Germany. Under his guidance, the school grew rapidly. More teachers were hired, all with fine musical credentials, and additional classes were added to the curriculum. Now the young people of Fresno could also study voice culture so their speech would be a pleasing attribute which they would carry through life.

The conservatory faculty was proud to offer young people a course of study that had not been available in Fresno. The frontier town with its unpaved streets was acquiring a degree of sophistication. That all of this was taken very seriously was evident in the conservatory's motto. It read, "To educate and not amuse."

# The Short Home

In 1925, the death of a well respected member of the Fresno community brought about an unusual chain of events. In that year, Mrs. Nellie Curtis Short, the widow of attorney Frank Hamilton Short, bequeathed her formal classical revival mansion and surrounding gardens to the city of Fresno. Her will was very clear in its intentions. The home was to be used by the city as an art gallery, reading room and lecture and concert hall. Another stipulation was that the house could never be torn down. The city accepted the gift and allocated $3,000 to maintain the home for one year.

After little community interest was shown, Mayor Al E. Sunderland appointed a committee of seven to find uses for the home. The Fresno Historical Society used two of the rooms for exhibits. Rotary donated thirty-two statues that could be displayed in the home and gardens. However, the lack of an organized art group made it difficult to combat general public indifference about using the home.

The Short family requested that the property be given back to them. The city tried to get them to modify the restrictions concerning the home. The family refused. Finally, in 1938, the Short family brought a title suit against the city aimed at recovering the property. A compromise was finally reached. The city was given $5,000 and the property was returned to the heirs of the Short estate.

After the property was sold several times, it was purchased by I. Magnin & Company in 1954. The structure was modernized, but the original brick outer walls remain. The magnificent ballroom is still intact on an upper floor. Little remains on the northeast corner of Calaveras Street and Van Ness Avenue to let us know that it was once graced by a luxurious mansion.

Arte Americas, a cultural arts center designed to make the Central Valley a place where Latino art and culture can flourish, now occupies the modern building on the site of the Short home. On the opposite corner of this downtown Fresno intersection, the Fresno Metropolitan Museum receives visitors eager to experience art and culture.

It is ironic that the city had to return this valuable property because no one wanted to create a center for the arts at this site. Today the neighborhood in which the Short home stood is again being considered as a cultural arts distict.

# Kings River Switch

In 1872, after the route for the Central Pacific Railroad had been chosen by Leland Stanford, the line was built through the valley. As it progressed on its southward march from Lathrop, a new railroad town just south of Stockton named for Mrs. Stanford's family, railroad stops were chosen and new towns sprung up.

In late April of 1872, Fresno Station was founded. The new line continued south, reaching the Kings River in May. By mid-summer it had been completed as far south as Goshen.

In 1873, it was decided that a switching point should be established on the line near the Kings River. It was appropriately named the Kings River Switch. Goods could be unloaded from the train and grain could be shipped off to markets from the "Switch."

The first people to settle near the "Switch" were Andrew Farley and Josiah Draper. When they arrived they each took a quarter section of land, Farley on the west side of the tracks and Draper on the east. Thomas Cowan arrived soon afterward and settled northwest of Draper's land. The little settlement began to grow.

In 1874, a post office was established and the town was officially named Wheatville. Farley, who had opened a general store, became the first postmaster. Draper built a hotel. A blacksmith shop and several saloons were also opened. The new town acquired quite a reputation. Since most of the buildings were marked by bullet holes, Wheatville came to be known as "the toughest place" between Los Angeles and San Francisco.

By the end of 1874, another name change had taken place. Now the town was known as Kingsbury, named for a man who was a clerk for the Central Pacific Railroad. Soon the name was changed to Kingsburg, the name that has endured.

Today, Kingsburg is a city noted for its clean, tidy streets and Swedish atmosphere. It has come a long way since the days when it was called Kings River Switch.

# The Great Camp Pinedale Offensive

After the outbreak of World War II, there was a shortage of facilities to house soldiers in the Fresno area. Hammer Field, a two million dollar bomber base, was established at Shields and Clovis avenues. Many soldiers were housed at that site. Other soldiers were billeted at Camp Pinedale, a United States Army Signal Corps training school, which was located at Herndon and Palm avenues.

Camp Pinedale was rather primitive. The buildings were made of clapboard, faced with tar paper and had hard concrete floors. Many of the men were housed in tents. The sanitary facilities were of the nineteenth-century variety. Needless to say, living there was not a pleasant experience.

As the months wore on, calisthentics joined marching as the soldiers endured their training. Grenade course trials followed and then, in September of 1943, the real test came. A number of units were going to be dispatched to the San Joaquin River bluffs, where a simulated attack would take place.

The troops were marched for eight miles over open fields dotted with barns as they headed for the bluffs. During this year the rains had been generous and the San Joaquin River channels were filled with water. The troops crossing the river had to wade through water that was chest high. When the signal for attack was given, the soldiers bravely forded the rushing water. On reaching the other side they broke out their gas masks and, donning them, scrambled up the steep bank to the top of the bluffs. The sandy soil made this difficult, but the tenacious soldiers did not give up until their destination was reached. Exhausted and panting for breath, they slowly made their way back to camp.

Today, the San Joaquin River bluffs are lined with luxurious homes. Few residents are probably aware that at one time their neighborhood was the locale of that bone-wearying event historians may one day call "The Great Camp Pinedale Offensive."

# An Old-Fashioned Pharmacy

When you walk toward the middle of the 4200 block of East Tulare Street, a neon sign over the Vista Pharmacy catches your eye. Could it be original? As you enter the store and see two art deco counters containing 1930s glass blocks and walls lined with shelves that date back to an even earlier time, you just know the sign has to have been in place since the store opened.

Before you can ponder any longer, a friendly voice calls, "Hello, may I help you?" You look up to see the smiling face of Jim Winton, the proprietor of Fresno's oldest family-owned drugstore, celebrating over sixty continuous years at this location.

City planners told Jim's father, J. Martin Winton, that he was making a big mistake by locating his drugstore in the middle of the block. Only corner drugstores succeed, they said. But, he knew something the planners had not considered, that offering the public good service in a friendly atmosphere was more important than location. Indeed, it was the key to the future.

Throughout its history, the Vista Pharmacy has offered free delivery service to Fresno residents. From opening day, September 9, 1932, and throughout the 1930s, boys on bicycles sped through the streets of Fresno delivering medicine to customers. The bicycles were later replaced by three-wheeled motorcycles.

On the evening of one of the big Roosevelt-Fresno High football games, one zealous delivery boy made an unscheduled round of the track at Ratcliffe Stadium on his motorcycle bearing the Vista Pharmacy sign in all its glory. It caused quite a sensation.

Today, three cars and four people are required to keep deliveries going out to customers. They travel 90,000 miles a year.

One special feature of the business during the 1930s through the 1950s was Pete Hill's ice cream parlor next door. It was a popular neighborhood place that shared an interior door with Vista until a fire marshal insisted the door be filled in.

Today, in spite of the large chain stores which are flocking to Fresno, the Vista Pharmacy bustles with customers. Many have a special loyalty. One patron remembers the time years ago when he could not afford to pay for medicine for his three sick children. Although he was a first-time customer, he was given the medicine. He promised to pay as soon as he could. He kept his word and has been a loyal customer ever since. His three children, now grown, are also.

As it continues its years of service to the Fresno community, the Vista Pharmacy is making history as well. Jim's son, James Michael Winton, has graduated from pharmacy school and has become the third generation in this family business—a legacy in the truest sense.

# A 20th Century Fur Trapper

When one thinks of fur trapping, one's mind goes back to another century when our country's frontier was unexplored except by the few whose dreams gave them the courage to blaze a path through an unknown territory. Indeed, by the nineteenth century, fur trapping had become a major industry in the west. But would one ever guess that during the twentieth century, from 1910 to 1961 to be exact, a fur trapper named James Walter (Shorty) Lovelace plied his trade in the area that is today a part of Kings Canyon National Park? As incredible as it may seem, Shorty spent the greater part of his life trapping in the Sierra Nevada.

Born near Three Rivers in 1886, by his late teens Shorty had become an alcoholic. He finally decided that the only way he could conquer his addiction was to live away from civilization. He turned to the mountains for refuge. In 1910, he moved his operations to the upper Kings Canyon region where he had the unique distinction of being the only Caucasian to ever inhabit this part of the Sierra on a long-term year-round basis. Within five years, he was trapping along most of the watershed of the south fork of the Kings River from an elevation of 4,600 feet to above the 12,000-foot line.

He built a succession of approximately thirty-six small cabins and shelters, each a day apart, throughout the 200-mile area of his operations. Many of them were kept fully stocked with provisions in case he got snowed in. All but one of these sites consisted of either a small one-room log cabin or a shelter housed between large native boulders. The design and use of these cabins and shelters was very close to those used by fur trappers in the Rocky Mountains in the 1820s. This very simple type of dwelling worked well for a trapper who spent the winter months in the isolated mountain areas.

Each spring Shorty, so named because he stood five-feet, four-inches tall, would come down from the mountains briefly to bring out his furs for trade. In 1940, when Kings Canyon became a national park, Shorty moved his fur trapping operations to the north fork of the Kings River, outside the park. He did not leave the mountains until 1961, two years before his death.

Today, nine of his cabins and shelters comprise the Shorty Lovelace Historic District. Listed on the National Register of Historic Places, visitors to this part of the Sierra have the opportunity to see these reminders of a man who chose to leave civilization and live at one with nature.

The first Swedish immigrant to settle in Kingsburg, Frank D. Rosendahl, had studied landscape gardening and horticulture in Stockholm. Before settling in Kingsburg, he played a role in the design of New York's Central Park and of Golden Gate Park in San Francisco. After settling in Kingsburg, he was made a justice of the peace, thus, he was given the title Judge. His brother, the Reverend E. G. Rosendahl, followed him to this small town in 1888. Other Swedish immigrants soon followed.

The first real estate agent in Kingsburg, A. A. Smith, sold a number of properties to a group of Swedes who had settled in Ishpeming, Michigan. At least nine members of this group purchased properities adjoining Sierra and 18th avenues. Led by Andrew Ericson, they represented the principal early Swedish colony.

As other Swedes flocked to Kingsburg, their influence was greatly felt. Once known as the "toughest city between San Francisco and Los Angeles," the community became more sedate as these sober, hardworking people became integrated into the life of the town. By 1921, 94 percent of the population within a three-mile radius of Kingsburg was Swedish.

Today, a visit to downtown Kingsburg is a delightful experience. With its large, brightly colored dala horses on the light standards lining Draper Street and the charming shops to be explored, the city has truly carried out its Swedish village theme.

Although Kingsburg is always an enjoyable place to visit, the four-day Swedish Festival, which is held each May, is the highlight of the year. Beginning on Thursday evening with a Swedish pancake supper, continuing with a smorgasbord dinner on Friday night, a parade on Saturday and ending with a church service on Sunday evening, this event reminds Kingsburg residents of their unique heritage and gives the residents of the Central Valley another reason to value the rich and varied ethnic traditions that are a part of life in this corner of California.

# Raisins, Raisins & More Raisins

Several years ago, a traveler from Fresno was visiting the northernmost reaches of Europe, near the Arctic Circle, where a people called Laplanders live. Invited into a small hut, he was amazed to see a red box with its unmistakable trademark of a girl in a red sunbonnet sitting on a table. "Amazing," he thought, "even in this far corner of the world Sun-Maid raisins are enjoyed!"

This sun-dried fruit, which most valley residents take for granted, is processed and packaged using the most demanding quality control standards in the industry. Its packages are translated into nine different languages and are shipped to more than twenty-five countries all over the world. This is quite a story for a cooperative organization of raisin growers that was established more than eighty years ago.

During the turbulent early years before the establishment of this raisin cooperative, raisin growers had a struggle selling their crop to packers who dealt on a commission basis. Working together seemed the only way. Early attempts met with failure. M. Theo Kearney, Fresno's mysterious raisin baron, became president of the California Raisin Growers Association. He tried to organize the growers. His efforts met with some success, but ultimately his squabbles with the growers and then his death in 1906 left the situation unresolved.

Finally, in 1907, Peter Droge, owner of the La Paloma Vineyard, evolved a plan for a new growers cooperative to be known as the California Associated Raisin Company, which ultimately became the Sun-Maid Raisin Company.

Today, the success of this local company can be measured in its total production figures. During peak periods, more than two million fifteen-ounce cartons are shipped all over the world. In addition to standard raisins, golden raisins, Zante currants and seeded muscats are boxed and shipped to stores. A special cereal-size raisin is sent to cereal companies so that millions of consumers can enjoy them in their bran cereal at breakfast. All of this shows there is a Sun-Maid raisin for every use. As the brightly colored boxes travel to markets far and near, this Central Valley fruit lives up to its trademark name of "The World's Favorite Raisin."

# Fashions & Foibles

For the young matron of 1880 Fresno, fashion was very important. Even though the streets were unpaved and travel was by wagon or horseback, women followed the style of dress that was popular in other, less rural, parts of the country. Long dresses with tight sleeves and high collars were worn even when the temperature soared over a hundred degrees. Tight corsets that were pulled even tighter and then laced to hold them in place allowed women the opportunity to appear in public in much admired tiny-waisted dresses. Such apparel also gave women an excuse, or more likely, a reason to faint at appropriate times. Such displays were often accompanied by nervous flutterings and usually occurred when a gentleman was present—thus becoming a part of the courtship ritual.

Hairstyles also followed the dictates of fashion. A woman never allowed her hair to be cut during her lifetime. As she reached her eighteenth birthday, she ceased to wear her hair down and began to pin it up in an elaborate style. This necessitated the use of large tortoise shell combs and bone hairpins to keep it in place. Such hairdos were lovely to look at, but not always practical for the young matron in a frontier town.

One young lady in particular, Belle Ellen McKay, lived with her husband at Church and Elm avenues in Fresno Colony. One Saturday evening, as a respite at the end of the week, she decided to go horseback riding with her visiting brother-in-law. Their horses galloped along as they circled the colony area. "How wonderful," she thought, "to be so carefree and to feel the wind in my hair." Upon arriving home at dusk, she realized her hair had fallen down and all her bone hairpins were gone! As dawn broke on Sunday morning, Belle could be seen walking along the horse path looking for her hairpins. She certainly could not attend church until they were found and her hair was once again properly held in place. Fashions may change, but one's adherence to them goes on forever.

In the spring of 1956, Alan L. Funch Sr. (right) and an unidentified man discuss the sign advertising the new shopping center, Fig Garden Village, that was being built at Palm and Shaw avenues.
*John Frigulti photo. Courtesy of Fig Garden Management Office.*

In the early 1900s, George Sherman purchased a large acreage of grain north of Fresno. He built a fine home and planted peaches and grapes as supplemental crops. His holdings did well and he continued to farm his property for many years.

In the years following World War II, Fresno's growth moved northward. By the beginning of the 1950s, residences were being built north of Shields Avenue and, by 1960, Shaw Avenue had been crossed.

In the early 1950s, the only major shopping area in Fresno was downtown. By this time Sherman's daughter, Ellen, had married Allen Funch. They dreamed of creating a shopping center on the

Sherman property. Comprised of quality specialty stores that were operated by the owner of each business, this project would indeed be unique. They hired architect John E. Fennacy to design the three main buildings which would be the core of the development.

In the spring of 1956 construction began. By the fall of that year the building that would house the grocery store and six other small shops was completed. Other buildings were added one at a time. A large drugstore was built on land that had been the site of George Sherman's home.

Today this center, Fig Garden Village, bustles with activity. Wide, covered walkways, beautiful stores and fine restaurants draw people from all over Fresno. Still owned by the family that farmed this land almost one hundred years ago, the "Village" takes its name from the fig gardens that surround it. However, during the years this property was a farm, not even one fig tree was grown on the property.

Christmas 1957 at the newly built Fig Garden Village.
*Courtesy of Fig Garden Management Office.*

# The Sample Sanitarium

The old building in the 300 block of North Fulton Street stands vacant, boarded up against would-be plunderers, its tile roof the one last vestige of the stateliness it once possessed. Graffiti adorns its walls as it stands silent, amid a few last palm trees, awaiting a new freeway to complete its swath across the land to the north.

This structure, one of only two original hospital buildings left in Fresno, was once an important fixture in the exclusive North Park area. Administered by Dr. Thomas Sample and his efficient nurse, Miss Zerlang, this edifice was a refuge for the ill. Dr. Sample, a son of pioneer David Cowan Sample, was an old-fashioned doctor in the best sense. He treated all who came for help, regardless of their ability to pay.

The third-floor surgery room was the birthplace of many Fresnans who were born during the 1930s and 1940s, and they quite likely feel a pang of regret every time they drive past the empty building.

The once-proud Sample Sanitarium faces an uncertain future. Not protected by inclusion on the city's historic list, it may be razed unless someone rescues it and converts it to an office building or finds some other type of adaptive reuse for the structure. There is a sadness about this stately edifice as it awaits the future and what that may hold.

# The Home of Clovis Cole

The name of Clovis Cole, who was known as the "Wheat King of the Nation," evokes thoughts of a city northeast of Fresno named for him. This was most appropriate because he donated land from his 50,000-acre holdings for the railroad and town-site of present-day Clovis.

Cole came to Fresno County in 1873 and lived here until his death in 1939. What most valley residents may not know is that he built a home in Fresno.

After the depression of 1893 and a severe drought, he scaled down his wheat ranching operations. He moved with his family to Fresno, where, in 1916, he built a home on U Street. He hired the Hansen Construction Company, one of Fresno's leading builders, to do the project. The two-story structure was of neoclassical design and featured a hipped roof with a small cantilevered balcony on the second floor. Two fluted Roman-style columns extended from the porch to the roof and gave the home an impressive facade.

After Cole's death and then his wife's death nine years later, their daughter, Ida, and her husband moved into the house. In 1958 the property was sold to Caltrans for a freeway project right-of-way. In that same year the home was purchased and moved to its present location on the 3600 block of Kerckhoff Avenue.

The Clovis Cole home is listed on Fresno's Official Register of Historic Resources. It stands as a reminder of Clovis Cole, the man for whom Clovis was named. It is interesting to note, Cole's father, S. H. Cole, served as the chairman of the board of trustees of Fresno from 1891 to 1893, thus making him the mayor of Fresno.

# The Fresno Adventist Academy

When one thinks of the name of Moses Church, one conjures up visions of canals bringing water through our county, thus creating endless possibilities for agriculture. Did you know that Church's contributions reached far beyond that?

On a Friday evening in March of 1888, Mrs. Ellen G. White, national leader of the Seventh-day Adventist Church, paid a condolence call on Church, who was mourning his wife's death. During the visit, she proposed the idea of building a church, a school and a mission house in Fresno. Church not only supported the idea, but he became the guiding force behind the project. Two days later, the members of the Seventh-day Adventist Church, who had been meeting in various locations, pledged $30,000 for the project.

The church building was completed later that year. Built of brick with a clock tower, the handsome edifice dominated the southeast corner of O and Mariposa streets for many years.

It wasn't until 1897 that the church school began. In that year, twenty-five children were enrolled. They met in the back rooms of the church building. Curriculum included the three R's and the Bible. The girls were taught sewing, tailoring, darning, and patching while the boys learned chair caneing and shoe repairing.

In 1903, the first eighth grade graduating class consisted of nine female students. Three years later, in 1906, the school's campus moved to North Fruit and Napa avenues. Some of the students drove horse and wagon to school, which required them to make sure that their horses were watered and fed during lunch hour. By 1908, the school had grown—thirty-eight students were enrolled in the first five grades and twenty-one in the upper grades.

In 1917, George Driver donated five acres of land at 841 West Belmont Avenue for a new campus, and the ten-grade Fresno Academy opened in 1919. In 1929, the school was named Fresno Union Academy and offered grades one through twelve. Forty years later, the campus was moved to 5397 East Olive Avenue and the name became the Fresno Adventist Academy.

In 1997, the academy celebrated its 100th birthday. Still thriving, with 300 students enrolled, it is an lasting legacy from Moses Church, whose vision for Fresno reached beyond agriculture.

For sixty years, photo enthusiasts have flocked to a store at 69 East Belmont Avenue for their supplies. Actually, the store was first located at D and Mono streets in the basement of the family home. After returning from an eleven-year stint in the Navy, Peter developed some of the photos he had taken during those years and showed his fifteen-year-old nephew Rueben how to make a print. Pleased with his efforts, Peter took out a business license for one dollar and opened his business. He charged his customers twenty-five cents to develop and print a roll of black and white film. Rueben often delivered the orders.

Three years later, in 1940, Peter Horn moved his business to the Belmont location. A few years later he asked Rueben to become a partner. The building on Belmont was originally a three-bedroom home with a hardware store in front owned by the Goodenough family. Later, it was a pet store.

In 1952, John Horn, Rueben's younger brother, began working in the family business. becoming a partner in 1958. In 1961, Peter Horn died. In the late 1960s, Bradley, Rueben's son, began to work in the business and also became a partner.

In 1959, Horn Photo, out of 12,000 dealers across the country, was named Polaroid dealer of the year nationwide. The business has been a Kodak dealer for over fifty years.

In 1991, the business was sold to Stan and Shelly Grosz. Bradley left the business to go into commercial photography. Rueben decided he wanted to retire. Shelly worked in agribusiness as an accountant. Stan is a livestock photographer. They decided to buy the business on the condition that John Horn would stay on as manager, they could keep the Horn name, and the coffee pot would remain as a central part of the Belmont store.

As Horn Photo begins its sixty-first year of business, they have opened new store in Fig Garden Village called Horn Photo/Kodak Image Center. The central feature of the store will be presentation of the photograph using frames and gift items. The store will also feature cutting edge technology including digital restoration of old photographs. As technology evolves, the store will continue to evolve with it. The two other stores will remain. The store at Fresno and N streets will continue as the lab where custom printing and film processing will be done.

One thing will remain constant, however. The Belmont store will remain the full camera shop. With John Horn behind the counter and the ever-present coffee pot ready for the customers, both long-time and new customers will find a full line of camera, filters, darkroom equipment, and accessories for their photographic needs.

One of the privileges that comes to citizens of a city of great ethnic and religious diversity is the opportunity to share unique components of each culture. Special foods, festivals, music and religious holidays all contribute a unique flavor to our community. However, there is another aspect to cultural diversity that is very rewarding. In times of travail, groups who have little in common will offer to help each other in ways that forge enduring bonds. Fresno boasts many such instances.

In the early days of Fresno's history, the Unitarian Church held great influence in the community. Founded by pioneer families, such as the Rowells, it was a flourishing congregation. In the early part of this century the church opened its doors to Fresno's only Jewish congregation.

Before a suitable temple was built at the corner of N and Calaveras streets, the congregation purchased the Methodist parsonage on N Street for use as an annex for its Sunday school. At this time the members of the Unitarian Church, after some years of declining membership, were without a building. Temple Beth Israel was able to return the Unitarians' hospitality by offering them the use of its annex for their place of worship. The offer was gratefully accepted. In 1938, after the Congregational Church had a serious fire, its members held their worship services at the temple until they were able to repair the damages to their structure.

More recently, Rabbi Kenneth Segel traveled to a meeting of the National Jewish Congress and spoke eloquently in support of a resolution concerning the Armenian genocide that Senator Robert Dole had introduced in Congress. After gaining the support of this organization, Rabbi Segel and the Reverend Roger Minassian, then pastor of Pilgrim Armenian Congregation Church, went to Washington, D.C., where they lobbied in support of the resolution. Rabbi Segel gave a number of talks on the capitol steps to rally others to support it. The Armenian National Committee honored the rabbi as its Man of the Year. His efforts created a closeness between the Armenian and Jewish communities in Fresno that will be felt for many years. Enduring legacies have resulted from special acts of humanitarianism such as these.

Travelers journeying through the Central Valley in 1926 had few choices about routes. Highway 99 was the only major roadway. It was three lanes wide. The center lane was used only for passing. It was dangerous and slow because the speed limit was thirty-five miles per hour.

However, on March 26 of that year, drivers in Madera County were witness to a thrilling, high speed chase. A chauffeur-driven sedan had just left the city of Madera when, suddenly, the driver began to drive faster and faster. Traffic officer M. A. Harrison, riding in a roadster rather than a motorcycle, began to follow the sedan, which by this time was speeding up to eighty miles an hour.

As they reached the Herndon Bridge at the Madera/Fresno counties line, Harrison pulled the sedan over to the side of the highway. He issued a ticket to the chauffeur, Robert Gates, who was outraged that he had been cited by a policeman riding in a car. He declared that he had been fooled and that if he had known he was being chased by a policeman, he would have driven the car even faster and gotten away.

At that point Officer Harrison decided to look into the car and speak to the owner. To his surprise, seated in the backseat were heavyweight champion of the world Jack Dempsey and his wife, Estelle Taylor, who were very nice about the situation. Harrison issued a ticket to Gates, but both he and Dempsey were charged with reckless driving because, as Harrison's employer and owner of the car, Dempsey was responsible was well.

A complaint was filed with the Madera court the next morning. Dempsey posted one hundred dollars bail and left for Los Angeles, agreeing to return for trial on May 25. "Will he return?" was the question asked by residents of the Central Valley. The reply was pronounced loudly by Madera Judge Leroy E. Bailey, "If he does not, he must remain forever out of California."

# The Champ Wins Again

On a June morning in 1926, heavyweight champion of the world Jack Dempsey, dressed in a blue suit, walked sharply into Judge R. G. Cornell's courtroom in Chowchilla. On this occasion, court was being held in the local dance hall to make room for the largest crowd of onlookers to ever attend a trial in Madera County.

Dempsey had arrived to stand trial on charges that stemmed from an incident during which his chauffeur drove over eighty miles an hour with Dempsey and his wife in the car. Dempsey was being charged with allowing his chauffeur to speed.

Round one was lost when the judge denied an attempt by the defense attorneys to have the case dismissed. Round two began when Dempsey pled "not guilty" and requested a jury trial. By noon jury selection was complete. Round three began at 1:00 p.m. as testimony opened. Dempsey took the stand and testified that during the high speed ride he was sitting in the back seat with his wife. He was not aware of the speed the car was traveling and was not conscious of any unusual vibrations in the car. During cross-examination he said that he had never traveled fast in his other car, a Rolls Royce, and there were no vibrations in that car because it was guaranteed to give a smooth ride.

Dempsey was informed that, if convicted, he faced a $500 fine, as much as 180 days in jail or both. Judge Cornell was accustomed to dealing with famous people. He had fined Tom Mix ten dollars and San Francisco Mayor James Rolph fifty dollars. The judge instructed the jury that the only point they had to consider was whether or not Dempsey intended the car to be driven at the high speed it was when traffic officer M. A. Harrison stopped the car and issued the ticket.

Round four began as the jury retired to a room at the back of the hall at 3:42 p.m. They returned at 5:20 p.m. Judge Cornell asked if a verdict had been reached.

The foreman of the jury stood. A hush settled over the room as the anxious crowd held its breath. Dempsey was asked to stand. The foreman's "Not guilty" echoed to the farthest reaches of the hall. The crowd surged forward to congratulate the champ, who returned their good wishes by treating the boys of Madera County to a free soda at a local soft drink parlor.

The champ won, if not by a knockout, at least by winning the hearts of all those who were there.

# The Messenger of the Gods

The archives of the Fresno City and County Historical Society houses thousands of photographs and documents that tell the story of the history of our county. Among the treasures are a myriad of unique oddities that surface from time to time.

One such curiosity is a photo of a Greek god that dates back to 1893. The story it tells is as follows. As William M. Hughes, the son of Thomas Hughes, was driving through Fresno, he picked up a stranger, took him home and gave him lodging in his basement. The man turned out to be an Italian sculptor with great talent. He told Mr. Hughes that he wanted to carve a statue out of redwood.

A huge Sequoia Gigantea log was obtained from the Wawona Grove in Yosemite National Park. From the heart of this log, the sculptor carved a detailed likeness of Mercury, the Roman god who was the messenger of the other gods. The statue, along with a large log, was placed on a railroad flatcar and shipped to Chicago. They both became part of the California exhibit for the World's Columbian Exposition in Chicago in 1893.

Many of the visitors to the exposition could not believe that the statue was carved out of a single piece of wood. They felt it must have been done in pieces and assembled. But it was carved out of a single log in the Hughes basement, the result of a chance meeting on the streets of Fresno.

# A Close Shave

The ten-story Helm Building, which today stands proudly on the corner of the Fulton and Mariposa malls, was erected in 1914 and was one of the first high-rise buildings in the downtown area. The bottom floor housed a number of businesses. If one wished to visit one of the many offices on the other nine floors, one entered the main lobby on the Fulton side, rode one of the elevators facing the door or ascended the staircase to the left.

At the time our story takes place, in the 1930s, the building had a unique feature. On either side of the elevator shaft was a sort of atrium covered by a skylight. Beneath the southern skylight there was a barbershop. Beneath the other skylight was the office of the owner of Ennis Finer China & Crystal.

On one fine summer day, the window washers were busy at work. For one window washer, in particular, the day was going well. He had completed the windows on several of the floors of the building. Thoughts of finishing early began to weigh prominently in his mind. Suddenly, he felt something slip. Oh, no! His strap and harness parted company, and the poor window washer plummeted downward—tumbling over and over. Just as it seemed he faced a certain death, he crashed through the skylight and landed perfectly seated in one of the barber chairs. He looked around, got up and walked away—in the words of an observer—"shaken, but unscathed and unshaven."

# DeVaux & Dempsey

A $680,000 business agreement made the headlines of the *Fresno Bee* on May 24, 1928. According to the article, prominent businessman and agriculturalist D. W. DeVaux and former heavyweight champion Jack Dempsey exacted an interesting trade. The Hotel Barbara in Los Angeles, owned by Dempsey, was traded for 250 feet of frontage property on Broadway in Fresno, 286 acres of farmland and $350,000 in cash from Mr. DeVaux. The farmland in Madera and Tulare counties was primarily planted in vineyards. The DeVaux home, now the site of the Fig Garden Swim and Racquet Club, was not a part of the transaction.

Dempsey, who was married to actress Estelle Taylor, made a number of prolonged visits to his Madera property, often training in Fresno. All this gave rise to speculation that he was going to make a comeback in the ring. However, the champ told reporters there would be no comeback; he was only training to keep his weight in check.

All went well for about three years. Then, in 1931, Dempsey divorced his wife. To pay court costs and the property settlement, the Madera holdings were mortgaged and sold for less than their current value.

Remembering the spectacular court trial in Chowchilla involving a speeding ticket that, even though he won, caused him some unpleasant publicity, and then reflecting on his present situation, Dempsey, the ex-Manassa Mauler, may have felt that the climate of the Central Valley did not bring him good luck. Even so, from time to time, he made an overnight stop in Fresno, usually staying at the Hotel Fresno near the Broadway properties that he still owned.

# A Farm House in the Tower District

As one leaves downtown and drives through the older sections of Fresno, one will often see a Victorian home tucked among newer structures. In the early part of this century, many of these homes stood alone on large acreages of land because they began as farm houses. As Fresno grew and the farm lands were subdivided, many of these homes were incorporated into the new neighborhoods that developed.

One such home in the Tower District, on the 900 block of North San Pablo Avenue, stands apart from the rest. Painted in several shades of blue, its scroll work, spindles, spools, and fish-scale shingles happily evoke another era. Built in the early 1900s by Mr. Joseph P. Vincent, the home stood on a twenty-acre parcel of land with an address on Bloomington Avenue, a street name which no longer exists. Behind the house stood a large water tank with a windmill atop, a must for any country residence at that time.

Mr. Vincent was a well-respected member of the Fresno community. He served in the post of county assessor, was a director of the horsecar lines, president of the YMCA, president of the Pine Ridge Railway and president of the Confidence Oil Company in Coalinga. In 1887, he was elected to the state assembly and made a notable contribution by helping to draft and enact the Wright Irrigation Law.

Mr. Vincent died in 1910, but today his home is listed on the Local Register of Historic Resources. It is a striking example of Eastlake Stick Style architecture and is a colorful addition to the Tower District section of Fresno.

The front parlor of the Joseph P. Vincent Home in 1910. As was the tradition at this time, the body of Mr. Vincent lies in state in a corner of this room banked by flowers. *Courtesy of Michael and Anita Clifton.*

# Rolinda, Robbers & Rails

There is a railroad track on the west side of the valley located parallel to and between Belmont Avenue and Whites Bridge Road. It extends to Kerman and beyond to Mendota, Firebaugh and Los Banos. Today it is little used; only occasionally do rail cars speed along its track. However, one hundred years ago this was not the case. It was then a well-traveled line.

On one hot August night a horrifying event occurred. At a place called Rolinda, six miles after the train left Kerman headed for Fresno, two masked men jumped on. One of them came over the tender, pointing a double barreled shotgun at the engineer and fireman. The other robber appeared in the gangway. The train came to a halt.

Still covering the engineer and fireman with his gun, the first robber ordered the men off the train. Placing a dynamite bomb on the side rod of the engine, they forced a young railroad employee to ignite it. With one explosion the train was disabled. Firing their guns to let the passengers know they should not get off the train, the robbers threw two dynamite bombs at the iron door sills of the express car, blowing holes, but none large enough for a man to enter. The bandit threw another bomb through a hole into the car and this time succeeded in his mission. Gaining access to the car, the robbers, at gunpoint, made one of the train's crew open the safe. Stashing the money it contained into bags, they forced the fireman to help them carry the bags to their waiting horses. They galloped off toward the Coast Range mountains.

The next day, the ruined railroad car was taken to Fresno where the curious flocked to look at it. Thus, the Great Rolinda Train Robbery of August 4, 1892, became part of the history of the Central Valley.

# Religion & Circuit Riders

The early mining camps of the Sierra were populated by rather wild folk more interested in gaining wealth on earth than treasures in heaven. Church buildings were usually not a part of the settlements of the early Gold Rush period. Fresno County's first seat of government, the town of Millerton, was no exception. In the entire life of this town, a church was never constructed.

Into this rather immoral setting of painted ladies, gamblers, and gun-toting miners, ministers of the Gospel appeared from time to time. Known as circuit riders, they were usually shown respect and were welcomed into homes, where they were given lodging and food. If a building was available, religious meetings were held in it. If not, a tent was used for a meeting place. The sessions, called revivals, often lasted for two or three weeks. During the gatherings, the circuit rider would preach sermons focusing on the evils of life, whipping those attending into frenzies of excitement. The repentant sinners often rolled on the ground, shouting wild supplications for forgiveness to the Almighty as their religious ecstasy reached a feverish peak. Many converts were made during these revivals.

After the circuit rider left, life usually returned to normal. There were some who, when pondering the glimpse of a reward in the hereafter, heeded his warnings of hell fire and tried to lead a better life. But, for many, the appearance of the circuit rider just provided much-needed entertainment which gave a dash of variety to the hard life of the mining camps.

# A Man Named Erclas

Many strange tales can be told of the lives of those who lived in the western wilds in those years before civilization tamed the frontier. The story of one such man, Erclas Herbert Love, emerges from the pages of a scrapbook which belonged to his niece, Loverne McKay, another gem from the archives of the Fresno Historical Society.

His story begins with his birth on December 11, 1842, at a place called the Old Black Swamp in rural Ohio. At age sixteen, he left home to begin a life of adventure in Canada. With the outbreak of the Civil War he returned to Michigan, where his family then lived. He and four of his brothers enlisted in the Union Army's 13th Infantry, Company H, from Kalamazoo, Michigan. He was three times wounded in action, but survived.

At the war's close, he told his family that the solitude of the wilderness beckoned him. He told his mother, stepfather and siblings goodbye and left for the northwest with a hunter and trapper named Sullivan, taking only clothing, a gun and a trunk full of books. He settled for a time where Spokane stands today.

For years, he roamed the hills of the northwest and British Columbia, trapping, fighting Indians and living off the land. His trunk of books was always close at hand. Through them, he became an educated man.

His family had moved to Fresno Station in 1873 and he briefly visited them there. After he returned to the wilderness, he located a gold claim on the shores of Lake Okanogan which he mined for a number of years. His reputation became legend in the northern wilds that were his beloved home.

In 1926 his health failed and he began the long journey to his family in Fresno. When he arrived at his brother A. T. Stevens' home, there was great rejoicing because his family, not having heard from him in many years, thought he had died. Although surrounded by his kin, he grieved for his beloved hills and his solitary life. He died within a few months and was buried by the Fresno Atlanta Post 92 of the Grand Army of the Republic at Mountain View Cemetery.

His legend lives on in the northern wilds. His treasured books are cherished and still read by his great-great niece in her Fresno home.

Erclas Herbert Love, Civil War veteran and reknowned Pacific Northwest Indian fighter. He was buried in Mt. View Cemetery in Fresno by the Atlanta Post No. 92, Grand Army of the Republic in 1926. Photo taken c. 1870.
*Author's collection.*

1984 line drawing from *Reflections of Coaling's Past.*
*R. C. Baker Memorial Museum, Inc.*

Soon after Coalinga was incorporated in 1906, the city fathers were aware that a school was needed for the growing community. After a site was chosen on Polk Street, a school was constructed in 1908. The highest quality redwood was used throughout the building. Modern, Greek, Gothic and Early California architectural styles were blended in a distinctive way to create a unique structure. Atop the very center of the building sat a bell tower that rose ten feet above the roof line. The original bell measured three feet in diameter and, when rung, its loud toll could be heard throughout the community calling children to school.

The building itself gave the citizens of Coalinga a sense of pride and belonging. When the school first opened, grades one through six were taught. Eventually, more modern buildings were constructed and, in 1942, Polk Street School became part of the Coalinga Recreation District. Historically, it served other uses as well. During World War I, it became an emergency hospital. In 1917 and 1918, it was used to house those suffering the scourge of the flu epidemic.

In 1982, it was purchased by private owners, restored and placed in the National Register of Historic Places. Sadly, the Coalinga earthquake of May 2, 1983, and the many aftershocks which lasted through September, caused irreparable damage to the building.

Today, the Polk Street School no longer stands. However, to many of the residents of western Fresno County, its memory lives on.

# A Fair "Scandal"

In the fall of 1920, the plans for the Fresno County Fair were getting underway. As usual, the fair would showcase the finest examples of the agricultural produce of the central San Joaquin Valley.

But, in 1920, the board of managers was planning another sort of exhibit as well. It seems that a parade would be part of the festivities and in that parade would be young women attired in bathing costumes.

When word of this intended event leaked out, the young men of Fresno County were quite delighted. However, for one group of stalwart folk the news was scandalous. A letter to the board of supervisors was dispatched on September 8 from two members of the Women's Christian Temperance Union of Fresno County. In strident terms it chided the fair's board for planning an event of this kind that they felt would be degrading to women and demoralizing to men. It urged the supervisors not to lower the standard of morals in Fresno County by allowing young women to parade in public in bathing costumes. Calling on the good name of Fresno, its mothers, daughters and womanhood in general, the plea was emphatically made.

History does not record whether it was heard or not. However, it reminds us that there was a time when modesty was still in vogue, when bathing costumes were acceptable in public only when the intention was to swim, and when a young woman still blushed becomingly when a flirtation was directed her way.

# The Jensen Ranch

Driving through the lush vineyards and rich farmlands of the rural areas of the Central Valley, one spots interesting farmhouses tucked away amid large green trees. Many of the farm houses are original to their site and were built around the turn of the century.

One such home, situated on a thirty-acre ranch on South Bethel Avenue near Selma, can be viewed at the end of a long driveway lined on the right side by one-and a-half acres of Malaga grapes. The rest of the farmland contains eighteen acres of Thompson grapes and eight acres of other varieties. The entire ranch is an agricultural preserve.

The home contains the unique history of a family. Built for his wife and children by a Danish immigrant named Christian Jensen, who had achieved the status of master carpenter, it is made entirely of wood, using a blending of architectural styles. A two-story tank house behind the home can be seen from a great distance. A necessary part of every farmhouse water system, the tank house still contains a 1,000-gallon tank.

Mr. Jensen acquired other acreage near Selma and chose to do most of his farming by hand, using horse-drawn equipment and plows. He was judged one of the best farmers in the area. Today, his home is listed in the National Register of Historic Places. It is significant because it is an example of an early family-owned farm house. Its greater significance lies in the fact that descendants of Christian Jensen still live within its walls.

As you travel south on Palm Avenue from north Fresno a very distinctive structure comes into view. It can be seen for several miles and, for the first time visitor, it can be puzzling. Looking like a series of round tanks fastened together, it seems out of place in its surroundings.

As you follow the curve of Palm as it comes to Belmont Avenue, the structure seems to have grown in size. And, when you reach the foot of Palm Avenue, it looms up and dwarfs everything around it. About the time your attention is focused on the structure's immenseness, a peculiar essence assails your nostrils. Then the mysterious structure reveals its purpose—it is a grain storage facility with an elevator and distribution system. Of course! The series of silos, common to the midwestern United States, is rarely seen in the west. This facility, with its aromatic and visual uniqueness, is the only one of its kind in Fresno.

Built soon after World War II, it was originally known as the J. B. Hill Feed Company—"Hilco" for short. The property on which it sits was purchased from the Pierce Lumber Company in 1937 for $40,000. The war intervened, but by May of 1946 the plant was almost complete, and plans were that it would be finished for the summer harvest. When the eight storage silos were completed, they held 230,000 bushels of grain. Each measured twenty feet in diameter and was 150 feet high.

At the base of the northernmost silo a large hopper was constructed for truck and train unloadings. A conveyor was planned to move the grain to an elevator of six buckets, which would hoist the grain to the top for distribution to the silos. Stored grain was drawn through a feed tunnel, under the concrete foundations, and either distributed to farmers or to the mill which consisted of twenty-four storage bins and various types of machinery.

For many years, neon lights outlined a chicken, a cow, a horse and a pig on the highest tower. During the holiday season, a crane hoisted a Christmas tree atop that tower which could be seen for miles around.

Today, the facility is called Zacky Farms, owned by brothers Bob and Al Zacky. It is an integrated grower, processor, seller and distibutor of poultry products. The feed mill provides feed for the flocks of birds that Zacky grows—twelve million birds at any one time. The commercial mill provides feed for dairies, beef cattle and pig farms all over the Central Valley.

When you drive by it is not uncommon to see trucks parked under the loading area where they receive their quota of grain. For those Fresnans who often drive by and whiff the singular aroma, it is a good reminder that Fresno is first and foremost an agricultural capital.

# A Royal Policy

Newcomers to the Golden State often feel that they are arriving in an area that doesn't really have a history, a place where everything that has happened is of recent vintage. But, once again, certain events remind those of us who live in Fresno, that, yes, indeed, we do have a heritage and a colorful one at that.

At a luncheon on the twenty-third of September, 1992, the Fresno insurance firm of Shepard-Knapp-Appleton was saluted by the Royal Insurance Company, one of the largest insurance companies in the world, with a home office in London. The reason for this tribute is that SKA, and its forerunner, B. F. Shepard Company, have offered Royal continual representation in the Fresno area for over one hundred years.

One of the early policies is framed and hangs in the SKA office today. Looking at it, one is reminded of the fact that 100 years ago downtown Fresno was a combination of rural and urban life. The policy was issued to Andrew Andreasson for fire insurance which would cover the structures on his M Street property. Located between Mono and Ventura streets, the wood frame house was insured for $750, the barn along with sheds and "additions there attached" for $150, and his furniture for $350. The policy's premium was $19.90 for three years.

As one drives down this block of M Street today, it is amusing to think of barns and wood frame houses situated on large lots dotting its length. It's a little hard to imagine, too, for Mr. Andreasson's land sits beneath Selland Arena.

# The Evinger Home

Just north of downtown Fresno, tucked between Van Ness Avenue and Fulton Street, on a quiet street named Amador, sat an unusual home. To the passerby, it certainly was eye-catching, because it was built entirely of brick. Its bright red color and the thick pillars surrounding its porch gave it an appearance of solidity and permanence. While the thick pillars were of a classical style, a very different architectural motif ornamented the remainder of the facade. Over the windows of the front room was a high, curved parapet that reminded one of the Alamo House on L Street nearby.

This distinctive home had a number of interesting residents after its construction in 1912. It was built by Simeon Evinger, who was a butcher and the president of the Fresno Meat Company. He later became a vineyardist. Another owner of the home was Angelina Doherty, whose husband was reputed to have sown the first alfalfa crop in Kings County. Bernard Goodman, the manager of the Kinema Theater, was also a resident. Many Fresnans will remember that the home was used as an antique store for a number of years.

Sadly, time has not been good to the Evinger Home. It fell prey to vandalism and neglect. Once a proud, unique part of Fresno's heritage, and listed on the Local List of Historic Resources, it has been demolished. With its demise, another of Fresno's architectural treasures has vanished forever.

The adventures of David Bice James, which are a part of the manuscript collections of the Fresno Historical Society archives, transport the reader to a period of history when life on the frontier was harsh, often lonely, exciting, and sometimes brutal.

James joined Indian Commissioner and Colonel George W. Barbour's party in Los Angeles. It headed for the untamed San Joaquin Valley in the early 1850s. General John C. Fremont and Major Jim Savage were part of this expedition as well. As they journeyed over the Tehachapi Mountains, they met a Frenchman who lived among the Indians at Tejon, which was then known as French's Ranch. Descending the mountains onto the valley floor, they saw antelope everywhere. Huge bands of mustangs galloped across the plains, running fearlessly free. When they reached the Tule River, a member of their party, Andrew Lane, killed a 500-pound elk.

Upon arrival at Four Creeks, they saw their first Indians—all armed with bows and arrows. Members of the expedition were nervous because word had reached them that this tribe had recently massacred all the settlers at the nearby town of Woodville. No trouble broke out, however. To help ensure their safety, they had a powwow with the Indians, giving them blankets and other items. As they continued on their journey, they crossed the Kings River and set up camp. Word of their gestures of friendship must have spread because two Indians appeared nearby, but did not enter their camp site.

A couple of days later they crossed the San Joaquin River at Cassidy's Ferry, just a few days after Cassidy had been killed by hostile Indians. At this point, James decided to leave the expedition. He turned his thoughts to gold mining, a contagious disease that was causing thousands of people to flock to California.

# Fresno's Greene House

In the early years of this century, two brothers from Pasadena, Charles and Henry Greene, began designing homes in a style that would carry their names into architectural history. Their basic concept was to unite the interior and exterior of their structures through the use of handcrafted building materials. For instance, large beams that supported overhanging eaves of the roof would be left exposed in the interior of the home.

Rather than trying to create a style of design that would not be compatible with the California climate, they were very aware of the special features of this state and mixed Oriental, Mission and Swiss Chalet forms to create homes that were comfortable for California's indoor/outdoor mode of living.

Although Fresno has many older homes that borrow from the Greenes' ideas, it can boast with certainty only one Greene and Greene home. Situated on a corner in the Huntington Boulevard section of Fresno, the Mundorff Home, designed in 1917 by Henry Greene, reflects many characteristics of their style. Built in a U-shaped design, with a sleeping porch at one end, it lends itself to the hot valley summers when the sleeping porch was an important feature. The brick that is used on the exterior of the home also is used in the fireplace inside. The home boasts a butler's pantry, a typical feature of Greene and Greene designs.

Listed on the Local Register of Historic Resources, this lovely home has a contemporary feeling that belies its age. With seventy-five-year-old maple trees providing a lush backdrop, this home adds beauty and charm to its historic neighborhood close to downtown Fresno.

# A Honeymoon Cottage in Kearney Park

When one thinks of Kearney Park in the year 1997, one sees a long boulevard that connects it to downtown Fresno, an expanse of lawns and unusual trees, and an imposing turn-of-the-century mansion in an oddly Southern-like setting. But for many Fresnans whose memories run deep in the community, Kearney Park conjures up personal recollections of a different kind.

One hundred years ago M. Theo Kearney's Fruit Vale Estate was just being developed. The park was being planted and the buildings of the town to the south of the park were being built. By 1900, many people called the estate their home. Some twenty cottages were erected along a little street behind present-day Kearney Mansion. Mr. Kearney's servants and certain farm workers were allowed to live here, paying a modest rent. As the years went by and the estate was inherited by the University of California, the cottages, now nestled in tall trees, continued to be occupied.

In 1936, on a cold and rainy January night, a young, newly-married couple arrived at one of the cottages to begin their married life. The husband worked for the Kearney Vineyards. As they entered their brown-shingled home, they walked directly into the living room. A pot-bellied wood stove stood in one corner, its glow providing a warm welcome. Two long windows hung with green flowered curtains gave life to the room. A cord with a light bulb hung from the center of the ceiling, giving needed light. As they walked into the kitchen where the bride's new four-and-a-half-cubic-foot Leonard refrigerator greeted them, they saw in another corner an iron wood stove of a decidedly earlier vintage. The sink, which supplied only cold water, had two well-used sloping drain boards. A service porch, a sleeping porch, master bedroom and bath completed the quarters. In the bath, the large claw-footed tub and lavatory with a pull-chain and tank above evoked a much earlier era. All this was theirs for seven dollars per month rent that was deducted from the groom's twenty-five-cent-an-hour wage. But, the little house had electricity and that was included in the rent.

As primitive as it may sound today, for the bride, Althea Wheat of Fresno, the little cottage in Kearney Park was a cozy, love-filled home, one that she remembers with great happiness.

# The Giffen Estate

*The Image Group from the Laval Historical Collection.*

On the southeast corner of Chestnut and Butler avenues a large structure sits amid fine landscaping. Built in an English Tudor half-timbered design, it boasts a tile roof, a tribute to the California lifestyle.

It was built in 1916 as a private family residence for Wylie M. Giffen, who farmed the land around it. Mr. Giffen had extensive agricultural holdings in Fresno County and, although he farmed thousands of acres of wheat and cotton, he is best remembered for his contributions to viticulture. In 1912, he could boast that his vineyards of Thompson grapes were the largest in the world. His muscat vineyard encompassed 1,320 acres, making it the world's largest also.

Not content to be involved only with farming, he became one of the founders of the California Associated Raisin Company. He also served as president and manager of the Sun Maid Raisin Growers Association.

In 1919, he became involved in land development in north Fresno. A partnership with J. C. Forkner resulted in the Forkner-Giffen Tract, which today is known as Old Fig Garden. During the years 1916 to 1923, Giffen and his family lived in the gracious home on Butler Avenue. In 1923, the land surrounding the home was subdivided.

Today, the residence has been carefully kept in its original state, including the stained glass skylight over the central hall. Home to the Mennonite Brethern Biblical Seminary, it is a well-preserved reminder of one of the largest farming operations in the world.

When last we left David Bice James he had just parted from Colonel George W. Barbour's 1850 expedition of the San Joaquin Valley.

The lure of gold proved to be stronger than his desire to explore uncharted lands. Heading toward the Sierra Nevada mountains, he reached the San Joaquin River. The year was 1851—the Gold Rush was already well underway.

He met two men named Jamison and Crumley who were mining on the river, making five dollars a day using rockers to extract gold from gravel bars on the water's edge. James needed supplies and walked twelve miles up a steep trail to Fine Gold Gulch where Cowen's store was located. Today the gulch is called north Fine Gold Creek. It empties into Millerton Lake near the mouth of the San Joaquin River channel.

James' purchases that day included a five-dollar shovel, a five-dollar pick, a two-and-a-half-dollar pan, a one-dollar plug of tobacco, a blanket and foodstuffs, including flour, onions, and tea. With sixty pounds worth of purchases on his back, he hiked back to the river and set up camp. Darkness was descending as he began to cook his dinner. He fried his bacon on the shovel blade over his campfire. He put his bread dough on a stick and placed it in the ashes to cook. An old oyster can was used to brew his tea. All that plus the sky for a roof and a blanket for furniture seemed to James quite enough for his new adventure.

When he awakened the next morning, another new experience awaited him, for curled up next to him and quite asleep was a very real rattlesnake. Now totally awake, he picked up his gold pan and sat down beside the river. It had looked so easy to him, but he soon found that he was working until his hands were bleeding and he had little gold to show for it.

After three weeks of back-breaking work, James decided he must be doing something wrong. He went to the camp of Jamison and Crumley, the men he had seen that first day on the San Joaquin River. When he told them how he used the gold pan, they laughed uproariously. "Stay away from the gravel bars," they told him. "Look instead for places in the river where the gold and black sand concentrate in crevices in the bedrock." Taking their advice, he went farther up the river to a canyon where the water came rushing through. He could see the gold shining through black sand that was lodged in areas above the water. Excited, he took off his clothes and with his pick over his shoulder and his pan on a string around his neck, he swam to a spot where he found a pot hole in the bedrock that was rich with gold. The gold was so coarse it looked like grains of wheat.

On that hot summer day in 1851, David Bice James struck it rich just a quarter of a mile from Fine Gold Gulch in the western foothills of the Sierra. Gold fever had paid dividends for at least one of Fresno County's pioneers.

In the years immediately after the Camp Barbour Treaty of 1851, which was supposed to settle matters between the local Indians of Fresno County and the new settlers, the plight of the Indians did not improve. It may be shocking for today's citizens of Fresno to contemplate, but in 1862 it was legal and not uncommon for an Indian who had committed a crime to be sold to the highest bidder for the length of time he would have served out his sentence in prison. This, of course, was slavery.

Another legal agreement that was allowed was called an "indenture." One such document exists in the archives of the Fresno Historical Society. The agreement was entered into by Ira McCray of Millerton and Jack, an Indian boy approximately twelve years old. Jack agreed to bind himself to McCray as a domestic servant and general laborer until he was twenty-five years old. In return, McCray would have "the care, custody, control and earning of him...during the whole term." Jack, in turn, had to promise to obey and serve McCray honestly and faithfully in all things. McCray, it was written, would treat Jack with kindness and furnish him with all the necessities of life. At the end of the indenture, when Jack became twenty-five, McCray would pay him fifty dollars and give him a horse. The document was witnessed by County Judge James Sayles, Jr. and signed by McCray. Jack, who was illiterate, signed his X.

For Fresnans of 1997 this may seem like something that could happen only somewhere far away. But for La-Ache, the Indian from Centerville known as Jack, this was an all too real fact of life in the Fresno County of 1862.

# Fresno's Japanese Bank

The visitor to West Fresno will find many hidden architectural treasures tucked away amid the typical plain structures that line the streets. However, the visitor also will find a number of buildings that jump to his notice. These will be so intriguing that he will find himself driving around the block, then stopping his car for a better look. And, most likely, he will want to know the story behind the structure.

One such building, on the southwest corner of Tulare and F streets, invites the curious to linger and to wonder. For this two-story brick structure, with a corner tower and tiled roof parapets, has a decidedly Oriental flavor, yet it is built in the Mission style. What is the story behind this unique edifice?

In 1908, the first Japanese physician in Fresno, Dr. Buntaro Okonogi, established the first financial lending institution for Fresno's Japanese population. Called the Industrial Bank of Fresno, it was housed in a new building on the corner of Tulare and F Streets which Okonogi had hired San Francisco architect John C. Dressel to design. This structure blended Mission style elements with Japanese inspired craftsman details to create a unique architectural statement.

Dr. Okonogi served as president and director of the Industrial Bank which made farm and building loans to West Fresno residents. For several years the West Fresno Branch of the Bank of Italy operated side by side with the Industrial Bank in the new building. Other tenants were the *Japanese American Newspaper*, Japanese Association of Fresno, T. K. Tomita-General Business Agency and George Photography Studio.

There have been numerous other tenants in the building over the years, and for a while it stood vacant and in threat of demolition. But, happily, it was saved and now houses an art gallery and is a focal point for the revitalization of historic Chinatown.

# The Streets of Laton

One of the most fascinating things about any community is the names of its streets. Ingvart Teilman, who laid out the town site of Laton in 1899, named the streets by numbers and letters—which was not much fun for the settlers and gives no sense of history or whimsy for future generations at all.

Over fifty years later, the Fresno County Board of Supervisors wanted to create some meaningful names for county roads. It was also important, they thought, to do away with duplication of street names in county communities—and since numbers and letters had been overused in valley cities—it was time to find real names for streets.

The supervisors turned to Fresno County Counsel Robert M. Wash, a knowledgeable Fresno County historian, to choose the names for the streets in Laton. Many of the names he chose give reference to the old Laguna de Tache Grant, which was made up of 48,000 acres of land that today would stretch from just south of Kingsburg to the Lemoore Naval Air Station.

Some of the street names he selected are: Del Rio Avenue, for Rio de los Santos Reyes, the nearby River of the Holy Kings popularly called the Kings River; Murphy Avenue, for the Murphy Slough; Castro Avenue, for the first owner of the Laguna de Tache Grant, Manuel Castro; Pio Pico Avenue, for Don Pio Pico, the man who gave Castro his Kings River land and the last Mexican governor of California; Tache Avenue, for the Tachi Indians whose name was given to the grant; DeWoody Avenue, for T. J. DeWoody who, in 1864, made the original survey of the Laguna de Tache Grant; Kingston Avenue, for the old settlement on the south side of the Kings River which has now faded into history; Bliss Avenue, for Oliver Bliss who operated Whitmore's ferry and served as justice of the peace at Kingston; and Tiburcio Avenue, located west of town and Wash's personal favorite, named for the bandit who raided Kingston in 1873.

Renaming the streets of Laton has had a two-fold effect: It has given the citizens of this community a better sense of their history and it has given the town itself a more colorful flavor.

# Christmas at Kearney

For thirty-three years Fresnans have made a special journey at Christmas time. Even though it means a short drive in the country, somehow that drive takes on a magical quality in December, that most magical of months.

For many, the drive begins at Fresno Street, just beyond A Street, where two pylons mark the entrance to an eleven-mile boulevard named after early-day land developer and premier raisin grower M. Theo Kearney. The palm trees, oleanders and majestic eucalyptus trees that line its way create a sense of timelessness to those who make this journey. A sense of the importance of the man who built this private driveway for himself leaves no doubt that along its way a memorable destination will be reached.

And, sure enough! Six miles down the boulevard a sign points to Kearney Park, a left turn is made, and suddenly the visitor is swept into a vista of green lawns and one hundred year old trees. At the fork in the road, the left branch is taken and, as the visitor begins to feel transported to another time and place, a large French Renaissance mansion comes into view framed by stately trees. The lights in the mansion beckon and as the visitor walks up to the house, music can be heard.

Entering the front door, the spell is not broken, for the sweet subtle scent of evergreens, the lush Victorian decorations and the sounds of Christmas music all blend to transport the visitor to the mystical world of Christmas long ago.

Those who make this journey for the first time find that they return the following year. Those who have always made the journey can explain why. For many of those who call Fresno County home, Christmas just isn't Christmas without a visit to Kearney Mansion.

# Elections in Early California

The process by which we elect candidates to public office in these days of ten-second sound bites, talk shows and round-the-clock news coverage involves the voting public in a very comprehensive way. For one who wishes to be informed, it is merely a matter of reading the paper or listening to radio or television—all in the comfort of one's home. But it was not always thus.

In the early days of California's statehood, there were a few major population centers where newspapers were printed. However, most of the state was sparsely settled, with quite a bit of travel time between towns. The Gold Rush of 1848, which launched California's bid for statehood, brought most of the new, burgeoning population to its borders. For those miners throughout the hills of the Sierra, the events of the world seemed far away.

For our gold mining friend, David Bice James, located in his camp on the San Joaquin River, there were no newspapers or mail or even stagecoaches traveling by. The outside world encroached on his life only when someone new wandered into his camp.

One day a party of seven men called to him from across the river. They looked like decent men, so he got into his dugout, made from a pine log, and rowed to the other shore. As they piled in his primitive boat, they told him that one of their number, H. Skelton, was running for the state legislature, and that they were on an electioneering trip. Among them were a judge and a doctor. Skelton offered James his hand. "I'm running on the 'Know Nothing' party ticket," he said, "and I'd appreciate your vote."

When they disembarked, they thanked James for his hospitality, and ventured on to Fagan's store. After a night spent playing poker and drinking whiskey at Big-Foot Miller's saloon next door, they returned to James' camp. He ferried them back across the river, and on they went through the rich fields of the gold country, seeking votes and adding an interesting chapter to the tales of our valley.

# The Rabbit Drive

The early settlers in the colony lands that dotted the Fresno area had some interesting problems as they farmed. Roaming bands of cattle would encroach on unfenced land and eat and trample an entire field. Grasshoppers would appear en masse and eat every morsel of green in sight, whether it was new cuttings, roots or grasses. Probably the worst menace was the jack rabbit. Not only did the rabbit devastate crops, but he bred prolifically. A few rabbits in a short time could create teaming hordes of bunnies that seemed to overrun acres of land. Poison and wire fences were used to try to stem the tide. Both failed.

To deal with this problem, farmers came up with an idea that in the present day and age may seem very harsh indeed. It was called the rabbit drive. In a short time it not only became a way to rid agricultural lands of jack rabbits, but also a sport engaged in by other members of the community.

A half-mile long corral with lateral wings that were covered with a three-foot high wire screen was built. The participants lined up in carriages, on horseback or on foot. Often to the accompaniment of a band beating out a quick march, these folks proceeded across the ground in an unbroken line. They would shout and holler.

The rabbits, hearing this, would go into a frenzy and in their panic to flee would be forced into the corral. The almost human-like cries of the bunnies would be mingled with the shouts of the participants. Many of the rabbits were killed by knocking themselves against the wire fence. Those that made it into the corral were beaten to death by the mob. Sometimes the carcasses of dead rabbits at the gates of the corral would be stacked several feet high. This succeeded in depleting the rabbit population for a while.

Coyotes, ground squirrels, gophers and rabbits all had a bounty on their heads with money offered for their scalps. This was part of a major plan, in the words of federal authorities, "for the destruction of agricultural pests serving no known purpose in nature's economic plan."

Result of an 1890 jack rabbit drive near Fresno in which 80,000 rabbits were driven into an improvised corral and clubbed to death. *Courtesy of the Kings County Museum at Burris Park.*

# Beans & Burros

The tales of California's rich gold fields are filled with many interesting tidbits of information. For instance, chili beans were the staple food, often eaten three meals a day, seven days a week. The energy they provided and the muscle they supplied, many felt, played an important role in the development of the mines.

It also is said that there existed an unwritten code of honesty among the men of the mining camps—one could leave one's gold dust out in the open and no one would touch it. Unfortunately, this rule existed only early on; later, a wise man hid his findings.

The unsung heroes of the early mining days also deserve recognition. These were the small burros, who, with their gentle dispositions, loyalty, and strength of spirit worked alongside their owners, toting supplies and proving their worth time and time again.

However, one burro of the San Joaquin River camps had gained a reputation that was a little unsavory. Bearing the interesting name of "Whiskey," this burro was known to steal anything in sight. The miners in the area hung everything out of his reach, just in case he decided to pay a visit.

At lunch time one day, a miner decided to bake bread. He put the loaf in his iron skillet, covered it and placed the skillet in the smoldering coals of his fire. He put more coals on the cover of the pan and left to work his claim while the bread baked. As he approached his claim, something caused him to turn and look back. He was just in time to see Whiskey knock the cover off the skillet, move it out of the coals, pick up the blistering hot loaf in his mouth, and run away. As the miner chased him, Whiskey dropped the loaf several times, always picking it up, and running on. Even though burros hate to cross running water, such was Whiskey's desire to keep the bread that he actually allowed himself to be chased over the river. The miner never did catch Whiskey, who had thoroughly outsmarted him. It was the miner's opinion that if there is any credence to be placed in the theory of evolution, "in a thousand years or more, burros will be reading newspapers and wearing pants."

# A Friday Evening in Fowler

Much has been written about women's study clubs in the tales of our valley, but what about the gentlemen among us? Did they not also yearn for intellectual stimulation and knowledge?

On October 29, 1910, eleven men, including Dr. W. T. Crawford, met in the Emporium Building in Fowler to materialize plans to create a club predicated on intellectual and social betterment of the members. Three days later an organizational meeting took place. The name of the club was chosen—the Fowler Friday Evening Club.

Every September, each of the sixteen members submits two topics for thirty minute papers. Nine topics are accepted. Seven topics are put in reserve. At each of the nine monthly meetings one member presents his paper. Another member opens the discussion. This person, who is called the opener, receives a copy of the paper in advance. The opener may enlarge upon or attack the paper's premise. The other members, who are hearing the paper for the first time, are each expected to discuss the paper for no more than five minutes. The discussion and debate can be spirited, but the club's most important unwritten rule is that whatever is said during the meeting must be maintained in absolute confidence. A certain formality is observed during the meetings— a dignity that evokes an earlier era, but one that members find heightens the level of intellectual discussion.

The fact that membership is limited to sixteen men is due to the era in which the club was founded. Women's suffrage and the development of so many exclusively women's clubs at this time led the men to create their own group.

Today, the Fowler Friday Evening Club is as actively involved in its intellectual pursuits as it was in 1910. Ten of its members live in Fowler or have close ties to that community; the others live elsewhere in Fresno County. On nine Friday evenings during each year, they meet for dinner and discussion. An old-fashioned club, you might say? The members are very pleased that it is so.

# A Valley Called Wonder

The valleys of the Sierra Nevada mountains hold many charms for the traveler. In spring, wildflowers carpet the meadows and, in fall, the trees become red and gold splashes of color against the brown hills. To reach one such lovely area, the traveler drives east on Belmont Avenue, north on Trimmer Springs Road and then east on Elwood Road. Upon reaching the valley the vista changes—groves of sycamore trees, oak-covered hills and a peaceful lake greet the traveler.

The beauty of the scene was first enjoyed by Yokuts Indians, who established eight villages in the valley. For a time, the peace of this secluded place was shattered by one of the infamous Dalton gang, Grat Dalton, who robbed trains in the area and escaped to his hideout on Dalton Mountain, which overlooks the valley.

In 1911, George S. Pierson, a veteran of the Spanish-American War, purchased 1,500 acres of land in this beautiful spot that he called Wonder Valley. He planned to raise cattle and horses. After a year had gone by, he decided to open his ranch to guests. The Pierson Dude Ranch became the first such facility in California. Word traveled quickly about the peace and beauty of this valley and soon such Hollywood stars as Hoot Gibson, Victor McLaughlin and Tom Mix were visiting the ranch often. Others came as well, not only from across America, but from seven foreign countries.

After thirty-seven years, the ranch was sold to Paul and Becky Webb. For the next twenty-five years the Wonder Valley Dude Ranch, as it was then called, became known throughout the country for its western hospitality and good down-home food.

Today, the ranch is operated by the Oken family. It serves as a setting for conferences, tour groups and children's summer camps. Each year Champ Camp is held in the middle of June. Children from all over California who are burn victims are brought by the California Burn Foundation to Wonder Valley, where they can enjoy all the ranch has to offer. Although visitors may meet up with a modern-day version of the Daltons, it's all in good fun. The real bandits are part of the past. Once again, just as in the days of the Yokuts Indians, the peace of Wonder Valley descends on all who visit there.

The story of one of Fresno's leading Bulldog supporters goes deep into the history of our community. His parents came to Fresno soon after the turn of the century. He was born in 1921 and attended local schools, graduating from Fresno High. While he was attending Fresno State College, the United States entered World War II, and he was drafted into the army. After serving for three and a half years, he returned to Fresno, intending to complete a degree in business at Fresno State.

During the war, his mother began teaching the hobby of ceramics in the garage of the family home on Adoline Avenue. She asked her son to delay his education to help her with her fledgling business. It was a successful venture and became so popular that the family opened a studio on Blackstone Avenue where they not only taught, but sold ceramic products as well. The studio was destroyed by a fire in 1953.

When the family rebuilt, they added a manufacturing component to the business. By 1961, Duncan Ceramics had become the largest manufacturer of ceramic hobby supplies in the world and moved into its present facility on East Shields Avenue. Bob Duncan served as president of his family's business from 1953 until 1980, when he became chairman of the board.

Duncan's commitment to excellence in business was equaled by his desire to contribute to his community. Fresno State College was now a university, and he felt that it could become much more of an asset to the area if the community became more involved with California State University, Fresno. He envisioned athletics as a way of accomplishing this. Long a fan of the Bulldogs, he became a trustee of the Bulldog Foundation and the driving force behind the fund-raising effort that resulted in a new football stadium on the campus. The adjacent athletic building was named in his honor.

His contributions to the university also are evident in his role on the school of business advisory council and the board of governors of the CSUF Foundation. The Leon Peters Valley Business Center is the result of a fund-raising drive that he co-chaired.

A Bulldog fan of the first degree, it is a sure bet that Bob Duncan can be found at each home game cheering on his favorite team. The community of Fresno will be cheering as well, not only for the Bulldogs, but for this man who sparked the spirit that linked California State University, Fresno to the citizens and businesses of the Central Valley.

# The Robinson Home

Tucked away on a quiet street corner of the 1000 block of South Orange Avenue in southeast Fresno is a tall, narrow Victorian home of Stick Style design. Nestled as it is away from the bustle of heavy traffic, it is largely unnoticed by most Fresnans. However, for those who venture off the main streets of our city and suddenly come upon it, the usual reaction is a gasp of surprise. The home stands out from its neighbors, not only because it is of an earlier period and design, but also because it has been restored and invites passersby to stop and admire.

Built in 1900 by Mr. and Mrs. Raymond Robinson, it was located just outside the city limits. Mr. Robinson worked for Griffen and Skelly, which later became the California Packing Company. He chose to build his new home with the fish-scale shingles, spools, spindles, brackets and colored glass windows that were so popular at the turn of the century. The trees, which today are approaching a hundred years old, were purchased from the Roeding Nursery.

Originally, the house was surrounded by a driveway and several acres of land. Today, it sits on a lot eighty-seven and one-half feet wide. The backyard has an intricate stone wall and a barbecue made of rock from the Kings and San Joaquin rivers. Designed and built by the Robinsons' son-in-law, each panel of stone creates a sunburst effect.

Until 1995, the home was one of Fresno's few bed-and-breakfast inns. Its owners welcomed visitors from all over the country, who had an opportunity to stay in one of Fresno's historic homes and experience the warmth and hospitality of another era.

California's Gold Rush was one of the most colorful periods in its history. Not only did it bring new residents flocking to the mountains of the Sierra, but it also underscored the era of the gun toting pioneers of the Old West, those who took the law into their own hands. Life was not easy in the mining camps of the gold country, and entertainment, aside from that offered by the nearby saloon, was scarce. A few fraternal orders were established, but these were not open to everyone.

During this time, a new institution appeared that was open to all. This new club poked irreverent fun at society's more serious organizations. Using a ritual brought from the East Coast, the Ancient and Honorable Order of E Clampus Vitus became so popular that new chapters soon could be found in all the mining camps. The club credo was "Credo Quia Absurdum" which means "Because it is absurd, we believe." It was further asserted that "All members were officers and all officers were of equal indignity." The initiation fee was enough gold dust to buy a round of drinks.

Today, the institution lives on with over two dozen chapters in California. The local chapter, which boasts more than 2,000 members, takes its name from Jim Savage who, in 1852, was killed at his trading post near the Fresno River in the foothill country of the Sierra. Those who join come from all walks of life. Although they enjoy the same rollicking good fun of the early day miners and poke fun at pompous self-importance anywhere they find it, the Clampers have a serious side as well. Initiation fees help to fund markers for historical sites. Among the numerous markers placed by the Jim Savage Chapter is in Kearney Park which commemorates the Fremont Expedition of 1844. By placing these informative plaques, the Clampers remind the citizens of the Central Valley of the colorful and important events that have shaped our history.

For this great service we can say, "Hats off to the Clampers," and for those who have served their chapter in the privileged role of the Noble Grand Humbug, we salute you!

For years riding had been a forgotten sport in the Fresno area. By the mid-twenties riding was making a comeback with the organization of the Boots and Saddle Riding Club. Mrs. Parker Frisselle was chairman of the group.
*The Image Group from the Laval Historical Collection.*

The early life of a woman who came to be known as the "first chatelaine of Kearney Mansion" centered around an atmosphere of wealth and privilege. Her grandmother's Piedmont home contained twenty-four rooms, including a tower room on the fourth floor that gave one a view of the Golden Gate Bridge. It took a staff of ten to care for the house and gardens. This young woman spent her summers on her father's 3,000-acre cattle ranch. Here she learned about ranch life and how to run a large home.

After receiving her education in San Francisco, she met Fresnan Samuel Parker Frisselle, who managed the Kearney estate for the University of California. They fell in love and married, coming home to Fresno to take up residence in Kearney Mansion. Newspaper accounts in these years just before World War I, described her as beautiful, an accomplished musician and sportswoman.

When she moved in, Kearney Mansion seemed to come alive. Her vivacious personality and creativity in planning parties became legend in Fresno. Invitations to her dinners became much sought after. She entertained not only celebrities like Herbert Hoover, but also University of California students, alumni and their families. The society pages of the *Fresno Morning Republican* and, later, the *Fresno Bee* featured stories of these events. On one occasion she opened one of the attic rooms for a display of drawings brought by each guest, who were instructed to come to the party dressed in artist garb. Prizes were given for the best pictures. Dinner and dancing followed.

Her interest in art was enhanced by two summer sessions at the California School of Fine Arts in San Francisco. She also took art classes at Fresno State College. One of the mansion's attic rooms provided a place for her to practice her skills. She received national recognition for a sculpture of American composer Charles Wakefield Cadman.

In 1929, she and Parker Frisselle divorced and she left Fresno. Her fondness for Kearney Mansion caused her to leave an important legacy to Fresno. During the 1970s, Dagmar Alix Bradford left her collections of memorabilia concerning her Kearney Mansion years to the Fresno Historical Society. More important, she took the time to share with the society's director the colors of the original wallpapers and carpets so that future restoration projects could be properly conducted. Her thoughtfulness has allowed the Fresno Historical Society to maintain Kearney Mansion in a way that undoubtedly would have pleased its original owner, M. Theo Kearney.

# A Twist of Fate

The tales of the valley often tell of ironic twists of fate—of rather incredible happenings in the lives of those who ventured west to make new beginnings in the world's richest agricultural region. One such story features Mary Brannan Roberts Donleavy, who founded the first orphanage in Fresno.

Shortly after her marriage to Joseph W. Roberts, they moved to Washington, D.C. The newlyweds found a place to live next door to a boarding house run by one Mary Suratt. The people who lived in Mrs. Suratt's establishment were friendly and hospitable and from time to time the young couple socialized with their neighbors next door. One man in particular stood out from the others, a young actor named John Wilkes Booth. He was very charming and Mary often danced with him. Although the country had just been launched into a civil war, life did not come totally to a standstill. The couple made other friendships as well, including a special one with President Lincoln.

As the war progressed, Mary's husband, Joseph, joined the Union Army and served until his death during the Battle of Bull Run. At the war's end, Mary returned to Washington. To celebrate, she attended a gala performance at Ford's Theater. She watched as her friend President Lincoln and his party entered the box, which was reserved for special guests. As the play progressed her eyes often looked in the president's direction to see if he was enjoying himself. She, along with the others in the audience, heard a gunshot and Mrs. Lincoln's scream. Horrified, Mary saw her dancing partner, Mr. Booth, jump from the box to the stage, brandishing a dagger in the face of the audience. Like everyone else who was at Ford's Theater that night, Mary was never able to forget what she had witnessed.

At the time of her death many years later in Fresno, she had probably been the last living person to witness the assassination. To her dying day, she believed that Booth was not killed after he shot the president, but had successfully made his escape.

# Mayor of Broadway

If one drives through the St. John's Cathedral district of Fresno, one will see a mixture of new buildings interspersed with a few historic homes that are the remnant of one of early Fresno's most beautiful residential neighborhoods. One home in particular catches one's eye. Located at the corner of Mariposa and T streets, a large Georgian Colonial home with four soaring chimneys and Ionic columns in front certainly makes the statement that a person of importance must have lived here.

When the home was built in 1906, white marble extended from the street, up the front walk and stairs right to the front door of the house. Upon entering, one's eyes followed the graceful stairway that rose to the second floor. It hung suspended without visible supports and seemed to float in space. Five fireplaces, including one in the paneled basement, provided warmth and welcome.

The original owner of this incredible home came west from Tennessee to California in 1849. He settled in Fresno in the 1870s and established a clothing business. He continued in that profession for over fifty years until his death in 1924. He was a charter member of Temple Beth Israel and played a major role in the construction of the temple at N and Calaveras streets. He also was responsible for making the present Liberty Cemetery available to war veterans. His interest in the civic affairs of the community led him to take an active interest in a project to widen Broadway and to modernize many of the buildings on that street. For this and for his many contributions to the city of Fresno, Sol Goodman was given the unofficial title of "Mayor of Broadway."

I Street (Broad-
way) in 1900.
*The Image Group from
the Laval Historical
Collection.*

# The Hanger Home

Until the summer of 1992, a lovely historic home on Van Ness Avenue fell slowly into disrepair. For most of its years it had added charm to its North Park neighborhood and was designated a local historic resource. Built around 1900, it was first the home of William H. Hanger, a vineyardist and agent for a local fruit packing company. It then had a succession of owners, including F. P. Black, owner of Black's Package Company; and Fred A. Berg, who had established Berg's Furniture Store in 1914. For a few years in the 1970s, it housed the Bay Berry Antique Store.

Then time and a freeway project made the once-delightful home undesirable. As other historic homes found owners and were moved, the Hanger Home continued to wait for the right party to show interest. And, happily, someone finally did. The Adult Literacy Council needed more space for offices. The City of Fresno donated a parcel of land at the corner of San Joaquin Street and Broadway. The cost of the move was donated and others from all parts of the community volunteered their help as well. The exterior of the house has been restored while the interior has been made to suit the needs of the council.

The Hanger Home has now joined the ranks of other relocated historic homes in Fresno.

In the days of the old wood stove, cooking was a much more complicated business than turning on today's microwave oven, but the wood stove offered some amenities that might be remembered with nostalgia. Central heating was unheard of early in this century, but the wood stove provided a heat that pervaded the kitchen and made it a wonderfully warm place to be. The stove also had a hot water tank with pipes that came through the outside wall. These pipes made a perfect spot to dry dishtowels. And thereby hangs a tale.

On one wintry Thursday evening, early in this century, the Emma Miller Study Club was meeting in the front parlor of the Millers' home on P Street. That evening the ladies listened in rapt silence as Emma Miller conducted a dramatic reading of Shakespeare's "Romeo and Juliet."

Next door, Wilbur McKay was just returning home. Young Mr. McKay was one who always moved and spoke in a slow, deliberate fashion. He climbed the stairs to his bedroom and, as he closed the curtains, he noticed a fire in the Millers' kitchen. Taking his time, he walked downstairs, out the front door and down the sidewalk to the Millers' front door. Beulah, the elder daughter, answered his knock. "B e u l a h...y o u r  h o u s e  i s  o n  f i r e," Wilbur said in his own slow, drawn-out, inimitable way. The two young people made their way to the kitchen to find that the dishtowel that had been drying on the pipe had caught fire and was creating a rather cozy conflagration in one corner of the room. Grabbing a bucket of water, they doused the flames and put out the fire.

Wilbur returned to his home and the ladies of the study club continued their evening of Shakespeare, unaware of the events in the kitchen. Life in turn-of-the-century Fresno was rarely dull!

# Producers Dairy

$A$s you go about your daily activities, it is unlikely that you think about the life of a dairy cow in the great Central Valley. In 1877 Fresno, before the city was incorporated, cows were a familiar sight. Mrs. Calvin Jones kept her herd in a corral next to her husband's flour mill. Today the site is marked by the Mason Building on the Fulton Mall.

Mrs. Jones' cows gave milk for her customers, but their lives were devoid of any luxury, and by the time their milk reached Fresno tables, it was often not drinkable.

Times have changed. The lot of the dairy cow is much improved, with ultra modern milking parlors, computers, and the strictest standards of quality control possible. Sixty-five years ago a group of men wanted to bring quality packaged milk products to the citizens of Fresno. They incorporated their new business, Producers Dairy, on December 22, 1932.

In 1949, a major interest in the company was purchased by Larry Shehadey, who soon became the general manager. During that year, a new plant was opened at 144 East Belmont Avenue that is still in use today.

In the intervening years, Producers Dairy has continued to grow and has seen a number of "firsts" in the valley—from the first half-gallon and quart-size single service packaging machines to the first dairy plant to own 100 percent refrigerated trucks. Producers' Bar 20 Dairy Farms and processing plants use the most modern techniques available to make sure the highest standards are maintained. The Fresno shopper not only has many items to choose from, but also knows that they are fresh and have undergone the strictest quality control.

With this in mind, the next time you venture out Whites Bridge Road and find yourself driving past the Producers' Bar 20 Dairy Farms, you should not be too surprised if you see a cow smiling. She definitely has something to moo about!

# A Fishy Prank

In the 1860s, Fresno's lovable practical joker, Fulton G. Berry, lived in San Francisco. He numbered among his many friends a writer named Mark Twain who, at that time, lived in San Francisco also. One of the interests they shared was the joy of fishing.

On one occasion, Berry invited several of his pals to spend a quiet day angling from the decks of his yacht. Twain had often said his life's desire was to catch a mess of red rock cod. Berry assured him his dream would come true. Since Berry knew there were no red rock cod in these waters, he visited the local market, picked out the biggest red fish he could find, and smuggled it on board.

The day was perfect for fishing—calm and still. Everyone except for Berry and Alexander Badlam, who was in on the joke, dropped their lines from the upper side of the boat. Badlam attached the red fish to his line and pulled it in amid loud excitement. He put the fish in a barrel of water and yelled to the others to stay where they were because, he said, the cod liked the shady places that the upper side offered.

Actually, the lines tossed from the upper side trailed under the yacht where Berry and Badlam could catch them. Grabbing Twain's line, they put the red fish on the hook and pulled furiously. "A whale," Twain cried, "I have got a whale!" When he landed the fish, his excitement knew no bounds. He marked its length in chalk on the deck, threw the fish in the barrel of water and cast his line again. Berry retrieved the red fish, rushed to the other side and grabbed Twain's line again. At least fifty times the joker put the poor tired red fish on Twain's hook; at least fifty times the chalk mark was made and the fish was thrown in the water barrel. In the excitement of realizing his dream, Twain did not catch on.

Finally, tiring of the prank, Berry and Badlam put a monkey wrench on the line. Twain pulled it on deck. He rolled up his sleeve and went to the water barrel. Plunging his arm in the water, he pulled up one very worn out red fish. Realizing he had been had, he said, "Boys, we have had lots of fun—let's go home."

The humorist had a sense of humor even when confronted with Fresno's ultimate prankster, Fulton G. Berry.

# A Sheep Man Named Kennedy

Robert Kennedy was born in Liverpool, England, on March 23, 1839. In 1863, he joined two friends, Henry Ross and John Treadwell, on a ship bound for Australia. During the trip, the ship's crew mutinied. The mutineers were rounded up and thrown in the brig, and the male passengers had to crew the ship until it reached Sydney. After four years of building a construction business together, the trio moved the business to San Francisco. In 1870, they dissolved their partnership, but remained life-long friends.

In 1869, Kennedy and Ross scouted the San Joaquin Valley on horseback looking for a suitable place to raise sheep. Soon after his 1870 marriage to Marion Ryce, the daughter of San Francisco's Andrew Ryce, Kennedy took his bride by boat to Stockton. From Stockton they drove their wagon and team of horses to Millerton, where he started his sheep business. Two years later, in 1872, he moved his operations to Tulare County just three miles southwest of present-day Dinuba. This profitable venture not only involved wool growing, but Kennedy also raised top grade lambs for market. He rented a portion of his holdings to farmers who raised wheat. In 1891, he sold part of his ranch to one of these farmers, Amaziah W. Clark. They created a partnership and expanded their business to include grain, alfalfa, and cattle.

In 1892, Kennedy moved his family, which by now included six daughters, into Fresno. He began to invest in business property and, among other holdings, owned the Sequoia Hotel. In 1895, Kennedy purchased the Colwell mansion on Q Street. A year later the Santa Fe Railroad tracks came down the middle of the street. The large home was moved to the corner of S and Mariposa streets, causing quite a commotion for the residents of the neighborhood.

Two of Kennedy's daughters were married in the house. One of these girls, Jessie, and her husband, F. Dean Prescott, moved into the house when Robert Kennedy and his wife moved to Berkeley in 1910 and lived there until their deaths many years later.

From builder to sheep man to investor, Robert Kennedy played an important role in the development of the central San Joaquin Valley.

When the automobile first made its appearance in Fresno soon after the new century began, it heralded a new era. Paved streets replaced dirt roads, gasoline exhaust replaced something more solid left by horses, and the luxury of riding slowly in a horse-drawn buggy was replaced by a vehicle that was touted to move people from place to place much faster. Indeed, the whole world seemed to be anxious for speed. The Victorian way of life was coming to a close. However, this new mode of transportation brought with it some problems. In the era of the horse, if a gentleman spent a little too much time in the saloon before heading home, his mode of transportation usually could find the way home safely without his owner's help. After all, the horse had a brain, too. Automobiles, for all their new fangled wizardry, lacked a brain, and a gentleman in a car, when faced with similar circumstances, was on his own.

In 1924, just twenty or so years after cars had been introduced to Fresno, Police Judge James G. Crichton had just about had enough of reckless and/or drunk drivers. He decided that the time had come to apply some creative remedies of his own. When a reckless driver came before his bench, he offered the following sentence which would be pronounced for a period befitting the nature of the offense: During the specified time period, the offender's vehicle would be left in the offender's garage stripped of license plates and registration. During that time the offender was deprived of all driving rights. If he told the judge that he did not like that sentence, the judge was only too happy to put him in jail and allow his family full use of his vehicle. The time that the owner was without a means of transportation was used to educate the driver about mixing alcohol and driving.

The results of Judge Crichton's experiment were noteworthy. The cases of drunk driving in the county were reduced dramatically and other communities throughout the country began to try his approach. From the vantage point of 1997, with the knowledge that this problem still has not been resolved, it might be tempting to hope that the next century might usher in a new era of horse-drawn vehicles.

# The Spencer Home

In a once-proud neighborhood north of downtown Fresno, many interesting homes still attract the notice of those who drive through the area. One does stand out, however, because it is a little different from the rest. Two stories tall and built of red brick, the home at the corner of San Pablo Avenue and Klondike Street has a timeless, solid quality. Only the porch details and the fish scales, eastlake spindles and jigsaw pieces of the front gable let you know that the home is of Victorian vintage.

Constructed by Wright H. Spencer in 1899, the home has double brick walls with a six-inch air space between for insulation—a popular method of building in the Midwest or East Coast, but unusual in Fresno County. Mr. Spencer had grown up in Caro, Michigian, a city his father had founded. This midwestern style of architecture must have reminded him of home.

Having learned the abstract business by working in his father's office, he continued in that profession in Fresno. His arrival in Fresno in 1888 coincided with a tremendous land boom. There were so many sales every day that title searchers were in great demand. He became a partner in a firm with Clark and McKenzie. In 1891, they merged with three other abstract firms, today known as title companies, to become the Fresno County Abstract Company.

In 1918, Spencer was elected county recorder, running with the motto "Thirty Years a Searcher of Records in Fresno County: honesty, efficiency, fidelity and courteous treatment." Mr. Spencer was active in local politics for many years and left a legacy of honest midwestern values to his community, both in his public life and in the home he built on San Pablo Avenue.

# The "Painted Dog"

The dry, semiarid desert climate of Fresno County may seem a long way from tropical India, especially the romantic 1880s India of the British colonial period. And, indeed, it is. However, there is a link and wouldn't you know, it involves a bulldog!

Long before he became a Fresno County supervisor in the early 1920s, Robert Lochead served in Her Majesty's Army in India. He owned an English bulldog who became the mascot of the regiment. As the only one of her breed in this foreign colony, she became well known outside the regiment as well. Her exploits in the combat arena were well documented and earned her soldiers a little extra spending money. When it was time for Lochead to leave India he decided to leave the dog behind. He gave her to an attorney for a railroad company. The bulldog was not pleased and ran away, returning to her regiment of soldiers. So afraid were they that she might be taken from them, they decided on an interesting scheme—they painted her so that any attempt to find a dog fitting her normal description would fail.

The story of the "Painted Dog" was told to the young writer Rudyard Kipling who was living in India. So enchanted was he with the tale that he used the character of such a dog in *Soldier's Three*. And thus, the stalwart English bulldog, the pride and joy of Lochead's days in India, lives on in the literature of our western culture. Even Lochead's accomplishments as a Fresno County supervisor had a hard time beating that.

# The Home of Mr. Main

As you travel through the areas of Fresno that have developed since the 1940s, it is not uncommon to notice intriguing bits of architecture tucked away amid newer homes. As you drive north on Fruit Avenue between Clinton and Shields avenues, you have to be watching closely or you will not even notice a two-story brick home on Princeton Avenue, surrounded by mature landscaping. This home once had a Fruit Avenue address and, as late as 1945, there was nothing between it and the old St. Agnes Hospital, now Glen Agnes Elderly Housing. But, as the neighborhood grew and the land was subdivided, another house was built in front of it.

Once you notice the structure, it is hard not to be intrigued by it for it is so different from its neighbors. Not only is it an adaptation of the Colonial Revival style, but an all-brick house is not a common sight in Fresno. The design is very simple, however. In fact, the only unusual features are the round brick columns that support the porch.

The house was built in 1914 by Eugene Main, a stockholder and foreman of the Fresno Brick & Tile Works. When Mr. Main decided to construct this nine-room house for his family, he began by making all the bricks in the backyard. He did an excellent job. By his own account, the house contained only one bad brick. When he sold his home to another family in 1945, he took pains to point it out to the new owners. But, in spite of its one bad brick, the Main Home still stands, a sturdy, yet gracious reminder of Fresno's past.

# The Cobb Home

The Freeway 180 project through the North Park neighborhood of Fresno has forever changed the appearance of this area. While many of the homes have been torn down, a surprisingly high number have been saved, moved to new locations in other parts of Fresno or, in some cases, within their historic neighborhood. For one of the most magnificent of these historic homes, a journey of just a block and a half has brought it to a new site on Yosemite Avenue.

The Cobb Home, long a landmark on Fulton Street, has the look of a Southern plantation house. Three Ionic columns soar two stories high to the roof. A deep porch on the second story offers a place for the owners to relax on a hot summer night. A finely detailed railing surrounds the porch, adding an elegant touch to the design.

The house was constructed in 1913 by Charles H. Cobb, the second man to engage in the automobile business in Fresno. He was the owner, with his brother, of a livery stable at the corner of Kern and Fulton streets. He began selling cars in 1907. He was the first president of the Fresno Auto Dealers Association, a board member of Chapman College and a state senator from 1926-30.

Today, the home has added significance for its association with the Cobb family. It is this family that donated the fountain in front of the new city hall, giving present and future Fresnans something beautiful to enjoy for many years to come.

In February of 1860, Elisha Cotton Winchell was appointed the first county school superintendent.
*Courtesy of William B. Secrest Sr.*

# The Honorable Elisha Cotton Winchell

The tale of one of the earliest residents of Fresno County, the Honorable Elisha Cotton Winchell, begins with his birth in West Springfield, Massachusetts on July 25, 1826. After his father suffered business reverses in 1835, the family moved to Illinois, and then to Missouri in 1838. Elisha decided to study law and was admitted to the bar in 1848. He opened his own practice in a town forty miles west of his parents' home.

Stories of the young state of California fascinated him and he became determined to settle there. He set out on his journey with three friends, a wagon, six horses, provisions and his law books. They had a harrowing trip, especially across the deserts that dot the landscape between the Rockies and the Sierra. After three months of traveling they were still 600 miles from Sutter's Fort. Finally, they were forced to abandon their wagon because the horses were too weak from hunger to pull it further. They struggled through the Humboldt Valley, a 300-mile trip. Everywhere they looked were scenes of devastation—dead and dying animals and property that had been left along the side of the trail. Five months after their journey began they reached the Carson River. They followed it to the Carson Canyon and across the state line into California. They made their way to Sutter's Fort.

In January 1851, Elisha Winchell opened a law office in Sacramento. The next year he was made justice of the peace. Three years later he was elected to the post of assessor for the city of Sacramento. During this period he married Laura C. Alsip. Their first son, Lilbourne Alsip, was born in 1855.

The Gold Rush was still in full swing. Winchell had read about the southern mines in Fresno County. He decided to move his family to Millerton and open a practice there. They arrived in May of 1859 and settled into a large adobe house at Fort Miller. A year later they moved into another adobe in the complex, which had at one time been used as the hospital. It was here that their second son, Ledyard Frink, and two daughters, Iva Mary and Anna Cora, were born. In 1861, they moved to a valley south of the fort and built a home. Winchell planted grapes and 600 fruit trees, which he obtained from a nursery in Sacramento. They provided the only fresh fruit in that area.

The family moved to Fresno when the county seat was relocated. Winchell continued to involve himself in important community activities.

Probably one of his most lasting contributions to Fresno County, however, was through his son Lilbourne, whose photographs of Tehipite Valley are among the earliest ever made and who wrote *History of Fresno County*, published in 1933. The writings of Lilbourne's wife, Ernestine, about the earliest years at Millerton have provided researchers with a wealth of knowledge that might otherwise have been lost.

# The Forces for Righteousness

Tales of the valley have told of the wild, untamed frontier town of Fresno Station with its rough, unpolished inhabitants and the saloons that existed on every street corner. However, beneath this layer of wildness, there existed a group of people who tried hard to wake up the evil forces in their town and call them to a better way of living.

In 1881, just nine years after the railroad created Fresno Station, the White Ribbon Reform Club was founded. Based on other groups of this name in California, the members of the local club took as their creed the following: "Knowing that intemperance is the greatest of all evils; filling prisons and poorhouses; causing children to cry for bread...and destroying the souls and bodies of men and women...we do band ourselves together to rescue drinking men and women and to destroy the liquor traffic in our community."

Serious in their pledge, the group of 258 people met once a week. Dues were fifty cents for men; women were exempt from payment. With Judge Sayle presiding as president, the first meeting opened with singing and prayer. A program was presented and then a number of hymns closed the meeting.

The list of members was impressive. Judge Gillum Baley, that stalwart founder of Fresno's first church; Mrs. James Faber, wife of Fresno's first resident and businessman; Mr. and Mrs. S. A. Miller, he the owner of the *Fresno Republican* and she Fresno's first telephone operator; Clark and A. T. Stevens, brothers and owners of the Black Hawk Stables at the corner of Fresno and L Streets: J. W. Shanklin, who would later become city clerk, and his daughter, Clara, were just a few of the dedicated members.

However noble their cause might have been, the forces behind the saloons were mightier still. The club did not last long. However, other similar clubs sprang up from time to time, each one stronger than the last. By 1919, the temperance forces throughout the country had made their voices felt. In that year an amendment to the Constitution brought Prohibition. The White Ribbon Reform Club and all the hundreds of forces for righteousness had won the day—at least for a little while.

# Justice in Fine Gold Gulch

In the days of the mining camps of the Gold Rush, when life was often lived not by rules, but by necessity, the legal system that we know today often did not exist. In the region of Fine Gold Creek, which today flows into Millerton Lake, justice existed in the form of John M. Hensley. A landowner who had large herds of sheep in the area, he spent his time conducting his operation and overseeing the men who tended his flocks. These men decided, quite on their own, to make him justice of the peace, to serve as the virtual ruler of the area.

Since there was no elected officer in the region, everyone accepted his role. People came from all over, bringing their problems and disputes to Mr. Hensley, asking him to mediate and to pass judgment on their disagreements. In each instance, Mr. Hensley listened carefully to the evidence and then decided the matter fairly, using common sense. The miners and shepherds understood this and never asked for an appeal of his decisions.

In many sections of California during this period, lawlessness often was a problem. But, on the Fine Gold River, if knives or guns were drawn, a word from Mr. Hensley restored the peace. As time went on, he not only was the voice of justice, but he also became the one who created laws as they were needed. For those who lived and mined in this part of Fresno County, Mr. Hensley was a legend who ruled wisely and well.

# Stop, Go & Move On

On January 8, 1927, the *Fresno Morning Republican* reported an event that stirred much local interest. Mrs. V. Phillips-Carter, a former Fresnan and wife of the former chief engineer and manager of the Madera Irrigation District, had invented a new traffic signal—one that would help those afflicted with color blindness.

The new signal was based on the premise that wavy lines can be seen by those who are color-blind. A long wavy line with arrows at each end was placed above the red stop sign on the signal. When the red light went on, lights cut off and on behind the line, giving the appearance of a wavy line. This line looked very much like the gesture of someone waving his arms to stop. When the green "GO" light went on, small lights cut off and on, making it appear that a ring of light was revolving in a circle. The moving circle would suggest going forward and joining the flow of traffic. Again, a person who could not see colors would be immediately aware of the moving line.

Mrs. Phillips-Carter proudly introduced her improved traffic signal at a convention of the California State Traffic Association where it was greeted with great enthusiasm. Not content with one successful invention, Mrs. Phillips-Carter also devised an arterial highway stop sign and a railroad crossing warning. Both were so well received that they were installed in many counties throughout California.

In the world of traffic engineering Mrs. Phillips-Carter's inventions were applauded and must have given her great satisfaction. However, one must wonder if deep in her heart of hearts there was a thought that gave her even greater happiness. For a woman of the 1920s, who was only beginning to gain a glimpse of the freedom for women yet to come, she knew that through her invention she was the one who would be telling motorists, male and female alike, when to stop, when to go and when to move on—not bad for a female from Fresno.

# The Knapp Cabin

Not all of the buildings in Fresno County that are listed on the National Register of Historic Places are grand homes or important commercial properties of another era. Indeed, several of these designated historical structures are of humble design, but have a significance that goes beyond their exterior appearance. It is the story of one of these that will be told.

In the years just after World War I, a wealthy Santa Barbara gentleman by the name of George Owen Knapp became acquainted with a summer recreation area that was developing along the South Fork Canyon of the Kings River. He built several cabins on Bubbs Creek, an eastern tributary of the South Fork. By 1925, the altitude proved to be too high for his deteriorating health. He decided to built a cabin at a lower elevation near Cedar Grove. Since he and his guests preferred sleeping in the open, the cabin was designed to store supplies and equipment.

It was a simple structure made of local materials. The poles that comprised the frame were cut in the nearby forest. The boards for the cedar walls also were cut in the immediate vicinity. The dirt floor of the one-room cabin rests on an accumulation of stones, rocks and gravel left thousands of years ago by the Kings River glacier.

Today, the Knapp Cabin is still standing, managed by the National Park Service as a historic structure. As humble as it is, its significance lies in the fact that it is one of the few existing tangible reminders of the early recreational use of the Kings River canyons before the Kings Canyon National Park was created. As such, it tells a story that goes far beyond its humble appearance.

# A Tale of Two Trees

Highway 99 stretches through the great Central Valley with monotonous regularity. Mile after mile it extends through the flat country, occasionally curving gently to break the tedium. Those who travel this highway try to look for landmarks along the way—something to talk about, something to recall a former trip, or something that, perhaps, will create a memory for a future holiday journey.

Such is the nature of this drive that many may have noticed something rather interesting in the median strip just south of Avenue 11 between Madera and Fresno. In this small elongated section of dirt sit two trees. The southernmost tree is a palm. Just north of it sits a deodar cedar. A rather strange twosome one might think and yet, by their very existence, they tell a story that could happen only in California.

Sometime during the 1920s or 1930s the trees were planted at this spot. Legend has it that they were either planted next to the old two-lane Highway 99 or near an old grocery store that was torn down when the roadway was widened. Whichever story is true is not as important as the fact that they were planted at a spot that marks the center of California. The palm tree symbolizes Southern California and the deodar cedar symbolizes the northern part of the state. Ironically, it was also the halfway point on the old Highway 99 that stretched from Oregon to the Mexican border.

Recently, Caltrans, in its efforts to provide safety to motorists in our state, proposed installing a three-beam guardrail along the median for four miles. The trees were in danger of being cut down. Once highway officials were told the legend of the trees, they worked out a plan to save them. Next time you travel along Highway 99 between Fresno and Madera, the trees will be there for your enjoyment, making your journey more interesting and providing a story for generations to come.

# A Caveman Named David

When one thinks of cavemen, one's mind goes back to ancient times when dinosaurs roamed the land, men wrote on walls, women cooked over open fires and the invention of the wheel was a new idea which, it was hoped, would make everyday life easier. Those days are lost forever in the mists of the past. Or are they?

A reading of the *Fresno Morning Republican* on June 27, 1929, gives the old adage "There's nothing new in the world" new meaning. For there on the pages of this well-known newspaper is an article on the valley's "Caveman."

It seems that halfway between Exeter and Lindsay, where the floor of the valley gives way to low-rolling foothills, a seventy-two-year old gentleman named David H. Wade made his home in an abandoned mine shaft that had been carved out of the hillside. Wade had a hard life. A serious accident, followed by financial reverses, caused him to decide to live a nomadic life. He purchased a pack of dogs and made a living by ridding farm properties of jackrabbits, which were a major problem for valley ranchers.

This life suited him well until one day when two of his dogs were poisoned. Feeling that society did not want him, he moved to the mine shaft. Using a cot for a bed and a cook stove made out of old oil cans, he and his dogs created a cozy home. On occasion friends brought him fresh fruit and vegetables. Otherwise, his diet consisted mostly of rabbit.

Many months passed. Wade was happy with his life. Then one day he fell ill. His friends took him to the county hospital in Visalia where he received the care he needed. However, he dreamed of returning to his cave home. His dogs were given to friends where they could be properly fed. But at least one of them shared the dream of his master. The loyal and faithful hound left the safety of his new home and returned to the cave. There he kept a quiet vigil, waiting for his master to return. Whether he did or not has been lost in the annals of time.

# A Ghostly Steamship

Many romantic stories were told of the days when steamships plied their way along the sloughs and rivers of the Central Valley. However, the names of some of the sloughs themselves conjured up thoughts of another kind, referring as they did to unpleasant physical conditions. Bog Slough, Cold Slough and Big Salt Slough did not exactly sound welcoming to those wishing to travel their waters. And, perhaps, they were not always friendly.

A steamboat captain tried to pilot his vessel, which was filled with lumber, from Mendota through the sloughs to Summit Lake, located between Mendota and Tulare Lake. The steamboat became grounded in Bog Slough. As the water receded in the summer heat, a tule fire which swept through the area burned the part of the boat that remained above the water line.

In the intervening years, as valley river projects have brought dams to the foothills, the sloughs ceased to exist for months at a time. The winds of more than one hundred valley summers have changed the topography still more. Among those whose memories go deep into the history of our valley, a story persists of a wreck of a steamboat that is buried in the valley's west side.

In the late fall of 1931, reporters from the *Fresno Republican* decided to investigate. Their lengthy search turned up only the ruins of an old dredge at the point where Cold Slough and Murphy's Slough met. "Could this be the remains of the steamship?" they wondered. They decided it was not. But, the ghostly remnants of the romantic steamship eluded their search. And still today the mystery remains—another legend of the valley lost in the mists of the past.

# Camel's Thorn

When a shipment of alfalfa seed arrived from Turkestan in 1931, the authorities allowed it to be admitted to California. Never in a million years would they have guessed that the seed carried with it another seed that would be the cause of many sleepless nights for our local farmers. The other seed was thought to be an unidentified legume, but, instead, it was camel's thorn, one of the most notorious weeds known to man. By the time its true identity was discovered, it had wreaked havoc in Riverside County and was well on its way to disturbing the peace of farmers in Fresno, Kings and Kern counties. Its rapid spread was attributed to its tasty qualities. A close relative and look-alike of the sweet pea, its small leaves, red flowers, and delicious green stems appealed greatly to farm animals who had been eating it with their alfalfa. However, when the weed dried out, it was full of spiny thorns. It grew in such density and became so impenetrable a mouse could not get through it. It also had the disagreeable habit of creating a huge root system close to the ground with a new root springing up at frequent intervals. Each new root had a taproot ten to eighteen feet deep. The nightmare was obvious.

There were two ways to eradicate this curse of weeddom. One could either apply carbon bisulphide to the stricken field, which would kill all plant life; or plow the afflicted land so that all plant life was turned under and then flood the land with water steadily for four months so the camel's thorn would be suffocated.

Fresno County agricultural officials decided to try the chemical method. With a $500 commitment from the board of supervisors, efforts began. Everyone truly hoped that the noxious weed would be gone for all time. Indeed, their efforts seem to have worked, for it has not been seen for a long time. For several years after this trying experience, the one flower local farmers wives did not grow in their garden was sweet peas. For some reason, the mere sight of them caused an otherwise even-tempered farmer to take on the appearance of one suffering from apoplexy.

# The Stoner Mansion

Tucked away in the Tivy Valley east of Fresno is a very special home. Sitting atop a knoll that offers a 360-degree view of this beautiful area, this home is an excellent example of an enlarged California bungalow style. Built in 1910 by Bertrand and Kitty Stoner, its foundation of river rock and mortar sits on solid granite. River rock, taken from the Kings River, is also used on the front porch and for a huge two-story fireplace. The four-gabled roof, trimmed with barge boards, is striking. Indeed, in aspect and appearance this home is set apart from its neighbors. It is the only home of its kind in Tivy Valley.

The Stoners were prominent members of the community and were connected with the development of the Kings River Thermal Tract that transformed the landscape into an agricultural paradise. Today the home has been carefully restored and is listed on the National Register of Historic Places.

A visit to Tivy Valley, with its rich orange groves and apple and walnut orchards, is a lovely experience. The breathtaking snow covered peaks of the Sierra, coupled with the gentle sounds of the nearby Kings River seem to create a symphony for the senses. When the modern world seems to close in on us with all its stresses and cares, it's a comfort to know that there are places of beauty nestled in the hills of Fresno County where tranquility can be found once again.

Tiburcio Vasquez was a colorful stage robber, rustler and thief who terrorized California from the 1850s until he was hanged in San Jose in 1875. He had this photo made to sell during his last trial.
*Courtesy of William B. Secrest, Sr.*

One of the most notorious bandits of nineteenth century California—he was second only to Joaquin Murrieta—was born near Monterey in 1835. He was of Mexican and Native American heritage. He launched his life of crime by getting mixed up in the killing of a constable. He was involved in horse stealing and served three jail terms for his efforts. After his release from prison, he and three compatriots held up the Visalia stage near Hollister. Two of the robbers were killed and the local marshal was wounded.

Unlike Murrieta, who was described as handsome and chivalrous, Tiburcio Vasquez was described as "coarse, treacherous and brutish." In spite of this he had the reputation of being a ladies' man. It was said that he was irresistible to the opposite sex.

Vasquez formed a gang and began to commit robberies in the Central Valley. The first raid on Firebaugh's Ferry netted them six hundred dollars.

In 1873, Vasquez and his men came to Fresno to look for others to join his gang. They stabled their horses at Russell Fleming's, without paying for the service. Fleming, who had been gone when they arrived, grabbed his gun when he returned and saw them. He demanded money from each of the outlaws. They jumped on their horses and rode off, calling to Fleming in Spanish, "Bueno hombre" (good man).

Soon after this the gang raided Jones Ferry, a little too close for comfort for the residents of Millerton. The gang made off with a thousand dollars.

The next plan was to rob the store of Jacob & Einstein in Kingston. Not only did the bandits rob Jacob & Einstein, but a store owned by S. Sweet and the local hotel. Everyone who got in the way of the gang was ordered to lie down on the ground and robbed. They made off with over twenty-five hundred dollars in jewelry and money.

The gang's final robbery occurred at Tres Piños. While the gang was inside a store looting it, Vasquez stationed himself outside and filled his time by killing several people.

Sheriffs all over the state were on the lookout for Vasquez and his men. Eventually, he was apprehended while eating dinner at a friend's house in Los Angeles. Sheriff W. R. Rowland of Los Angeles, who received the state reward for Vasquez' capture, called him "the most daring rascal since Joaquin Murrieta's time."

Vasquez held court while in jail, entertaining the tremendous crowds who flocked to see him. Tried for murder, he was found guilty and sentenced to hang. The bravado that was such a part of his character did not fail him. The day before his hanging, it is said he asked to see his coffin to determine if it was large enough to fit him.

He was executed on March 18, 1875.

# Budgets & Cents

In times of travail, history becomes a leveling agent that brings problems into perspective. These days, citizens are bombarded with news of budget crises at every tier of government. The city, county, state and federal governing bodies are all scrambling to allocate what little monies are available and are trying to deal with shortfalls.

In light of the money problems of our time, it might be of interest to refer to an article which ran in the May 8, 1935, edition of the *San Francisco Chronicle*. The news story tells of a meeting of the Fresno County Board of Supervisors. The agenda for this particular meeting contained a variety of matters including the ever-present necessity of finding money to fund the projects that were necessary to keep the County of Fresno and its government in good condition. At one point during the meeting, board chairman P. H. McMurty asked the county clerk if he had any matters to bring before the board. "I have the matter of a budget transfer, Mr. Chairman," he replied. The eyes of all the supervisors brightened. Perhaps there was additional money available that they did not know about. The clerk pulled himself to full height and said, "Mr. E. E. Quinnby of the county mechanical department desires a transfer of one cent from the general road fund to the general fund; the transfer is necessary for the payment of labor."

In the stunned silence that followed no one had the courage to ask what kind of work had been performed that required a one-cent remuneration. A roll call vote was taken, the transfer was made and the financial concerns of that particular meeting passed into history.

# The Hansen Home

The community of Selma was incorporated in 1893, joining Fresno as the only other town in Fresno County to formally gain the status of a bonafide city before the turn of the century. As Selma developed from a small rural settlement into a city, a number of charming homes were built within its boundaries. A number of them still stand, including the Hansen Home.

Built in a vernacular Victorian style by first owner Mr. Misten, this two-story home was constructed with square nails. Pine was used for the frame and inner walls of the home, but the outer walls were all faced with redwood one-by-twelves which were grooved at the top. The front door was typical of the period. It contained a transom for ventilation and was decorated with spindles and beaded work. A barn, carriage house and springhouse also were constructed on the property.

In 1908, the home was purchased by David Brooding, who added a front porch with pillars which supported the resulting second floor balcony. Mr. Brooding also planted a number of eucalyptus trees, many of which still grace this property.

The Hansen family purchased the home in 1937 and faithfully maintained the property in keeping with its historic nature. In recent years, this property was nominated to the National Register of Historic Places. Its significance lies in its historic associations with the development of Selma and the excellence of its detailed craftsmanship. Because of its potential landmark status, the Hansen Home will be a part of Selma's future as well.

# The Sharer Home

For almost one hundred years, travelers driving east on Shaw Avenue were treated to a charming sight. As soon as Fowler Avenue was crossed, there on the right, nestled in trees and shrubbery was a lovely Stick Style Victorian home with Eastlake decorative elements. All the gable ends were covered with fish scale shingles. Open spindle work decorated the gables and veranda. The transom panels of the bay windows and the panels in the front door were made of stained glass, adding beauty and color to the design. Every detail of the house showed an appreciation of fine craftsmanship and a determination to create beauty in the flat farmlands of Fresno County.

In 1892, John William Sharer began construction of his home. He carefully selected the wood himself and hauled it on mule-drawn wagons from the Peterson Mill in the mountains beyond Toll House. Such an undertaking meant the lumber journeyed down the Tollhouse grade—not an easy undertaking. He managed to bring lumber not only for his home, but also for many of the other homes that were being built in the Clovis area. It turned out to be a profitable venture.

During the first ten years the Sharers lived in the house, they added on to it several times. A tank house and barn with a cupola, built by Clovis Cole, were also part of the property.

In the 1980s a developer purchased the property. For a time the future of the house was in jeopardy, but eventually it was moved around the corner to a site on Fowler Avenue just south of Shaw Avenue. In its new location it is being preserved for another generation to enjoy and appreciate.

On January 10, 1881, just south and west of Fresno, around Adams and Cedar avenues, a small settlement and post office were established. The postmaster, Judge J. W. North, was charged with naming the new town. His first choice was Washington Colony, but that was vetoed by the federal authorities. It seems the name was too common. His daughter, May, suggested that since there were so many oleander bushes in the area, the town should be named for this prolific plant. And so, Oleander it was.

The settlement began to grow. The combination of cheap land and plenty of water drew people who wanted to farm. By the late 1880s, Oleander also could boast a number of fruit-and raisin-packing companies. The arrival of the Valley Railroad in 1897 helped to spur the economy.

However, there was another feature to this settlement that made it a good place in which to live—it had a very active social scene. There were religious organizations: the Congregational Church, the Church Endeavor Society, the Ladies' Aid Society, the Salvation Army and the Danish Missionary Society. There was also the Oleander Athletic Association, the Good Templars Lodge, the Social Club, the Oleander Dramatic Society and the Hoot Owl Club, which drew those interested in fishing and hunting.

It is interesting to note the presence of another organization that was an unusual and rather secretive one—the Old Maid's Club. This group was made up of ladies who felt that the marriage state was an unhappy situation and that those women who entered it would have to relinquish their independence. This was not for them! They chose to live pure and happy lives as single women. Needless to say, their number was small and rather select.

Most of the members of the community preferred the many ice cream socials and dances provided by the Social Club and the Ladies' Aid Society. On one of these occasions, the dance floor was waxed too well. The dancers that evening who managed to stay on their feet created a variety of new steps. It seems that life in the early years of our county could be rather fun. For those who lived in the settlement of Oleander, it was certainly much more than raisins and packing houses.

# The "Grapevine"

Webster's dictionary defines a nickname as a descriptive name applied to a person, place or thing. Those who drove on Highway 152 before a major project leveled the road between Los Banos and the Pacheco Pass will remember quite clearly the stretch of highway known as the "Washboard." For several miles, the road became a series of peaks and valleys that undulated like the washboard Grandma used on laundry day. It was a test of skill and endurance for any driver, and few shed tears when the new road was finished.

Another well-known stretch of highway bears two nicknames whose meanings may not be quite as evident. The names "Grapevine" and "Ridge Route" have both been applied to the highway that wends its way through the mountains from Los Angeles to the Central Valley. In the 1880s, the old stage road followed a path through the mountains known as the Ridge Route. When Highway 99 was constructed, it followed the course of this old road. Quite naturally, the nickname of Ridge Route remained.

But where did the name Grapevine come from and what stretch of this highway can properly bear that name? For the answer, one must journey back to the year 1772, when Don Pedro Fages, the military commander of Alta California, led an expedition in the Central Valley. As he began to descend the Tehachapi Mountains, he noticed a profusion of wild grapes growing luxuriantly from the top of the steep grade to the base of the mountain. By 1806, this was called Cajon de las Uvas, the Canyon of the Grapes. With the completion of I-5, the freeway was popularly called the Grapevine.

Today, both the Ridge Route and Grapevine are appropriate names. But, according to the California Highway Patrol at Fort Tejon, Grapevine enjoys the widest usage. Both names conjure up a part of California's past and remind us that we have a rich and romantic history, one that is worth taking time to explore and savor.

# The Owen Home

A lthough Clovis Cole is best remembered for his contributions to the community that would bear his name, he lived in Fresno from 1916 until his death in 1939. Indeed, from 1891 to 1893, his father Stephen served as Fresno's mayor.

Cole's sister, Carrie, married Charles Owen, a pioneer grain farmer in the Big Dry Creek area, who also owned and bred thoroughbred horses. His knowledge and ability in this field was known throughout the state. The Owen family had come to Fresno County in the 1870s. Owens Mountain, north of present-day Clovis, is named for them.

In 1902, Charles and Carrie Owen decided to retire from ranching and built a lovely home on the 2000 block of East Washington Avenue. Situated on a corner lot, it has entrances on both frontages. The roof line is marked by gables that face both streets. Typical of the period, the house is wood framed. It has a simplicity that reflects a transitional architectural design. The ornate Queen Anne style was becoming less popular; it was being replaced by the more spare look of a neoclassical row house.

On December 20, 1902, less than a year after the Owens moved into their home, Charles Owen was killed in a train crash. Tragically, he was returning from a business trip to San Francisco to attend the Christmas wedding of his daughter.

Today, the Owen Home is listed on the Local Register of Historic Resources; however, it is part of the Lowell/Jefferson Redevelopment Project area. As such, it faces an uncertain future. In a time when so many of our turn-of-the-century middle class homes have been lost, it may be hoped that this one will survive to remind future Fresnans what their city looked like in the early 1900s.

# The Rooster Crows at Midnight

The year was 1936. The month was October. The air smelled of a thousand small burning mounds of sycamore leaves. The nights were cold and crisp. Autumn was wrapping Fresno in the panoply of fall colors that only such nights bring. In this normally most tranquil of months, one would think that nothing could disturb such a beautiful season. But, all was not well.

As the smoke hung heavy on the evening air, Fresnans who lived on White Avenue between Thesta and Clark streets took a deep breath as they prepared for another night of disturbed slumber. What, one might ask, could cause such a nuisance that it was repeated every night? What could cause such neighborhood consternation that a group of citizens would finally petition the city's governing body to put a stop to it? Well, as those who grew up in the country know, it could be only one thing.

In the wee hours of early morning, long before daylight would break across the sky, a group of very cocky, vocal roosters would crow their hearts out to their captive audience. Their cacophony of sounds would soar across the stillness to waken every creature— man and beast alike. No living thing was spared their prideful cries. Windows might bang, neighbors might scream, dogs might howl, but nothing could pierce the din of their wailing symphony.

The pleas of the inhabitants were heard by the city fathers, but it was a police captain who offered an interesting suggestion. Build the chicken coops so low that the roosters will not be able to hold their heads up high enough to arch their necks and crow to the world. Keep them humble, he said, for it is only when they feel pride that they crow.

History does not record whether or not his suggestion was followed. But, one could hardly argue that it showed merit. For, as it has been shown many times in the tales of the valley, those who crow loudest often find a dose of humility waiting at the next turn in life's road.

# Checkerboards & Courthouse Park

During the years between the two world wars many of the early residents of Fresno had reached retirement age. After spending so many years in downtown Fresno, both living and working there, it seemed only natural to look to Courthouse Park as a place to gather with their friends. The shade trees, the expanses of lawn and the wooden benches provided a perfect setting for sharing political discussions, ball scores and the latest business news. Something else developed as well—spirited checker games. Each day the games went on from early morning until dinner time.

The checkerboards had been constructed by A. Fahler. However, by 1937, only three wooden checkerboards were left—hardly enough to keep the group of twenty-five players busy. Also, the stands for the boards were worn out, forcing players to hold them on their laps, or set them on the nearest trash receptacle during play. This was hardly appealing to the players.

Finally, the situation could be tolerated no longer. The checker players banded together and took their case to the board of supervisors. They were told that Mr. S. M. Ellis, who supervised the courthouse and its park, did not have money for this kind of expense in his budget, but that the matter would be considered. Two weeks later the supervisors voted to build an area on the north side of the park that would include new tables and checkerboards. The players were delighted. This assured them that their games, which had become part of the special flavor of downtown Fresno, would continue until the sound of the last checker being played could be heard throughout Courthouse Park.

Life for those who live in the great Central Valley is not totally unlike the rest of the world. There are those special days, filled with magic, when everything goes right and the world seems a glorious place. And, then there are those other days—days in which absolutely everything goes wrong and one wonders why one got out of bed that morning.

It was one of those days that Fresno Police Chief Truax was experiencing on December 10, 1936. Up until then, it had been a record-breaking month. His officers had tallied up fifty-seven arrests for speeding and reckless driving. My, but they were proud. Not only were the city's coffers going to benefit, but this kind of performance showed how dedicated his officers were.

He couldn't help but think that the two new police cars the city had purchased were partly responsible. They were so efficient—certainly worth buying. And then the unthinkable happened. A woman motorist who was stopped for speeding complained. "I was only traveling twenty-nine miles an hour," said she. "I was watching my speedometer and I will swear to this in court!"

Word of this was immediately dispatched to the chief, who ordered a check of the speedometers on the new police cars. The report came back. They were as much as ten miles an hour too fast. Whoops! To be wrong was bad enough, but to be caught by a woman driver! This was not a good day.

At a hastily assembled press conference a red-faced police chief announced that the fifty-seven motorists who had been arrested for speeding would have the charges against them dismissed. Those who had already paid their fines would be reimbursed. After all, this was only fair because the speedometers in the new police cars had never been checked. It was assumed that since the cars were new they were in perfect working order. It probably also could be assumed that the poor police chief wished that he had stayed in bed on this most embarrassing of days.

# Mr. Dillion's War

In these times, one often reads stories of past wars in the newspapers. They are usually contained in an interview with a veteran of Vietnam, Korea or World War II. For the reader, these accounts evoke memories of those times and, perhaps, of personal experiences as well. When reading an old newspaper from 1929 and suddenly happening on an interview with a Civil War veteran, one's reaction is a mixture of surprise and regret. Amazement to realize that the year of the stock market crash was not so far removed from that terrible war, and regret that one had not been able to ask many questions of the gentleman himself. History often leaps off the pages and catches us unaware.

For the 1929 reader of the *Fresno Republican*, W. H. Dillion recounted his experiences as a soldier with the 129th Cavalry. He enlisted in 1863 at Monmouth, Illinois. After completing training in Chicago and Saint Louis, his division traveled by the river to New Orleans. Most of Dillion's time was spent scouting and raiding in Louisiana, western Texas, Arkansas and Mississippi. He hardly ever ate in camp and often did not eat at all. Sometimes he had sweet potatoes and a little bit of meat.

The most difficult battle that he fought in was at Liberty, Louisiana. The Union artillery pounded the enemy for three hours. In another instance, during the Davidson Raid, his "division was in the saddle for thirty-seven days, tearing up railroads and destroying…Confederate property." At the war's end, his unit was ordered to Mexico to get Emperor Maximilian, who was executed before they had traveled very far.

After his discharge, Dillion decided to come west to Selma, where he became a farmer. In 1919, he moved to Fresno and brought with him many stories of the heartbreaking Civil War that pitted brother against brother, but, in one of the great ironies of history, resulted in truly uniting our country for the first time.

# Happy Birthday, Fresno County Free Library!

In 1993, the 100th year of the Fresno County Free Library, it behooves each of us to think about the special role this institution plays in our lives. Where else can you go and find so many opportunities beckoning? If you wish to travel to Greece, visit mysterious Tibet, or wander through the great museums of the world, all these options are available simply by taking a book off the shelf.

Perhaps an engrossing novel suits your mood, or a complex Agatha Christie, or maybe a biography of Harry Truman or the latest history of Gettysburg. Maybe a real treasure awaits on the new non-fiction shelf. Whatever your interest or pleasure, just the right book can always be found.

For the serious researcher, the library offers a wealth of opportunities. The reference department has materials on the shelves for delving into the most obscure subject, and, for students who just need to check facts for a term paper or class project, the appropriate books are there to be used. Did you know that this department has phone books from most of the major cities in the United States? A quick trip to these shelves can put you in touch with long lost friends or help you plan your next trip.

Do you like local history? A visit to the California History Room on the second floor of the downtown library will open a wealth of reading possibilities. Here, books on every facet of the history of Fresno County sit on the shelves awaiting interested readers. In this place, microfilm of early Fresno newspapers is also available. If you want to find out what happened in Fresno on any given day, this is the place for you. If family history is more your cup of tea, this room offers shelves of books on genealogy. Volunteers from the Fresno Genealogical Society stand by waiting to help you.

Whatever your interest, whatever your need, the staff at the library can point you in the right direction.

As you hurry home with your newly checked-out books firmly in hand, the anticipation of much enjoyment is uppermost in your mind. Happy Birthday, Fresno County Free Library and thank you for providing us all with many rich and happy hours.

Catherine Morison Rehart

In the years between the two world wars, a beautiful red-haired actress was making a name for herself in stage performances all across the country. A native of Clovis and a daughter of the mayor of Fresno, Ninetta Eugenia Sunderland was praised by critics for her fine acting ability and excellent speaking voice. She played on Broadway with some of the greatest actors of the time including Otto Kruger, George M. Cohan, Victor Moore and Walter Huston. Her talents were recognized by Walter Hampden, a famous Shakespearean actor, who allowed her to travel with his repertory company.

In 1927, she was scheduled to appear in a local dramatic presentation. Her father was delighted and took advantage of the opportunity that his term of office as mayor allowed. He made plans to present her with the keys to the city, because he said that he remembered the many times she let him in the house when he forgot his.

Despite her fame and her marriage to actor Walter Huston, Nan Sunderland did not forget her home. A graduate of Fresno High School, she attended Fresno Normal School and reigned as Raisin Queen. Many years later she established the Huston-Sunderland Scholarship at California State University, Fresno in memory of her husband and her father. Each year the scholarship provides an outstanding student entering the school of art or drama with $600. A fine legacy from a beautiful lady.

Symbolic of Victory — Netta Sunderland
waved the American Flag as World War I came to
an end.
*The Image Group from the Laval Historical Collection.*

# Problems with Nudists

In the fall of 1938, avid readers of the *Fresno Bee* had something to snicker about. It began with the first of a series of articles regarding a film at the Rex Theater. According to the article, this movie, entitled *Fun With Nudists*, showed the recreational activities of "clothesless cultists." Evidently, the frolicking of these avid seekers of oneness with nature by shedding the garments demanded by civilization was, in the words of the reporter, "too Parisian for Fresno audiences."

After the film was confiscated, a special showing in the projection room of a private photographer was arranged for the district attorney's investigators and for members of the police vice squad. After viewing the movie, they said that it was not suitable for Fresno audiences. The theater manager was arrested and charged with indecent conduct. After posting $200 bail, he was released pending his appearance before Police Judge M. K. Gibbs. All of Fresno waited for this event because if he pleaded "not guilty" the movie would have to be shown before the court. History does not record the final outcome of this case. It must be assumed that it was settled out of court, which for some of the citizens of Fresno was perhaps disappointing.

In those primitive days before television, an event of this kind would most likely mean that on at least one cold, winter day, Judge Gibbs' courtroom would experience standing-room-only crowds. Those who managed to brave the crowds would have a story to tell for many years to come—a story that would probably grow longer and more sensational with each telling.

In mid-September in the year 1938, the *Fresno Guide* published some of the entries in a writing contest the newspaper was sponsoring. The theme of the contest was "What I Would Do For the Good of Fresno If I Were Mayor." An interesting question at any time, the answers that were published in some cases reflect the tenor of those times; other answers show that certain problems still have not been solved.

For instance, one writer stated the need to "bring a union depot to Fresno, ordering abandonment of the Santa Fe tracks through the residential district to eliminate about 40 dangerous crossings."

One writer wanted to eliminate all gambling houses in the city, while another wanted all illegal establishments to be classified and licensed and allowed to remain in operation. One writer had another way of dealing with the problem: "Order a complete probe by efficient fact-finders from out of town into Fresno's 'underworld' and back up their findings with fearless prosecution."

Public transportation was a problem then as it is now. The suggestion was made that the rail lines be removed, buses be installed and city streets be improved. The establishment of municipal parking lots for automobiles was encouraged.

In those days before backyard swimming pools were common, one person suggested building a public swimming pool that all Fresnans could enjoy. The more frequent use of the Memorial Auditorium for public entertainment was suggested.

Most of these ideas seem to be understandable to today's Fresnan. One suggestion, however, is of the kind that could cause a gentlewoman to protest mightily. Discharge, someone suggested, from city payrolls all married women whose husbands have jobs. Suddenly, the Fresno of 1938 seems light-years away from the Fresno of 1997.

# Josephine Ruth Gibson

As one drives through the residential neighborhoods of our city, it is not uncommon to see an elementary school complete with children happily playing in its adjacent yard. The school usually bears the name of a prominent, deceased Fresnan that is easily recognizable. However, sometimes the name is not well known, and a little research is necessary.

One such school, on Barstow Avenue, bears the name of a woman who came to Fresno from Maryland in 1920. She graduated from Fresno Normal School with her teaching credential two years later. She briefly taught in Kings County, but soon returned to Fresno to teach at a small country school called Bullard Elementary. With a teaching staff of three to oversee one hundred students, this school had a definite rural flavor. Some of the students came to school on horseback; others were driven in horse-drawn buggies.

This lady had studied foreign languages at several colleges, including Stanford, and, under her guidance, a sixth grade pilot program in languages began at Bullard. Although the study of science was a part of the curriculum, she felt that the study of humanities was more important. Her philosophy of teaching was that it did not matter if a student attained a high grade, but whether that student obtained knowledge.

Her career at Bullard began in the classroom, but she also served that school as principal. She is remembered as a just and kind teacher and administrator who truly cared about the future of her students. A fitting tribute to her educational legacy to her community was the naming of the Ruth Gibson School in her honor.

A drive out Belmont Avenue to McCall Avenue will bring the traveler through an area of Fresno County that is rich in the history of horticulture. It was in this region that Francis Eisen's grapes dried on the vines, starting the raisin industry. It was at nearby Fancher Creek that Frederick Roeding opened his nursery, offering varieties of trees for the farms that were developing all around. And, it was also, of course, in this area that Mr. A. Y. Easterby grew his fields of wheat, which started the whole business of agriculture in the Central Valley.

Not surprising then that horticultural history is still being made in this corner of our county, because—as the poet might say—the roots run deep in this region. For it is here, on McCall Avenue just north of Belmont, that Henderson's Experimental Gardens was located. Mr. Henderson started this business in 1926, after working with the world famous horticulturist Luther Burbank in Santa Rosa.

All of the valuable lessons that Burbank taught him plus all that he learned through many years of hard work in the garden business were carried on by Don Kleim, who went to work for Henderson in 1946. Kleim carried on the business after Henderson's death in 1972 until his own death on November 6, 1996.

Plant materials were sent to Kleim from all over the world to test in this climate. Some of them were considered unworthy of propagation by most nurseries because they were hard to grow here and would not sell quickly. Kleim, using methods of hybridization and selection, created varieties that can be grown in our Central Valley. As a result, the avid gardener could not only find a wealth of varieties of common trees like maple and dogwood, but also unusual plants that he was assured would grow well in his garden. In 1993 almost two hundred plants were in the process of experimental work. The gardener could find hardy varieties of popular plants as well. Most fascinating of all, Henderson's Experimental Gardens had a world-wide reputation.

Following Mr. Kleim's death, his wife continued to operate the gardens. They are now for sale and, for now, the future of this one-of-a-kind horticultural paradise is uncertain.

# A Weighty Subject

In the late 1950s and early 1960s, in those halcyon days just before Fulton Street was transformed into a mall, autumn brought all kinds of activity to downtown Fresno. Shoppers, anticipating Christmas, filled the stores. The streets bustled with cars and people—everyone on his or her own private mission of commerce.

For one store, Ennis Finer China & Crystal, which was located on the street floor of the Helm Building, the arrival of autumn also meant that the year's largest shipment of quality crystal would soon make its appearance via the United States Postal Service. And, one fateful year, true to tradition, the crystal arrived and was waiting in the basement of the Helm Building to be unpacked.

Unfortunately, the Otis Elevator Company chose this particular day to test the weights on the Helm Building's elevator. As the Otis truck, bearing two thousand pounds of elevator weights, began its backward descent into the basement, the weights began to shift. As the driver watched in horror, the weights parted company with the truck and shot with great force directly into the boxes which held two thousand pounds of expensive crystal. The devastation, to say nothing of the noise, generated by this spectacular crash was something to behold. However, according to Bill Ennis, "All was not lost...it had been a slow day and we finally had a cash sale."

# The Great Emancipator

As the tales of the valley unfold, some offer surprising moments in the lives of the people who were brave enough to make the arduous trip to the Fresno of the 1870s. One such couple had been born in slavery on the plantation of Harry Smith in North Carolina in the late 1830s.

Douglas and Elizabeth Hargrave met and later married on the plantation in 1876. They had not known they were free until two years after the Emancipation Proclamation was signed. They continued to work on the plantation because there was nowhere else to go.

In 1878, they enlisted with a group of black workers to go to Raymond, California, to work in a granite quarry owned by Harvey Knowles. Mrs. Hargrave cooked for the work crew. After six months, they moved to Fresno where Mr. Hargrave found work as a carpenter. His skills were put to work helping to build the Second Baptist Church.

Several years later the couple were instrumental in the organization of the Mount Pleasant Baptist Church. They were valued members of the Fresno community until their deaths. Mr. Hargrave died just before his 100th birthday. Mrs. Hargrave died in 1942 at age 102.

During their long lives they witnessed many changes and experienced many joys and sorrows. But for Mrs. Hargrave, her most treasured memory occurred when she was a young girl. On a beautiful North Carolina morning, President Lincoln stopped for a brief rest at the plantation where she lived. The memory of seeing that great man remained clear in her mind until the end of her days.

# The Raisin-The Profitable Mistake

Picking and drying raisin grapes, c. 1890.
*Courtesy of Joan Emerson.*

Raisins have long been the leading agricultural crop of Fresno County. The sweet, early ripening grape which makes delicious raisins was the result of Fresno's hot dry summers and cool moisture-free nights.

During the latter part of the 1870s, vineyards flourished. More and more acres went into production as people arrived in Fresno eager to enter the industry. One of the early vineyards was called Hedge-Row. It was owned and operated by four women schoolteachers from San Francisco, Minnie F. Austin, Lucy H. Hatch, E. A. Cleveland and Julia B. Short. In the first year their vines produced thirty twenty-pound boxes of raisins. Eight years later, they packaged 7,500 boxes. After ten years, the women were able to retire. This is only one of the early success stories.

How did the raisin industry get its start? It happened by mistake. The summer of 1875 was extremely hot and some of Francis Eisen's experimental grapes dried on the vine. He picked them, packed them and sent them to San Francisco, advertising them as a "Peruvian Importation." They caused quite a sensation and the rush to raisin farming began.

A group of women packing raisins, c. 1900.
*Courtesy of Joan Emerson.*

# The Corset Lady Cometh

For ladies who lived in Fresno over one hundred years ago, life was not filled with the comforts that we know today. Indoor plumbing was not universally known, and for those who lacked that luxury, water for bathing, cooking and cleaning had to be hand-pumped from the well in the back yard. Meals were cooked over a wood stove and air-conditioning was nonexistent in the long, hot, valley summers.

The fashions of the time were not well-suited to this way of life. Collars were chin-high, sleeves reached to the wrist and skirts were floor-length. It would not do, after all, for a gentleman to glimpse an ankle. Victorian mores frowned on such a thought. Not only was wearing apparel uncomfortable, but what was underneath was even more so. Tight corsets that were laced until a woman could barely breathe were the height of fashion. These articles of torture could be purchased at Kutner-Goldstein or through a catalogue. Or, one could arrange an appointment with the corset lady who would come once a year to one's home to take proper measurements so that the corset would fit perfectly.

The corset lady had to measure her customer very carefully because every curve had to be accommodated in the design. The garment was made of a heavy cotton fabric. Whalebone stays of different lengths and widths were used to give support and to create the hourglass shape that was so popular at the turn of the century. Eyelets were sewn into the garment so that laces could be inserted. It was the laces that would be tightened to create the tiny waist that was so fashionable. The job of constructing a corset was not an easy one. The corset lady was an architect of sorts— designing a structure that would accommodate her customer as comfortably as possible, given the constraints of fashion.

It is not often that one hears modern women long for the "good old days." One overwhelming reason is the nightmarish stories they have heard their grandmothers tell about the fashions of yesteryear and the horrors of the laced corset.

# The Kutner Home

A rather recent and welcome addition to the city of Fresno's List of Historic Resources is a distinguished looking colonial revival-style home with white clapboard siding. Built in 1910, in the North Park neighborhood just north of Divisadero Street, the Forthcamp (Fulton Street) address was a prestigious one. Most of the residents were leading business and professional people. Mayor William F. Toomey lived across the street. In its long history, this home has had only three owners and contains many of its original features.

The first owner, Louis Kutner, came to Fresno to join his brother in the family business, Kutner-Goldstein Company, as its treasurer. He planned and built his new home on a scale that would rival other residences in Fresno. It contains a large entry with a stairway, a big dining room with wood paneled wainscoting, and five bedrooms. In 1913, he added a ballroom for entertaining. Mr. Kutner and his family occupied their home for ten years and, in 1920, moved to San Francisco. The home was purchased by the Milan Vucovich family, who occupied it for the next seventy-one years.

Today, the name of the street has been changed to Fulton and the area has undergone a difficult period due to a freeway project. However, it is poised for rebirth, due to the efforts of many people who, like the new owners of the Kutner-Vucovich Home, Virginia and Kevin Robinson, are committed to preserving and restoring their unique and important structures. When the freeway project is completed and the dust settles, North Park will shine once again as an important and historic Fresno neighborhood.

# The Gregory Home

Deep in the northern portion of the Forkner-Giffen Tract, which today is known as Old Fig Garden, is a classic tri-level home. Its U-shaped design allows the perfect setting for a courtyard and fountain. The first owner of the home was Fred W. Gregory, the sales manager for J. C. Forkner Fig Garden Incorporated. He sold many of the parcels of land in the development. Legend has it that the first land sales were made from folding tables that were set up in tents along the boulevard. Here Forkner and his salesmen transacted their business.

The first five homes were built along Van Ness Boulevard in 1919. The Gregory Home is the only one of the five that looks much as it did then. The home has many interesting features including arched windows in the master bedroom, which also contains French doors which open onto the second story balcony, a bay window, wainscoting in the dining room, and an unusual child's room which has windows on two sides that make you feel that you are in a tree house

Before joining J. C. Forkner's operation, Fred Gregory had been in business for himself. At the turn of the century, he was the owner of Gregory and Company, a store on Mariposa Street which sold phonographs, White sewing machines and bicycles. In 1901, he began to sell automobiles, too. In 1903, Frank A. Homan joined the firm and, in 1908, he bought out the business which was then known as Homan and Company. It had become the largest sporting goods store in Fresno.

Mr. Gregory had moved to San Francisco, where he engaged in running a hardware store. After the 1906 earthquake he moved back to Fresno and went into the fig packing business. Then, in 1919, he went to work for J. C. Forkner.

Today, the Gregory Home still stands. Carefully restored, it is a part of the history of Forkner's successful dream of turning bare land into a beautiful landscape of homes and trees.

# The Alta 2

The tales of the Central Valley have recorded the stories of early explorers and their findings. However, in June of 1938, four intrepid adventurers of the twentieth century variety set out in a fifteen-foot skiff named the *Alta 2*, determined to travel the waterways of the valley from Bakersfield to San Francisco. The rains and heavy snow of winter had caused such flooding that the travelers hoped their exploits would point out the need for flood control measures. These men, father and son Frank and Don Latta, Ernest Ingalls and Richard Harris, left Bakersfield on June 19 with Kern County Chamber of Commerce representatives standing by, and began their journey through the valley's sloughs and waterways. Sometimes traveling on farmland that had been inundated by flood water, the foursome made their way along Buena Vista Slough to Fowler Lake across the flooded lands of Liberty Farms. They traversed Tulare Lake to the mouth of the Kings River. From there, they guided their skiff through the lower and upper Stratford Weirs to the San Joaquin diversion point. Here they entered the San Joaquin River and sailed to Stockton, where they were greeted by a reception committee from the Stockton Chamber of Commerce, who, with the local yacht club, provided a convoy through the Carquinez Straits to Treasure Island in the San Francisco Bay.

On June 31, twelve days after their skiff was launched, the crew of hardy sailors tied their boat at a Treasure Island pier. Members of the San Francisco and California chambers of commerce were there to greet them and applaud their adventure. A gala reception was planned, but the crew was more interested in clean clothes, a steak dinner and a soft bed—all of which were provided.

More important, they had proved their point. If the flooded lands of the Central Valley could be traveled to this extent, surely flood control projects were needed. Frank Latta was interviewed on NBC radio about his findings and gave a report to the Kern County chamber using film of the trip and the problems of many of the farmers he interviewed along the way. He and his crew, by demonstration rather than just using maps and graphs, made a tremendous impact on the valley. It was a turning point, a watershed experience in the history of the valley.

# The Storm's Eye

On March 15, 1938, the term "the eye of the storm" took on new meaning for a Mr. O. A. Flint, a Del Rey dairy farmer. At precisely 3:30 on that morning, the milkers had just gone to work when a massive windstorm hit the valley with a vengeance not often seen. One milker was adjusting the milking machine when a cow suddenly was blown on top of him. As he freed himself and jumped back, an entire row of eleven cows fell domino fashion, one on top of the other, as if an invisible force had mowed them down. By the time the milker was able to throw off the power switch, three of the cows were dead. The other nine went into shock.

This, however, was only the beginning. As the wind howled, the roof of one of the barns blew off and sailed majestically into a neighboring farm. A number of trees were uprooted, while many of those that stayed in the ground had their tops twisted out.

While this sort of thing might be expected during a windstorm, something else occurred that never could be explained. In farmer Flint's milk shed, there were ten empty sacks which had been neatly stacked on the ground. After the storm ceased, they were found just as neatly stacked, in perfect order, but they now were in Flint's yard.

As the farmer surveyed the damage and the loss of three valuable cows, he could only guess that his farm had been at the exact center of the storm. This was poor solace for the nine cows who were left with a bad case of the jitters. One cannot help but wonder how such excitement affected their ability to provide milk. Probably it will never be known—but, as one has often seen as the tales of the valley unfold, life's unexpected events often bring with them enough humor to overcome any obstacles that suddenly land in one's path.

# A Clubhouse on Calaveras

On May 14, 1938, the Fresno Society for the Hard of Hearing opened a new facility for those in the community whose hearing was impaired. The clubhouse, at 245 North Calaveras Street, was given to the society with funds generously donated by Mrs. Mary Huntzicker, in memory of her son, Ernest, who had been killed in an automobile accident in 1934.

One special feature of this building, which made it unique among other structures in Central California, was a group hearing-aid system which consisted of wires that were incorporated into the building at the time of construction. The wires were connected to individual hearing aids which were placed throughout the main room for use by visitors. These hearing aids were part of a master system which had a microphone that picked up sounds within twenty or thirty feet, amplified them and distributed them to the individual ear phones, thus making it possible for the hard-of-hearing to enjoy the meetings and programs at the clubhouse.

The system was tried out for the first time at the dedication ceremonies. On that memorable evening speeches were given by several people followed by a musical program featuring pupils from the Severance School of Dance. For those attending this event, the new equipment made it possible to enjoy the evening more completely. A major step forward had been made in making life richer for those in the Fresno community who were hearing-impaired.

# The Dance of Love

The journey down love's highway is not always an easy one. However, the obstacles in the road sometimes help to create stronger, and certainly more determined relationships. And so it was for famous dancer and former Fresnan Billy Carroll in the fall of 1940.

Carroll began to study dance in Fresno at the age of twelve. When he was fifteen, he left for Los Angeles and, within two years, signed a contract with Sir Victor Sassoon to appear at the Cathay Hotel in Shanghai. A few years later he joined the Russian Ballet and studied dance under the famous teacher Dimitri Folkine. After two years, he left to embark on a career that would take him around the world.

While dancing in Calcutta, he met another dancer, named Conchita, the niece of the Maharajah and Maharanee of Kucia and the daughter of an Indian mother and an English father. Her Hindu name was Kallecheta which means Black Panther. Her English name was Gladys Bond. The two became dancing partners and eventually gained world renown with a repertoire of more than forty exotic and authentic dances. They also fell in love.

All went well until they decided to come to Billy's home in Fresno to be married. When they arrived at Terminal Island, where the bride tried to enter under the non-quota group, the authorities detained her. After waiting for more than a month, she developed a severe toothache and was allowed to go into San Pedro to visit the dentist. Then it was back to Terminal Island to await permission to travel with her bridegroom to Fresno where a wedding would be held. Meanwhile, Billy Carroll waited in Fresno with his family, fully confident that she would be released soon. After the wedding, the couple was under contract to appear at the Biltmore Bowl in Los Angeles.

History does not record the outcome of this story. Did Conchita get off Terminal Island or was she destined to spend the rest of her life waiting for her love? Carroll was sure all would go according to their plans. For this young Fresnan who had gained international fame, the obstacles in love's path made him even more determined to marry the young woman he love.

# Life in Jail in 1888

In August of 1888, Fresnans were aware of a new building in Courthouse Park—a new jail. This new structure was the subject of quite a bit of conversation, until the mounting curiosity finally sent a reporter from the *Fresno Morning Republican* to see what life was like inside the new, improved facility. His findings were rather interesting.

The jail housed twenty-six prisoners. They all got up in the morning whenever they liked, except for those who worked on the chain gang. For these unfortunate souls, if they were not up by 7:30, not only were they denied any breakfast, but they also were not allowed to eat until 4:00 in the afternoon when dinner was served. The breakfast menu consisted of beefsteak, fried potatoes, bread and black coffee with sugar. When dinner time came, the men ate pot roast or stew with beans and bread. If Charlie, the cook, was in a baking mood, apple pie was served for dessert. The men on the chain gang who were up in time for their breakfast received a third meal. For them, a lunch was prepared at noon.

According to the report published in the *Republican*, eating seemed to be the main event of the day. Certainly the new building was more secure than Fresno County's first jail at Millerton. There the facility was so poorly built that the prisoners would break out whenever the mood struck them so they could frolic in the foothills, but they always returned for their meals, which were excellently prepared by cooks in the local hotels. Good food, it seems, has historically been as important as security in the jails of Fresno County.

In September of 1897, a lady traveled from San Francisco to Fresno to visit this city in which she had been a teacher for one term in 1874. Her memories of the Fresno of 1874 were good ones and her intention was to visit her friends who remained here and to see how the city had grown. When she had left, the courthouse was not yet built. Fresno consisted mostly of primitive wood frame structures which stood out starkly against the harsh landscape which was devoid of vegetation. She returned to find a city that had fine Queen Anne buildings, busy streets and a large populace. She drove through the colony farms and was amazed to see the vineyards and fruit trees that created a lush landscape.

Many of her friends remained in Fresno from the early days, including the family of Mr. J. W. Ferguson, publisher of the *Expositor* newspaper. She had lived with the Fergusons while she taught school. The contact with the newspaper business interested her and she had become a journalist herself.

After leaving Fresno in 1874, she married J. J. Owen, the founder and editor of the *San Jose Mercury*. After selling the newspaper, Mr. and Mrs. Owen moved to San Francisco, where Mr. Owen became involved with several publishing ventures. After his death, Mrs. Owen, recorded in history only under her husband's name, continued in the publishing business and, at the time of her Fresno visit in 1897, was the editor of a monthly newspaper in San Francisco called the *Petit Courier*.

Her pleasure at finding that Fresno had grown into a fine city during her absence caused her to write in her newspaper, the *Petit Courier*, that she really was not surprised. She remembered that the character of the people who lived in Fresno in 1874 ensured a great future for the town for they were energetic and ambitious. She also remembered that they were sociable and kind. All of these excellent qualities still existed, she felt, and she predicted that Fresno would become the metropolis for the empire that would develop in the Central Valley. And, as all who live here know, Mrs. Owen's prediction became reality.

When the needs of a community dictate that the use and storage of water would be better served by the construction of a dam, a number of things have to be considered. These are dealt with in studies which keep the engineers, planners and many governmental agencies busy for a number of months. But then the human element comes into play and, almost always, it presents the most interesting problems. The solving of these often brings up tales of the past.

In the case of the Friant Dam project, the new lake that it would create was going to cover the site of Millerton, Fresno County's first seat of government. Almost all of the buildings were gone, having been moved to Fresno Station in the 1870s and '80s. The old courthouse was dismantled, stored and rebuilt a number of years later at Mariner's Point, overlooking Millerton Lake.

But communities are more than buildings, and the United States Bureau of Reclamation officials were faced with a number of graves in six burial sites that had to be moved. Many were the resting places of early pioneers. Many others were of Indians who had been laid to rest long before the coming of the white man.

It was the policy of the government to locate the next of kin and offer this person two alternatives. The first was to move the remains to a suitable place above the water line of the newly created lake, without cost to the family. With the second, the government would turn the remains over to a designated undertaker for burial wherever the relative chose.

If the relative desired to be present at the time of disinterment, this was arranged. If not, an official was present to take a careful inventory of everything found at the burial site. It had been rumored that a valuable ring was present in one of the graves.

The government officials did all they could to locate and identify every grave and ease this difficult situation as much as possible for the families involved.

# Long Skirts & Leering Eyes

The files of the *Fresno Bee* and its predecessor, the *Fresno Morning Republican*, are filled with a rich legacy for the researcher—a chronicle of daily life in our city that transports the reader into any era of his choosing. These precious tidbits reveal more about life in Fresno than all the pages of the history books combined.

In 1888, two articles appeared in the *Republican* which dealt with women's skirts and modesty. In the first, a young man who termed himself a man of modest character used the pages of the newspaper to send a message to "a certain young lady who lives just east of O Street." He implored her to please wear hose when she watered her front lawn, especially in windy weather. If she did not, the young man wrote, the sight of her well-turned ankle would cause him to walk with his face turned to the other side of the street in order to hide his blushes.

The other story, written by a young woman who called herself a "Shop Girl," contained a plea of another sort. "Since I was not born with a silver spoon in my mouth," she wrote, "I am compelled to work for a living and must travel the public thoroughfares of this city twice a day." In so doing she had to elbow her way through crowds of men who had the unfortunate habit of chewing tobacco and spitting it on the sidewalk. The refuse thus created caused her to have to lift her skirts in order to keep them clean. The "corner loafers," as she termed the men who loitered about, were apt to comment rather loudly on the vista thus created. She had had enough.

Her fervent demand that the trustees do something about this horrible situation which the fair young ladies of Fresno had to endure made interesting copy for the readers of the *Republican*. Among other things, it certainly lets the readers of 1990s Fresno know that not all of Fresno's male population in the 1880s were of a modest bent.

The legends of the valley include the stories of many hardy men who made the mountains their home. Miners, trappers, explorers, and loggers—all made their own unique contribution to the story of our area. One of these hardy fellows stood alone, however, creating his own special legacy.

Traveling overland from Iowa at age eighteen, he arrived in California in 1874. He worked as a ranch hand near Le Grand for a time and then moved up to the position of foreman for the owner of a 49,000-acre ranch west of Fresno.

In 1887, he left the valley for the mountains. Locating at Poison Meadows near Pine Ridge, he operated a sawmill there until 1915. During this time, he traveled the Sierra from Yosemite to Kern County, often taking private parties on long pack trips to the high country. On his early trips to Yosemite in the 1880s he visited friends who lived in a small cabin at Nevada Falls. Their name was Snow, which provided him with the foundation for his claim that in summer and winter, he always found snow at Nevada Falls.

It was not until his eighty-fourth year that he decided to publish the poems that were the product of his life in the Sierra. The pages of his book, *Under The Trail*, were filled with poems with such titles as "Yosemite," "Life's Trail," "My Old Coffee Pot," and "The Saga of a Tree." A tribute to his horse, Kit, also was included. The poems, published in 1940, are a singular legacy left by John Epler Sage, pioneer and poet of the Sierra.

# A Triple Celebration

Most families feel fortunate if they are able to be together to honor one special occasion. For Mr. and Mrs. John E. Sage of Selma, April 5, 1940, brought their family together to celebrate not just one, but three special events. On that day Mr. and Mrs. John E. Sage observed their fifty-eighth wedding anniversary; their son-in-law and daughter, Mr. and Mrs. J. H. Wright, observed their thirty-eighth anniversary; and their grandson, Lewis Wright, married Frances McGill in the United Presbyterian Church in Fowler. On this extremely happy occasion, all of the members of the family were present.

An event such as this brings up memories of the past which, in this case, were chronicled in the *Fresno Bee*. The marriage of Mr. and Mrs. Sage had taken place on the home ranch of Mrs. Sage's parents, Mr. and Mrs. C. H. Robinson. Their ranch property is now the site of the city of Parlier. On their honeymoon trip, in 1882, they traveled 800 miles to Bakersfield, Los Angeles, Orange, San Juan, San Luis Obispo and Tulare Lake. The mode of transportation was a spring wagon. Not surprisingly, it took the couple eight weeks to complete the trip. They spent every night camping out and cooking their own meals. Only one night of the trip was spent indoors, at the Wright House in Los Angeles.

Memories are precious legacies of family life and, on the auspicious occasion of the triple celebration in the life of the Sages of Selma, it may be hoped that many more memories were created that are spoken of with joy even today.

# An Unidentified Prospector

Of the many graves that had to be relocated when Friant Dam was constructed, one stood apart from the others. It was fenced with wooden boards and lacked a headstone, and the officials from the United States Bureau of Reclamation had to ask the local residents of Friant for clues to the identity of the person buried at this site.

The story that was uncovered was not untypical of the lonely life of those miners who came west to seek their fortune when the streams and hills of California were filled with gold. The man was a prospector, the locals said, an old man who had lived and mined in the hills for several years. He had a companion who was a miner as well. One day in 1907 the old prospector came to Friant to get his mail. He left and was never seen alive again.

After two days had gone by and he did not return, his companion began to search for him. He was finally found in a cabin where he had taken refuge. He had died of a hemorrhage. His companion buried him near the cabin, using boards from that building to mark his grave. A funeral was held, with military honors because the old prospector was a war veteran. However, no one carved a headstone and his name was forgotten, lost forever in the mists of time.

# Roeding Place

$F$rederick C. Roeding, a native of Hamburg, Germany, arrived in San Francisco in June 1849 and headed for the gold fields. Not striking it rich, he returned to San Francisco and entered business. As one of his civic duties, he joined the famous San Francisco Committee of Vigilance.

In 1868, he became a major member of the San Joaquin Valley Land Association, commonly known as the German Syndicate. Using government agricultural college script, it soon purchased from the government 80,000 acres of land, reaching from near present-day Clovis south to near Easton, including the site of future Fresno and the Sunnyside area. The land was divided among its members and Roeding received as his share 7,040 acres. He ultimately sold all of this land except a small portion which he gave to the city of Fresno for a park and a small section bounded by present-day Kings Canyon, Belmont, Fowler, and Temperance avenues. This section he retained for his own development and home.

In 1883 under the management of Professor Gustavus Eisen, Roeding founded the Fancher Creek Nurseries on his land and planted many trees and vines. He built a two-story mansion with a circular pool in front almost in the center of the section just south of Fancher Creek. The ranch became known as Roeding Place.

Frederick Roeding lived on the ranch only a few years and then returned to San Francisco. His son, George Roeding, became the owner of Roeding Place and Fancher Creek Nurseries.

The home was built before electricity was available. Later George Roeding had electricity brought in. Soon after, on December 22, 1917, apparently due to an electrical failure, the grand old house caught fire and was destroyed. George Roeding had developed other nurseries elsewhere, and after the fire he left Roeding Place and made his home in the Bay Area, where he died in 1928.

Roeding Place was sold off and ultimately divided into smaller parcels. One of these along Kings Canyon highway became the well-known Golden Dawn Ranch, a portion of which has now become the Golden Dawn Subdivision. Things change with the passage of time, but the contribution of Frederick and George Roeding and their Roeding Place to the history of this area will live on.

Frederick C. Roeding, in 1903, offered seventy-two acres to the city of Fresno for a park. Five years later he donated another forty acres. George C. Roeding (left) was one of Frederick's five sons and did much to shape the park's future. The man on the right is unidentified.

The Image Group from the Laval Historical Collection.

# A Tract Home on West Griffith

When a structure is placed on the Local Register of Historic Resources it has to have been considered carefully to see if it meets the criteria requirements. If it does not, then it does not become a part of the list. However, in rare and unusual circumstances, the criteria requirements can be waived. Such was the case with a home in northwest Fresno.

It sits on a quiet street of tract homes and is neither fifty years old nor architecturally unique. But, its place in history is secure because the man who lived in it for the last ten years of his life was one of Fresno's most important literary citizens.

Born in Fresno in 1908 in an area of downtown called "Armenian Town," he spent a few of his younger years in an orphanage in Oakland after his father died. He returned to Fresno and grew up, going to local schools and selling newspapers on a downtown street corner. He left for San Francisco and, eventually, Paris and Hollywood. During his long career, he was awarded the Pulitzer Prize, the Drama Critics Award and an Oscar.

In 1963, he decided to return to Fresno and, for the rest of his life, spent six months of each year here, the other six months in Paris. He purchased the home on West Griffith Way and it was here that he wrote the literary works that filled the last years of his life.

Unlike Thomas Wolfe, William Saroyan found that he truly could go home again. His community revered him and Fresnans were proud that he chose to return to live among the people of the city of his birth. It was by the very fact that he lived and wrote in this modest tract home that it now takes its proud place on the city's Local List of Historic Resources.

# The Maracci Home

A large, Classic Revival-style home on the 900 block of North Van Ness Avenue is part of a once prestigious residential neighborhood and one that is still filled with well preserved structures. Designed in 1915 by Ernest Kump, Sr., a major local architect, it has a pitched roof with broad eaves and heavy double brackets. The exterior of the home is finished in stucco.

The home retains a number of its original features, including hardwood floors, natural finished woodwork and paneling, stained-glass windows, opaque glass light fixtures, glazed cabinets, and the hardware which is used throughout the house. At the rear of the main floor is a sitting room that features a large curved bay window.

Soon after the house was completed it was featured in *Architect and Engineer*, the premier architectural journal of that time. The article noted the lavender peacock tapestry design in the breakfast room. The living room and dining room contain such intricate details in the design of the woodwork and stained glass that the opportunity to view these two rooms alone is worth a visit to this structure. Used as an office, the Maracci Home is a proud part of the city's list of historic structures and an important part of the architectural fabric of Fresno.

# A Man & His Museum

W. Parker Lyon, Fresno's ex-mayor and museum keeper extraordinaire, made headlines in the *Fresno Bee* once again in June of 1938. It seems that just as he was preparing to set out on one of his hunting expeditions in search of relics for his Pony Express Museum located in Arcadia, California, he read an article that stated that Sutter's Fort in Sacramento was exhibiting the original Spanish batea, or gold pan, that James W. Marshall was using when he discovered gold in 1848. The mere fact that the museum had it documented did not dissuade Lyon from touting that, indeed, his museum contained Marshall's original gold pan as well. When asked how this could be, Lyon's reply was simple. Marshall was the only man in the world who could pan for gold using both hands at once—a fact that was underscored by the discovery itself. Only a man with that kind of energy, Lyon continued, could have made a find of that magnitude.

Having made this contribution to the history of California, Lyon shared news of the latest acquisition to his museum's collections, which was also a source of some anxiety. It seems that he had purchased an absolutely one-of-a-kind, two-story "Chic Sale" (outhouse) of the Grover Cleveland period of architecture that inspired awe in everyone who saw it. However, it was a bit of a problem as to how the move of this relic from Nevada would be accomplished. Lyon's first thought was to tie it on an airplane and have it towed through the air. The mere sight of this might well inspire more than awe and he decided that Interstate Commerce Commission regulations might well forbid using this method.

As he left on a buying trip to Nevada and Utah by way of the Mojave Desert, he left word that he had just about decided that his architectural masterpiece would arrive in Arcadia in a wagon drawn by a forty-mule team. Spectacular? Oh, yes. But, as the citizens of Fresno knew only too well, understatement and propriety were not part of the vocabulary of W. Parker Lyon.

# The Puppet Lady

During the years of the 1930s and '40s, the children of Fresno had a very special friend. Their friend worked as a clerk for the San Joaquin Power Division of the Pacific Gas & Electric Company. However, after working hours, she was transformed into the lady with the marionettes. Carefully carving and painting each one, she crafted almost fifty string puppets and thirty-six hand puppets. Her creative fingers also sewed costumes for them all.

Every Tuesday evening, her friend Bernaline Douglas would call for her in her automobile. After loading her puppet entourage in the back seat, they would depart for the Fresno County Hospital pediatric ward. Here, on a stage built by Robert Bell, she would take her marionettes through their paces, accompanied by records played on an electric phonograph and a script she had written herself. For the children, Tuesday became fun night, as they forgot their illnesses and were transported to the magical world she created for them.

During the summer, she put on monthly puppet shows in a neighbor's back yard. As many as four hundred people would come to the 100 block of North Blackstone Avenue to enjoy the wonderful entertainment she and her marionettes provided.

For those who experienced one of these events, Margaret Lindenmuth and her marionette family are one of the treasured memories of childhood—memories of warm summer evenings sitting out under the stars and of being enraptured by the enchanted world she created.

# A Ship Named McClatchy

On the night of March 17, 1944, an event of great moment occurred in Wilmington, Delaware. At exactly 11:30 p.m., a newly christened 10,500-ton merchant vessel moved out of its slip and into the Delaware River. It bore the name of a native son of California and was still wearing traces of vintage California champagne, a bottle of which had been ceremoniously broken across her bow. She was the 339th Liberty ship built by the Calship Company in its emergency wartime shipyards in Wilmington over a three-year period.

The company's choice of honoring a westerner and, in this case a journalist, was appropriate. Other like ships had been named for Horace Greeley, James Gordon Bennet, Joseph Pulitzer, Harrison Gray Otis and Lincoln Steffens. In this case, the new ship honored not just California, but, more specifically, the vast Central Valley.

The gentleman whose name now graced this ship was born in Sacramento on November 1, 1858, was educated in local schools and became the editor of the *Sacramento Bee*, a newspaper his father had founded in 1857. From that year until 1936, the newspaper had only two editors, the father and son. During the son's editorship, the *Fresno Bee* and the *Modesto Bee* were acquired. A broadcasting company comprising five radio stations throughout the valley also was formed. In 1935, the *Sacramento Bee* won a Pulitzer Prize, journalism's highest award.

Christening the ship, Eleanor McClatchy dedicated it to the principles that had guided her father throughout his career. His own brand of independent, fearless journalism led him to fight for what he considered was in the best interests of the people. Now a ship bearing his name was going to play an important role in the war effort. For those standing on the platform that night, watching as the champagne was broken over the ship's bow, no more appropriate name could have been chosen than the *S.S. C. K. McClatchy*.

# Mr. Blanding's Dream House

In 1948, a movie appeared in theaters all over the country that tickled the funny bone of everyone who has ever gone through the agonizing, yet exciting experience of building one's own home. The movie, *Mr. Blandings Builds His Dream House*, was developed from a book of the same name by Eric Hodgins. Hodgins had written out of his own experiences of constructing a home for his family that would embody all of his hopes and dreams.

This necessitated building a real house while the movie was being filmed. At each stage of construction, it was necessary to use two sets of carpenters, authentic ones and actors. The real carpenters would work furiously to finish the house to the stage required for a scene. Then the actors would step in for the filming and pretend to do the work the carpenters had done. For those who have ever built a house, the movie, starring Cary Grant and Myrna Loy, is a timeless and very funny work of art.

To promote the movie, sixty-eight "dream houses" were built all over the country, one right here in Fresno. Built by the firm of Taylor-Wheeler on the southwest corner of Palm and Terrace avenues, the Cape Cod-styled dream home included the most modern features of home construction. Furnished by Slater's Furniture, it was open for public inspection as a fund-raiser for the Fresno State College Religious Conference's student welfare fund. Fresnans viewing the house were amazed at the modern kitchen and the three baths that the house contained.

The home, which has played its own special role in Fresno's history, has maintained its charm and beauty. It stands as a symbol of the hopes and dreams of the imaginary Mr. Blandings and all those who undertake to plan and build their own homes.

# The Home of Dr. Burks

As one drives deep into the heart of Old Fig Garden, along that most beautiful of boulevards, Van Ness, the presence of the lush landscape and the numerous large homes that line its length quicken the traveler's expectation that every movement of the car will bring another vista to enjoy. As you reach Ashlan Avenue, your eye is immediately drawn to the northwest corner. Iron gates open into a park filled with oak and sycamore trees that are native to the valley. Framed by the landscape, an exquisite English Tudor Revival mansion sits in all its stately splendor.

Built in 1934 by Taylor-Wheeler Builders, the home was one of the finest residences ever designed by architect Henry Villalon of the firm of Villalon & Kump. Even though the exterior of this mansion pleases the eye at every turn, it is on entering that you are truly in awe of the workmanship to be found.

After stepping over the threshold into the entry hall, you find yourself looking at an exquisite stairway crafted from Philippine mahogany. The walls are paneled in the same wood, reminiscent of country homes in England. The study behind this entry is paneled in the mahogany as well. Legend has it that the men who constructed this home were not allowed to use the staircase, but had to enter the upper story through windows that they reached by climbing ladders on the outside.

The first owner of this impressive mansion, Dr. Floyd Burks, was the descendant of a pioneer Fresno County family. Beautifully maintained, the Burks Home stands not only as a reminder of an era in Fresno when the highest quality of craftsmanship was possible, but also as a legacy of beauty to the community.

# The Carriage Painter

In those days before the turn of the century and before the advent of the automobile, horses, buggies and carriages provided transportation for Fresnans. One of the threats to any good buggy or carriage was dry wood. The heat of a Fresno summer coupled with the lack of humidity in those early days would draw out the last bit of moisture in the wood of which the carriage was made. This created a situation that could cause serious trouble for the owner. If the wood cracked and broke while it was being driven, an accident would most likely result.

As the city grew and more and more people owned horses and carriages, the need for someone to tackle this problem became ever greater. As a resident of California for over thirty years and being well acquainted with its climate, J. B. Harrington opened an establishment that dealt exclusively with carriage painting, to provide this service for Fresnans. Harrington knew how important several heavy coats of paint applied evenly and with skill were to the wooden portions of carriages and buggies, and his business stressed strict attention to the smallest detail of painting these vehicles. A special dust-proof drying room also was available so that once painted, the carriages and buggies would be thoroughly seasoned before he returned them to his patrons.

Mr. Harrington did the painting himself. When the owner claimed his vehicle, he had a guarantee that the work Mr. Harrington had done would stand the test of heat, cold, moisture, or aridity. When the owner hitched his horse to his newly painted carriage and drove downtown, he could feel secure that his well-turned-out conveyance would last for a long time. Needless to say, Mr. Harrington, the carriage painter, was an important member of the Fresno business community of the 1890s.

# A. A. Rowell

Albert Abbott Rowell, the youngest of eight brothers, was born in Vermont in 1846. His family moved to a farm in Illinois when he was barely three years old. When the Civil War broke out, he joined Company G, 17th Illinois Volunteer Infantry, serving beside his brothers Chester and Jonathan. After the war's end, he came to the California community where his brother Chester, now a doctor, had settled.

A carpenter and builder by trade, he built Dr. Rowell's home on the corner of Van Ness Avenue and Tulare Street. Today, the six-story Rowell Building stands on the site. He also helped to construct Fresno's first church, the Methodist Episcopal Church South, and Fresno's first waterworks. He homesteaded a 160-acre farm west of Selma in 1878 and lived there until 1901. He was involved in planning the first irrigated colonies south of Fresno, including Washington Colony, and constructing the ditches that carried water to these developments.

His community interests centered around the First Christian Church in Selma, temperance work and membership in the Grand Army of the Republic. He held a leadership role in the Prohibition party in California. The owner of a number of commercial and residential properties in Selma, he had played a role in the development of that community.

At the time of A. A. Rowell's death in 1919, only one of the eight Rowell brothers, Milo, was still living. The Rowell brothers who came west made significant contributions to the development of the Central Valley.

# Space Ships in July

Midsummer, that hottest of times in the Central Valley, often brings out interesting phenomena. In the 1940s, when air-conditioning consisted of a swamp cooler that often only heightened the humidity and misery of a Fresno July, folks found that the out-of-doors was a far more pleasant place to be in the mornings and evenings. Sitting on the front porch or in the back yard under a tree with a cool glass of lemonade and, perhaps, the company of a neighbor, was a happy respite.

Of course, when one is outside, one tends to look up and notice things in the sky. In July of 1947, Fresnans were treated to a number of unidentified craft darting to and fro across the heavens. While fishing at Millerton Lake around 5:10 in the early evening, a Fresno man saw an object eight or ten feet in diameter following the line of the mountains in a northwesterly direction. Suddenly it flew northeast and disappeared.

A lady in the 200 block of North U Street was sitting on her porch enjoying the evening when three discs appeared in the sky. She watched them as they flew toward Clovis and disappeared. Several people in the 2000 block of Grant Avenue saw the discs, which they described as silvery and bright. They watched as they sped toward the mountains and the Millerton Lake area.

When questioned about these space craft, the Air Force reported these objects were probably "just plain jet fighting planes." They may have been, some folks thought, but those who saw the discs on those Fresno evenings were absolutely convinced they had seen flying saucers.

# The Most Beautiful Baby

More than a few folks have been awarded prizes for being the most beautiful baby in a contest, but how many people are there who not only have won the prize, but also were honored fifty and seventy-five years later? Well, the Central Valley has just such a person living in our midst.

It seems that at the Fresno District Fair of 1912 a contest was held to determine who was the healthiest, cutest and sweetest baby at the fair. Thirty babies were entered. The judges did not have an easy time of it; after all, most babies are cute, but the healthiest and sweetest, too—well, that took a little more time. Finally, the winner was announced. Her name was Verna Blaine and her mother was so excited she nearly fainted. The prizes of a blue ribbon, a gold ring with VB engraved on it and a silver baby spoon were duly presented. Mother and baby happily accepted them. But, our story does not end there.

After fifty years had passed, during which Verna Blaine's family had made many moves, the prizes had been lost. And then something rather wonderful happened. At the Fresno District Fair of 1962, director Arch Mathson welcomed both Verna Blaine Wilcox and her mother, Mrs. Katie Wolf. As they stood on stage at the open air theater, he presented them with a blue ribbon exactly like the one Verna had won all those years ago; an engraved ring, which was much larger than the original so that Verna could wear it; and a silver spoon. In addition, Miss Blaine was given a gift certificate from a downtown store for a fur piece.

And our story goes on.

At the Fresno District Fair of 1987, Verna Blaine Wilcox, who now lived in Clovis, was presented with a trophy by fair manager Ron Miller. The ceremony took place in the winner's circle at the race track. It was just seventy-five years after the first contest. In addition, Mayor Dale Doig issued a proclamation declaring that on October 1, 1987, Verna Blaine was appointed an Honorary Citizen of the City of Fresno.

# A Society Debut

The society pages of the *Fresno Morning Republican* during the early years of our century provide the reader with a myriad of fascinating information. Weddings, engagements, births, teas, and club meetings all chronicle passages in the lives of Fresnans. The articles about these events give the reader a glimpse of life and how it was lived. Not only do these stories chronicle the customs of the time, but the effusive language and extensive descriptions of every detail of the event transport the reader and often give the reader a chuckle as well.

And so it was that on May 14, 1919, Miss Cora Rowell, the eighteen-year-old daughter of Mr. and Mrs. Chester Harvey Rowell, made her debut into Fresno society at a tea given at the Sunnyside Country Club. Although the occasion was a formal one, "it was an affair of informal appointments." Mrs. Rowell, Miss Rowell and nine other ladies greeted the guests. The reception hall was decorated with pink peonies, Australian plum and potted plants. Miss Rowell "was lovely in a charming yellow georgette crepe with touches of Venetian blue ribbon and Venetian beads and handwork."

Several of the guests' costumes were described in vivid detail, giving the reader wonderful visual images. Mrs. George Roeding's ensemble "was most attractive, of orchid pink Russiana, embroidered in self-colored tones, with broad leghorn hat trimmed with orchid pink ribbon and field flowers."

The dining room was divided by a screen consisting of large rustic baskets of greenery and potted flowers, creating an area for the tea table and a separate area for the musicians.

As the ladies sipped tea and conversed, Miss Peterson sang "charming musical numbers" accompanied by Miss Hanner and Miss Worth at the piano. Over one hundred ladies enjoyed tea that afternoon. Miss Rowell then bade her guests good-bye and took her place in Fresno society.

# A Lyon & a Goat

During August of 1900, the Fresno Elks Club had a problem. The goat that they used as part of their initiation ritual did not have a place to live. It seemed that none of the members had either a large enough back yard or the inclination to have a goat living in close proximity to his home.

As he had on many occasions when a particularly unusual problem presented itself, and the good of the community needed to be served, W. Parker Lyon stepped in to help. Because he had a very large back yard and did not mind the presence of the goat, he offered to provide shelter for this most interesting of God's creatures. Delighted to have this problem so easily solved, Elk member Dave Adams offered to provide food for the animal. He gave Lyon a case of sample boxes of corn meal flour. He did not, however, remember to tell Lyon that the flour was self rising.

The goat adapted well to his new quarters and Lyon, launching into his new project with his usual zeal, began to feed the goat whenever he seemed hungry. The goat lapped up the corn meal flour as fast as he could, and Lyon gave him more and more. By the time the goat had eaten over a dozen boxes, Lyon began to wonder why the goat's girth seemed to be increasing. Indeed, the goat was taking on the look of a balloon.

As the twilight of a summer's eve began to cloak Fresno in shadows, it was said an explosion could be heard throughout the city. Residents ran from their houses wondering what had caused such a noise. As Lyon told his fellow Elks at their next meeting, a new goat would have to be obtained for their next initiation ceremony. The old goat "had busted," he said, "but it had been a dead swell affair."

# Beating the Heat

Today, as the heat of a Fresno summer soars, residents of our fair city retreat to air-conditioned houses, shopping malls, restaurants, and cars. We may all complain bitterly, but would any of us care to return to an age when air-conditioning did not exist, and when "keeping cool" was only a dream that would have to wait for winter to become a reality?

Long before the United States Weather Bureau began recording temperatures in Fresno County, Lillibourne Winchell, a resident of Millerton, and later Fresno, kept his own records. According to Winchell, the two hottest days he could remember were in August of 1856, when the army thermometer at Fort Miller recorded a temperature of 129 degrees, and on July 4, 1878, when the thermometer in a Fresno drug store hit 122 degrees. That Fourth of July was particularly memorable, he said, because on that day General Ulysses S. Grant was stopping at Madera on his way to visit Yosemite. Winchell could not leave work to see this great man. Instead, he spent the day in his roasting office writing a newspaper article. It was so hot he had to keep a blotter under his hand while he wrote so that the perspiration would not ruin his writing.

An article in the *Fresno Bee* dated July 7, 1928, noted that after the Fresno Weather Bureau began to keep track of the temperature, the highest temperature recorded each summer varied between 105 and 115 degrees. The writer noted that, perhaps, this is the solution for the heat—that if one wishes to feel cooler, just contact the weatherman because he usually says that it's cooler than it feels.

For those who complain about the heat, there is another solution as well—one that the early pioneers took to heart. As the heat of summer reaches the unbearable stage, just venture over the mountains, bundle up and revel in all the glories of the cold, damp coastal fog. It never fails to beat the heat.

The high cost of living is not a new topic of conversation. Indeed, it was a matter of grave concern immediately after the First World War. According to an article published in the *Fresno Morning Republican* in 1919, a survey conducted by the federal government showed that during the years 1916 to 1919, the cost of food had almost doubled. The following food items were priced as follows in 1916 and in 1919: Jelly went from 15 cents to 25 cents a glass; coffee increased from 25 cents a pound to 50 cents a pound; shortening, 95 cents a can to $1.60 a can; bacon, 37 cents a pound to 63 cents a pound; and cheese, 30 cents a pound to 50 cents a pound.

Even more telling were the price increases between 1913 and 1919. Butter, which in 1913 cost the consumer 80 cents for a one-pound roll, in May of 1919 was priced at $1.25 a pound. By September 1919, butter had gone up to $1.50 a pound. Eggs, which had sold for 19 cents a dozen in 1913, increased to 45 cents a dozen in May of 1919 and by September of that year were 65 cents a dozen. It now cost the homemaker more to feed her family than it did prior to the war.

And, from the perspective of 1997, one can feel sympathy for the plight of the homemaker even though it may be tinged with a little envy. For most of the residents of 1997 Fresno, a 50-cent pound of coffee is only a dream that will most likely never be realized.

# *Building Safety*

When the town of Fresno Station was established in 1872, many of the early buildings were erected in a haphazard, rather slapdash manner. Residents of Millerton who were settling in the new town dismantled their buildings and brought the lumber with them—lumber that had already seen its share of cold winters and raging hot summers. A few businesses began in tents, but most of the homes and commercial establishments were built of wood.

Initially, citizens did not have to worry about such mundane matters as building codes. Many structures were hastily erected. The lack of a formal fire department meant that many of these early buildings burned down. When they were rebuilt, the new structure was often not much better than the original. In the mid-1880s business blocks, which had far more sturdy construction, were built, but some of the early buildings still remained. After the incorporation of the city in 1885, more building standards were set in place. Also, there were city officials in charge of seeing that these standards were met.

On July 30, 1889, the fire marshal decided to visit the Fiske Opera House on L Street to check on the safety of the structure. He was inside only a few minutes when he hastily retreated to the sidewalk and declared the building unsafe. Part of his report stated: "The building has no foundations. It was built on the surface of the ground and the rains have washed some of the ground away and have allowed the walls to settle unevenly. It is the opinion of competent builders that the [opera] house will have to be taken down and rebuilt before it is safe." And so it was for many of Fresno's early buildings, as they came under the scrutiny of government officials.

# A Tree for a Horse

On July 30, 1889, a reporter for the *Fresno Morning Republican* was shocked to find eighteen ranch horses standing in full sun, tethered to hitching posts in front of the Southern Pacific Railroad tracks. This situation on a normal Fresno day would not be surprising, but on this particular afternoon the temperature had risen to 110 degrees in the shade. When the reporter investigated the matter, he found the owners of these animals cooling off in the nearest saloon, quenching their considerable thirst with several rounds of iced beverages, mindless of their horses' discomfort.

Horrified by this situation, he offered a suggestion in the next issue of the *Republican*. Plant shade trees, he suggested, rows of them in the open space in front of the railroad area. He further suggested that a row of trees be planted all the way around the exterior boundary of Courthouse Park. Hitching posts could then be installed, with a hitching line for teams of horses under the trees bounding Courthouse Park. In this way, the horses would not be neglected, indeed, they would be very comfortable; the owners could enjoy themselves without worrying about their horses, and the trees would help to beautify the city.

In those years before motorized transportation, life without horses would have been much more difficult. One might hope that the reporter's suggestions were followed and that Fresno's horses had the opportunity to relax in the shade during Fresno's good old hot summertime.

# The Projectoscope

In the May 14, 1897, edition of the *Fresno Daily Evening Expositor*, a story appeared touting the performance which was to be held that evening at the Barton Opera House. Mr. Edison's latest invention, a Projectoscope, was to be seen for the first time in Fresno. It projected life-sized figures upon a thirty-foot square screen, the only one of its kind west of the Rocky Mountains.

The article was sure to draw an audience. It listed the program as follows: "The great Corbett fight with knockout. Runaway at Central Park, showing horse and carriage running away. The boxing cats. Dentists scene, showing Dr. Colton administering laughing gas. Mounted police charge a mob—city of Dublin during riot. The hurdle race—taken in England. Cissy Fitzgerald's wink and dance. May Irwin and John Rice in their famous kissing scene, showing the only proper and correct way how to kiss. Major McKinley taking the oath as President of the United States, in front of the White House. The fire alarm—starting for the fire, showing the entire fire department led by the chief. Fighting the fire, representing the fire engine in full action. The Santa Fe limited express. The scene represents the eastern flyer emerging from the woods in the distance at full speed, going at the rate of sixty miles per hour."

With such a program offered on the new Projectoscope, ticket holders at the Barton were treated to an evening of breathtaking wonder at the marvels of Mr. Edison's latest invention.

# Colonel James N. Olney

As one thinks about the Civil War, the sites of the great battles of that war—Gettysburg, Vicksburg, Atlanta—seem a world away for those who have grown up in the western United States. It might surprise the residents of Fresno County to know that, although no Civil War battles were fought in California, an event did occur here which was a direct result of that war.

By 1861, the Mariposa Indian War was a memory in the Millerton area. Peace with the Indians seemed to have been achieved—at least the threat had lessened. With the onset of the Civil War another kind of threat to the peace developed. In states like California, which was part of the Union, Southern sympathizers organized groups called the "Knights of the Golden Circle," which incited violence and destroyed property, all in the name of the Confederate cause.

A chapter was established at Millerton. The group met on a regular basis at Gillum Baley's quartz mine not far from the Chowchilla River. They began storing arms there also, sneaking them into the mine a few at a time so that they would not arouse suspicion.

To further add fuel to this situation, a chapter of the Union League existed at Millerton as well. These pro-Union folk were rather anxious to take on the "Knights." A local character named Deaf Dick walked through the streets of Millerton yelling out his support for Jefferson Davis and the Confederacy. Even though Dick was a colorful character who was not taken too seriously, his pronouncements added to the tension. By 1863, it was feared that hostilities would break out.

Union Army Colonel James N. Olney, with Company A of the 2nd California Volunteers, was sent to Millerton to keep the peace. His unit came through the Central Valley on horseback. As they crossed the river near the Knights den, Olney ordered his men to draw their weapons because they were entering enemy territory. However, no one appeared to halt their progress. They continued on to Millerton where they were greeted with rejoicing by the populace. They stayed, and were joined by B, G and K companies. Their presence at Fort Miller kept the groups under control and for the rest of the Civil War-period, peace reigned at Millerton.

# Memories of Marching through Georgia

Today, most thirteen-year-old boys dream of baseball, the latest computer game and the exciting world that is opening up before them. But George W. Clark, a Fresno resident for twenty-two years, who told his story in the pages of the *Fresno Morning Republican* in 1928, at the age of thirteen was serving as a private in Company I, 30th Regiment, Illinois Volunteer Infantry of the Union Army. Uniformed and ready, he left his home to fight in the Civil War.

He fought at Vicksburg, where he saw, for the first time, a man shot to death. He also witnessed the aftermath of battle as the people of that city, who were starving and ill, surrendered to General U. S. Grant. He marched with the Union Army under the command of General William T. Sherman as they swept through the South all the way to the sea.

At Atlanta, where he was wounded, he witnessed the worst battle of the war. It would haunt him ever after. He remembered that after leaving Atlanta, the army was without food. The soldiers picked rice in the fields, shelling it themselves or paying former slaves ten cents a quart to shell it for them. On the remainder of the march with Sherman, he was part of a foraging detail which sought out food for ill and wounded soldiers.

At the war's end, Mr. Clark participated in the final review of Sherman's army in Washington, D.C. On that most memorable day, the army of soldiers marched down Pennsylvania Avenue in a line thirty miles long. The parade lasted all day.

As memorable as the war years were for Mr. Clark, he did have regrets. Most of all, he regretted that, because of the war, his youth had been lost to him and he had been robbed of his dreams.

# Coates & Traver, Architects

On a quiet corner in one of the Tower District's loveliest historic neighborhoods sits a beautiful Classical Revival home. Built in 1920 for Lee and Minta Blasingame, it was designed by Fresno architects Coates & Traver and was constructed by the firm of Shorb-Neads.

The Blasingame home was designed by the same architects who designed the original Fresno High School buildings located on Echo Avenue. William D. Coates, Jr. and Harrison B. Traver both studied architecture at the University of Pennsylvania and were affiliated with the Sigma Nu fraternity. A native Californian, Coates served as a State of California architect from 1909 to 1911. During this period, Traver also worked in the state architect's office. In 1911, the two formed an architectural partnership in San Francisco. Three years later they moved their practice to Fresno. From then until 1925, when they dissolved their partnership, they designed many important buildings including the Liberty Theatre, the Wishon home on Huntington Boulevard, the Hanford High School and the Porterville High School.

In 1924, the Blasingame home was purchased by Dr. and Mrs. Harry J. Craycroft. During the early 1930s, the Craycrofts rented the home to Elizabeth Ainsworth, the sister of author John Steinbeck. Mr. and Mrs. Walter Stammer bought the home in 1936. In 1973, the home was purchased by the present owner Sylvia L. Foraker. Like so many of Fresno's historic homes, this home has such amenities as a library, a butler's pantry and maid's quarters. These rooms harken back to a period of gracious living when elegance and manners were a part of everyday life.

# Akira Yokomi

Located on the corner of G and Kern streets, in the heart of West Fresno, is a store that has drawn customers from all over the Central Valley since it opened in 1950. Originally part of a grocery store on Kern Street, the Central Fish Company moved to its present location in 1979. Drawn to the store because of its well-deserved reputation for fine fresh fish, patrons also shopped there because of the wealth of diverse foods that could be purchased and for the vast array of Oriental goods that lined the shelves. The Central Fish Company was popular also because of the owner, Akira Yokomi.

Born in Fresno on March 3, 1921, Akira Yokomi was the second child of five children born to Sunayo and Fanpachi Yokomi. When he was in the third grade, the family moved to Fowler. After World War II and a tour of duty in the army, he and his family relocated to their farm in that community. Several members of his family moved to Los Angeles to learn the seafood business. Mr. Yokomi went with them, returning to Fresno only after he had worked in many facets of the business. He began the Central Fish Company in 1950. By 1979, when the business had outgrown its original building, the economics of the time seemed to indicate a move to another part of Fresno. But, he had a strong belief in the viability of Chinatown and by building his new store there, he made good on his firm commitment to the neighborhood. His decision brought scores of customers into that historic area—a fact that helped his neighbors as well.

For those who remember him and mourned his passing in June of 1996, an indelible image is etched in their minds—that of a man who never tired of his life's work, took joy in it and always had time to help those who were in need. In the words of his life-long friend George Teraoka, "He left a legacy of generosity." A fitting epitaph for a fine gentleman.

# The Ponderous Inkstand

An inkstand, an author and a fine autumn day all provided a link that stretched from England to Fresno.

One day in the autumn of 1875, author Robert Louis Stevenson visited the town of Wendover, England, about thirty-five miles outside London. While there, he stayed overnight at the Red Lion Inn and visited with innkeeper Joseph S. Holland and his children, Elizabeth and John. Stevenson expressed interest in Elizabeth's dolls, so she ran to get them and brought them to the famous man. Likewise, John had two whips, which he showed to Stevenson.

However, something else caught Stevenson's eye. A fine inkstand stood on a round table in the room. Although Stevenson thought that it was made of lead, it was made of pewter. It had a circle of holes around the top for holding pens, and right in the very center under a hinged metal cap was a china container that held the ink. The inkstand was attached to its own tray.

After his visit to Wendover, Stevenson wrote of this day in one of his *Essays on Nature.* The title of the piece was "An Autumn Effect." In it he described Elizabeth and John and the furnishings of the inn including, in his words, "the ponderous leaden inkstand."

Twelve years later, Mrs. Holland gave birth to another son, who was named Richard. He left home at the age of seventeen, going first to Canada and then enlisting in the Canadian Army in 1914 and serving for four and a half years in France. In 1919, he was mustered out of the service and came to Fresno to visit another brother, Charles. He decided to stay and make Fresno his home.

Sometime later the Rev. T. J. Barkle, representing the Stevenson House museum in Monterey, journeyed to England hoping to find the "ponderous inkstand" and acquire it for the museum. He met with Elizabeth, who told him that it had already been sent to her brother in Fresno, where it remains in his home in a place of honor. Even though he was disappointed, Barkle said that his trip had not been wasted. It seems that while he was in Wendover he acquired some lumber that had been used in building the *Mayflower*. Although not of the same literary value as the inkstand, it, too, could be said to have a history all its own.

# Melons in August

In the year 1906, a fruit merchant named J. N. Hovsepian arrived in Fresno from Diarbekir, Turkey. He brought with him Persian melon seeds that he planted, thinking they would grow well in the Central Valley, where the climate and soil were similar to his native land.

The plants did not bear fruit. To find out why, he wrote to Diarbekir, where these melons were a staple crop. The answer: For his Persian melons to propagate they had to be planted next to the pomegranate melon, which the planters called the "male." The two plants had identical yellow blossoms, but the pomegranate melon blossom was smaller with a strong, musky fragrance. When the two types of blossoms were fertilized, the result was a superior, delicious melon. To Mr. Hovsepian, the Fresno-grown melon tasted even better than the melons he had eaten in his native Turkey.

Until 1912 the market for these melons was modest so not many were grown. In 1914, Hovsepian shipped all the melons he could provide through the Wells Fargo Express Company and created a market for them in the East. His melons became popular items in the best hotels in Chicago and New York, where they were priced at fifty cents a slice.

By 1915, more than a ton of Persian melons a day was shipped to the East during the season that lasted from August to October. Approximately a dozen farmers were engaged in farming Persian melons, which are close to a cantaloupe in looks and flavor, but are bigger and have a thinner, lighter skin.

Like the discovery of the Capri moth that was needed to fertilize the Smyrna fig, the introduction of the blossom of the pomegranate melon made history of a sort. Without this necessary component that fertilized the seed of the Persian melon, one of the leading agricultural products of the valley might never have been. How awful it would be to miss out on the joy of a delicious slice of cold Persian melon on a hot summer day!

# Opening Night at the Barton

On the evening of September 30, 1890, the cream of Fresno society donned their finest evening attire for an event unparalleled in the history of the city. Arriving in elegant carriages, they swept through the doors of the Barton Opera House—a sea of black and white tuxedoes, frock coats, tall hats, swishing sumptuous gowns and elaborate hairstyles graced with ostrich plumes. The occasion was the opening night of the Barton Opera House.

The man responsible for Fresno's most luxurious house of entertainment was Robert Barton. On this evening he and his family sat in a place of honor in a box seat framed with elegant gold-fringed drapes. Mrs. Barton was attired in apricot silk décolleté, with diamonds at her neck. Mr. Barton was in black and white evening attire, their two older sons were in dark suits, and the youngest son, Leland, wearing black velvet, was sitting on his father's knee.

The featured program for the evening was a humorous play, the *Seven Ages of Man*. Mr. Barton chose this entertaining comedy because he felt it recognized the lively spirit of those who supported the new theater. Indeed, the citizens of Fresno seemed to feel that with the opening of this elegant establishment their city was experiencing a cultural coming of age.

The economic boom Fresno had experienced for the last several years and which encouraged Robert Barton to build his opera house began to decline in the next year. The collapse of the boom brought about his early death, on May 26, 1891, at the age of fifty-one. His sons took over the management of the opera house for the next twenty-one years. During that time, they brought the finest plays, actors and musical artists to its stage.

The Barton Opera House retained its exceptional distinction well into the twentieth century, but probably never quite recaptured the elegance of its opening night when the air was filled with excitement and anticipation.

The Barton Opera House opened September 19, 1890, on the northeast corner of Fresno and J (Fulton) streets with an audience of 1500. The opera house had a plush interior with many small lights on the high domed ceiling The box seats on each side of the stage were lavishly decorated.
*The Image Group from the Laval Historical Collection.*

# A Dog & a Quack

In the spring of 1885, the Fresno courts were kept busy trying to arbitrate a series of disputes between two citizens of Fresno stemming from a an interesting encounter.

It seems that on a fine day in February, a doctor by the name of M. Myers was passing by the store of fruit dealer Nick Petkovich. As the doctor approached the door of Mr. Petkovich's establishment, Mr. Petkovich made a noise like a duck, saying, "Quack, quack, quack." The doctor, infuriated at this presumed insult, began to exact revenge by throwing apples, bananas, coconuts, oranges and other pieces of fruit at the fruit dealer. As Mr. Petkovich turned to run, his dog came to his defense and dug his teeth into the doctor's leg. Dr. Myers extricated himself from the jaws of the dog, expressed his feelings about the fruit dealer to all who could hear, and fled the scene.

Aside from the colorful scene this presented to all those who happened to be shopping on this particular block of downtown Fresno that fine winter day, it began a series of legal actions that kept the courts and a number of lawyers busy for quite a while.

First, Mr. Petkovich purported that on the evening of the initial incident the doctor threatened him with a pistol. As a result, he sued to have the doctor placed in custody in order to keep the peace. The case was brought to trial, but a decision was not rendered.

Then, Dr. Myers sued the fruit dealer for damages to his leg as a result of the incident with the angry dog. The doctor then sued Mr. Bebora, Petkovich's partner, for perjury. Petkovich, in turn, sued the doctor for the same thing.

Unfortunately, history does record the outcome of all these lawsuits. One is tempted to hope they were all was settled out of court. Whatever happened, it must be surmised that they kept the conversations lively in that part of downtown Fresno during the spring of 1885.

# Father of Raisin Day

It was an imaginative idea and the persistent pushing of that idea that launched the annual celebration of the raisin. Indeed, if it had not been for the indefatigable efforts of the man whose brain child was marketed to the country, this event would never have happened in the first place. So it was that James Harsburgh, Jr.'s name has gone down in history as the "Father of Raisin Day."

The Raisin Day Festival, which he suggested in 1909, became a major event. It was held annually until 1932 and made the raisin and Fresno known throughout the country.

It turned out, however, that Mr. Harsburgh, the general passenger agent of the Southern Pacific Railroad, was a very private man. Although he was happy to receive thanks individually from the raisin farmers and community leaders, an effort to publicly honor him was met with frustration.

After the first successful Raisin Day, a lavish banquet was planned in his honor. A hotel was booked and speakers were scheduled. Indeed, every effort was made to pay tribute to this man. Only one thing stood in the way of making this a memorable evening for Mr. Harsburgh—he politely refused to attend. The banquet was canceled.

The Raisin Day Committee met to come up with another idea. This time they decided to present him with a fine clock. They bought the clock and asked Mr. Harsburgh to come to a meeting of their committee. They promised him that they would not hold a formal event of any kind. They would just hand him the clock and say, "Thank you." But Harsburgh, with his abhorrence of public recognition, was afraid that it was a ruse and that when he appeared he would be surprised with some sort of public display. So, he politely declined to come.

Finally, in desperation, the committee came up with a new idea. They appointed William Robertson, one of their group, to tuck the clock under his coat and go to Harsburgh's office. When he got there, Harsburgh was in his office, but unavailable. Robertson explained his problem to Harsburgh's secretary and asked him what he felt was the best way to give the clock to his boss. The secretary thought for a moment and then said that he would find a way to get Harsburgh out of his office for a few minutes. Then Robertson could go in and place the clock on his table, then run like crazy in case Harsburgh came back in too soon. And that's what they did.

A few days later, a letter arrived from Harsburgh, thanking the committee for the clock.

Anyone glancing through the files of the *Fresno Morning Republican* will find many fascinating bits of trivia leaping off the pages. For instance, do you know why Fresno Street is so much wider than Mariposa Street? The original plan of the owners of the Central Pacific Railroad was to donate four blocks, totaling twelve acres of land, for a courthouse park at the corner of Fresno and O streets. Fresno Street was designed in such a fashion that it would provide a sweeping, impressive approach to a future courthouse that would stand at the highest point in the county seat. When the city fathers convinced the railroad that this site was too far from the business district, the plan for Fresno Street remained unaltered.

The courthouse was constructed in 1874 at the new site chosen for it at Mariposa and L streets. Over the years a great deal has been written about the beauty of the exterior of this building. Let us take a moment to learn about the interior make-up of this most famous of Fresno structures.

The courthouse, in 1874, contained the offices of the county judge, treasurer, district attorney, surveyor, and superintendent of schools. It also provided offices for A. M. Clark, who was the auditor, clerk and recorder; Scott Ashman, who was not only the county sheriff but the tax collector as well; and T. W. Simpson, who held the dual post of assessor and coroner.

The back half of the first floor of the courthouse contained the jail. It also provided an office as well as living quarters for janitor Charlie Overhulser. He enjoyed his quarters next to the jail and the sheriff's office. Charlie Wainwright, the deputy clerk, had an apartment next to the janitor's. In 1882, Zack Hall was sheriff. He and M. K. Harris, who would later become a superior court judge, also had bachelor lodgings on the first floor. These socially prominent young men took their meals in private homes nearby.

The second story hall of the courthouse extended through the entire building, had no doors, and was reached both in the front and rear by broad flights of shallow wooden stairs. By the late 1880s, when the trees had begun to shade the windows of the second floor, the stairs and hall became a popular place for court-ing couples on warm summer evenings.

It is no wonder that this building held so many memories and is so sorely missed.

The year was 1866. It was a peaceful summer morning in the town of Millerton. The air was fragrant with the mingling smells of scrub oaks, the warm earth and the river that flowed nearby.

Otto Froelich was busy behind the counter of the general store of George Greiersen & Co. with his first tasks of the day. Greiersen was the postmaster, and Froelich was preparing a shipment for the Wells Fargo Express. It was a time-consuming, exacting, responsible task because on this particular day it was gold dust that had to be mailed for several customers. Froelich bent over his task, folding the heavy brown paper and wrapping the small packages of gold dust, sealing each one with hot wax, and stacking them in the strong, iron Wells Fargo box.

The boy who ran errands for the store stood nearby, holding the letters and papers that Froelich had given him to deliver to the town's residents. Whether it was Froelich's task that fascinated him and caused him to linger or the warmth of the summer morning, the boy made no effort to leave the store. Froelich ignored him, concentrating fully on the job at hand.

Meanwhile, just outside the open back door of the store, a biddy hen was scratching in the dirt. The open door with its view to the cool interior of the store beckoned and she hopped inside. She moved along the floor, pecking as she went. "Get out!" Froelich yelled. "Shoo!" he ordered. The hen's response was to climb on a stack of goods on the main counter. Froelich came up behind her and tried to grab her tail feathers. This affront to her dignity caused her to fly to the top shelf, filled with heavy crockery.

Froelich, frustrated at being pulled from his important task and terrified that the hen would cause damage, lost his temper. He grabbed the iron weights that sat next to the scales on the counter. He threw a weight in the direction of the hen—it missed but succeeded in hitting a number of dishes. Another weight was thrown, with the same result. This time the hen settled on top of a large china pitcher. Froelich manage to dislodge her by breaking the pitcher to smithereens. The hen decided that the better part of valor was to leave this crazy place, but not before she and Froelich had managed to break a good part of the china in the store. She escaped unscathed, having never been touched by Froelich or the weights. Froelich returned to his now-increased work load. What became of the errand boy? Laughing with great delight, he swiftly left on his appointed rounds.

One of the things we can count on in this life, besides death and taxes, is that fashions will change. The extent to which fashions may change can be demonstrated by the fact that the names of certain items have long been forgotten. A case in point is the "fascinator." Does anyone remember that once important item in a lady's wardrobe? Probably not.

In the 1880s it was considered unseemly for a lady to attend a function of any kind without a head covering. An elegantly trimmed bonnet or hat was a necessity for attendance at church, a play or other entertainment. Indeed, to attend one of these events bareheaded would have been considered ill-bred, even rude.

However, there was one occasion where hats posed a definite problem for the ladies. Dances and balls were favorite gatherings for the young and old of our city. How would one step out in a lively quadrille or allow a gentleman to sweep oneself around the room in an elegant waltz all the while trying to successfully balance a hat on one's head? Not easily, one would assume. So the fascinator was invented and was worn in place of a hat.

This item of apparel was usually handmade, fashioned by each lady to accentuate her dress. Made of lace or crocheted in the shape of a diamond or triangle, this dainty item covered the head with long scarf-like ends that draped about the neck and shoulders. A young lady usually added a touch of pink or blue to her fascinator. An older lady of forty would choose hints of lavender or violet if she made a white fascinator. An elderly lady would use black yarn, perhaps adding a fringe in white or purple.

Although the fascinator was designed to add to the wearer's beauty, it had the added attraction of keeping her warm as well. Now consigned to history, for a short time it was a necessary item in every lady's wardrobe, having been created to solve a most important fashion problem.

# An Opening Night to Remember

On the night of January 8, 1929, the citizens of Fresno saw searchlights streaking across the dark winter sky. Enormous feelings of excitement pervaded the city. This was an evening that would long be remembered in the annals of our history.

All day long movie stars had been arriving by train and by airplane. They had spent any spare time they had sightseeing, providing an opportunity for Fresnans to catch glimpses of many famous faces.

The evening began with a dinner at the Hotel Californian. Here, the city fathers, community leaders, motion picture directors, studio executives, and movie stars were hosted by the Warner Brothers organization, the company that had recently purchased the Alexander Pantages Theatre on Fulton Street. This evening marked the opening event for this, their first big theater outside of Los Angeles.

Following dinner, everyone drove to the theater, which was now renamed the Warner's Theatre, through streets lined with hundreds of Fresnans, cheering and hoping to see their favorite stars. Inside the theater, Edward Everett Horton and Patsy Ruth Miller, co-stars of *The Hottentot* that was being shown on this opening night, were introduced to the audience. They were followed by Joan Crawford and her husband, Douglas Fairbanks, Jr., Myrna Loy, Loretta Young, Monte Blue, Johnny Arthur, Alice Day, Bull Montana and many others.

During the 1960s the theater was sold. The new owners changed one letter of the name—the "e" became an "o." From then on, it was called the Warnor's Theatre.

The historic theater has seen many colorful opening nights. Many famous people have graced its stage. Probably none of these openings generated more excitement than the fabulous gala event on the evening of January 8, 1929.

In the early 1870s a railroad line was being built through the great Central Valley. It brought not only a transportation line and new towns, but it brought tremendous changes in the operation of such things as mail delivery. Up to this time, the United States mail was sent from San Francisco by steamboat to Stockton. Then it was sent by a horse-drawn stage, which traveled through the foothills to the county seat at Millerton with a stop first at the Big Dry Creek post office. An extensive system of stages served the foothill communities along the San Joaquin and Kings rivers.

The Butterfield Overland Mail Company and, later, the U. S. Mail Telegraph Stage Line also carried the mail from San Francisco to points south. These companies also carried passengers. A look at their schedules gives one pause. A trip from San Francisco to Visalia took thirty-six hours.

When the railroad line reached the newly created town of Fresno Station in 1872, the mail was carried on this new form of transportation. Then it was the job of Russell Fleming to drive the stage from the new community, bringing mail and goods to Millerton. Fleming was made postmaster of Fresno Station in August of 1872. He resigned within a short time and Charles W. DeLong was appointed to the position on November 14, 1873, operating out of Otto Froelich's store on Mariposa Street. This store also housed the town's only fire-fighting tool, a Babcock extinguisher. Since DeLong was put in charge of this important piece of equipment, he was, in a sense, the fire marshal as well.

Within the next few years, as Fresno grew, DeLong would find himself relocating the post office from one store to another—a total of six moves. The last location was DeLong's own store that he moved into in February of 1876. Here, the post office remained until the job of postmaster was given to Otto Froelich in 1880.

During those early years of our city it might be said that the United States Post Office was a well-traveled institution.

Fresno's Flag.
*City of Fresno,
Department of
Admisistrative
Services*

Did you know that Fresno has its own flag? Not only does the city have a flag, it is flown outside city hall along with the United States flag and the flag of California.

In 1962, the Downtown Association sponsored a competition to find a design for a flag for our city. Local citizens rallied to the cause, sending in over six hundred entries. A panel of judges including Mayor Arthur L. Selland; Councilman Paul G. Wasemiller; Edwin M. Eaton, president of the Fresno Historical Society; Floyd Hyde, president of the Fresno Arts Center; and Karney Hodge, president of the Downtown Association, chose the winning design that had been submitted by Lanson H. Crawford.

Three vertical colored bars divide the flag. The left section is colored a deep brown, symbolizing the fertile soil of our valley. The middle section is light blue, denoting sunny skies and the water that gives our area life. The right section is green, symbolizing the verdant trees and fields in and around our city.

On each of the three sections a design is superimposed. On the brown section is a geared wheel denoting Fresno's position as the agribusiness leader of the nation. On the blue center section the word "Fresno" appears in brown to carry out the theme of agriculture. Growing up out of the center of this word is an ash leaf, the source of our city's name. The green section on the right is centered with a golden sunburst indicating that which gives life to the orchards and fields that surround Fresno. The symbols in both the right and left sections also contain white, a reference to the snow in the Sierra that is the source of our water.

Fresno's flag was adopted on May 10, 1962.

In 1873 an event of great moment occurred in the life of Moses J. Church, the great canal builder; he became a convert to the faith of the Seventh-day Adventist Church. Three years later, in 1876, he led in the effort to bring the first missionary of that faith to Fresno Station. In April of that year a tent was set up in Courthouse Park and the citizens of Fresno were invited to attend the meetings that were held there. Those who repented of their sins were baptized in the waters of Dry Creek, the only body of water that was accessible for immersion.

Two years later, in 1878, Church built his flour mill at the corner of Fresno and N streets with its accompanying ditch that ran down the middle of Fresno Street. The water in the ditch had been used to provide power for the mill. Just above the mill, at a spot where clean water ran through the ditch and into the mill, Church erected a baptismal chamber between the mill's banks. Built of lumber with steps and a platform, it was open to the sky. This rustic baptistery served the people of his faith until 1889 when an imposing Seventh-day Adventist Church was built at the southwest corner of Mariposa and O streets to serve the congregation.

During the early 1880s, the Baptist congregation met in Courthouse Park at a spot where Dr. Chester Rowell's statue stands today. They also used the waters of Church's mill for their baptismal rites. In the mid-1880s, the Baptist Church was built at Merced and J streets. The Baptists discontinued their use of the mill ditch for baptisms.

In 1892, when the ditch was filled in by irate citizens tired of the city's laxness in dealing with other problems caused by its existence, the ditch itself ceased to exist.

During the years when Fresno State College was located in the heart of Fresno's Tower District, it was surrounded by neighborhoods of stately homes, bungalows and small businesses. The campus had a beautiful theater and a large auditorium in its Administration Building. Plays were presented and were attended by people from all over Fresno, but particularly from the surrounding neighborhoods. In good weather, nothing gave more pleasure than to walk to the campus with its lovely ivy-covered brick buildings and large trees to enjoy a night at the theater or a fine musical concert given by students of the college's department of music.

On the night of February 1, 1938, one such event took place. The Pianoforte Club, made up of alumnae of the music department, presented a benefit concert in the college auditorium. Four concert grand pianos filled the stage. Professor Miriam Fox Withrow, a brilliant teacher and gifted pianist herself, came out onto the stage followed by eight women musicians who immediately sat down—two at each piano. Miss Withrow took up her baton and sixteen hands began to sweep over the four keyboards, filling the auditorium with glorious music. According to the *Fresno Bee* music critic the next day, "It was a classic recital brilliantly played"—the women "demonstrated a highly schooled piano technique and their work showed strength, color and finesse." For those in attendance, listening to the perfection of eight people playing with such precision, yet with grace and warmth, made the evening memorable.

The concert program included works by Bach, Gluck, deFalla, Rachmaninoff, Bax and Rubinstein and ended with a sweeping rendition of *The Blue Danube Waltz* by Strauss.

For pianists Helen Schorling, Helen Kazato, Harriett Ratliff, Rhoda Hammatt, Frances McLaughlin, Clarice Roberts Hartman, Barbara Blake and Catherine McKay Morison, it was an evening of pure joy not only to play together again as they had in college, but also to know that the concert raised money for the college that they loved so well.

# A Hidden Treasure

When one drives east on Fresno Street through the downtown area, the historic Water Tower looms up, begging passersby to look and wonder about its story. The history of this, Fresno's most famous symbol, has been told in another of our tales. What has not been told is the incredible experience that awaits the visitor who enters this structure.

After parking in the adjacent lot and stepping out on the flat hard soil, a careful look at the ground is important. Why? Because the ground is not only historic, but is a potential archaeologist's dream. The lot is edged in bricks and concrete with a few steps going down on the Mariposa Street side of the lot. This is part of the foundation of Moses Church's flour mill that was built in 1878. Under the parking lot, the basement of the mill still exists. The land on which the Water Tower sits was next to the mill and, as far as anyone knows, has never held any other structure

As you walk around to the front door of the Water Tower, your eye is immediately drawn upward to the windows and balcony. When you walk through the front door, you notice a wooden door in the wall on either side of the entry. When opened, these doors reveal walkways that go around the base of the building to the back door. They also allow the visitor to see that the interior wall is made entirely of brick, 128 inches thick and straight. The exterior wall is also brick, but it curves in to meet the interior wall at a point about thirty feet above the ground. Stepping out of this walkway, you are in the interior chamber of the building. In the center of this room two large pipes extend upward from a point beneath the floor all the way to the large holding tank above. One pipe brought in fresh water, the other was the return pipe.

Steps on the east wall lead to the second floor. At this point, the visitor finds that he has entered a huge area that can be described only as breathtaking in its magnificence. The large round windows above the front door bathe the room in light. The visitor's eye goes immediately up the brick walls to the curved dome fifty-two feet above. At their thickest point, the walls are twelve feet thick. The dome curves so perfectly, each brick fitting into the other with such precision, that one can only admire the craftsmanship of the men who did the construction work in 1894 and of the architect who designed the plan.

A long metal stair scales one wall, going up to a door in the wall. Through the door there is another set of stairs going through the turret and up the side of the holding tank above. This is also the way to the door that leads to the outside balcony. At one time the Water Tower's holding tank held two million pounds of water. The weight of the water caused the bricks in the dome just below it to compress and form a tighter fit.

After leaving this impressive structure, a visitor has an even greater appreciation for this local treasure. Not only does it deserve its National Register designation, it deserves to be treated with respect and dignity. As it enters its second century as the foremost symbol of Fresno, one hopes that it will forever be a cherished reminder that it is water that is the lifeblood of our community.

# The Courthouse Elevator

In 1937, the historic courthouse in downtown Fresno was undergoing another renovation. Although, like many old buildings, this one had charming nooks and crannies and all sorts of architectural surprises, it also was a maze of corridors and offices—the sort of place where one could easily get lost.

The country was still in the throes of the Great Depression, and Fresno, like other cities throughout the country, had undertaken projects to put people to work. Allied Architects was hired to design buildings for the Works Progress Administration. Many of these buildings stand in the Civic Center area as a testament to these programs.

It was to the Allied Architects that the county of Fresno turned to do the courthouse renovation. New doors were put in place and partitions were moved, thus creating new office space. When the work was finished, the interior of the building had a new, more efficient look, with the added benefit that offices were easier to find.

One other feature of the courthouse was changed as well. The ancient elevator, whose outstanding feature was that it moved more slowly than a tortoise on a hot August afternoon, was replaced. There had long been a legend that happily engaged couples on their way to the third floor to obtain their marriage license from County Clerk Ernest Dusenberry had found plenty of time to quarrel, call off the wedding and reconcile, all in the space of time that it took them to get to the third floor. Dusenberry, who gave a recipe book to each bride, probably thought it was a good thing because it gave couples time to think things over. However, for those in a hurry, the new elevator gave them something to smile about.

When one enters the front door of the main branch of the Fresno County Free Library, one's eye is immediately drawn to a striking mural portraying the universe of books. The mural is based on the Dewey Decimal System, a system of categories used by most United States libraries. This system divides subject matter into ten different areas of knowledge. Each area is symbolized in the mural by human figures, plants, animals, objects, signs and vowels.

The first section of the mural is a tree blooming with printer's marks symbolizing accumulated and published knowledge. A Greek philosopher facing his image in a mirror symbolizes philosophy and psychology in the second section. Next, a scroll that carries the words Know Thyself symbolizes the carry-over of philosophic thought into religion. In the fifth section an eagle, representing the government, spreads his wings in protection of the family and the other elements of our social structure. The philology section contains the word "book" translated into ancient and modern languages. Science is represented by a man surrounded by the symbols of the traditional branches of science holding an atom in one hand and reaching for the stars with the other. In the seventh section, hands are depicted doing a number of tasks symbolizing the useful arts. The fine arts part of the mural shows costumed figures engaged in various activities related to this subject. A Pegasus, the mythological winged horse, symbolizing poetry and well-known characters from classical works of literature, rounds out the literature section. Finally, in the history panel, the figures representing War and Peace dominate. Additionally, likenesses of several outstanding figures from history are contained in this section.

The mural, titled Bibliocosmos, is made up of 416 pieces of enameled copper of many different sizes. The work of artists Jackson and Ellamarie Woolley of San Diego, it is a colorful reminder to visitors of what a library contains. It is also a work of art that is worth a visit to the library just to look at and enjoy.

# The Central School

The destruction of many of our historic buildings in past years evokes feelings of guilt and sadness for Fresnans of today. It might be interesting to learn that this is not a new feeling for the citizens of our city. Surprisingly enough, this very subject came up for the first time when our city was only a few years old.

In 1879, the Central School (later called the Hawthorne School) was erected on the site of the present-day Veterans Memorial Auditorium. For twenty years it served the students of Fresno well. However, at the Fresno High School graduation ceremonies in 1899, State Superintendent of Public Instruction Kirk said that the school building had fallen into disrepair and was in disgraceful condition. In fact, he called it an eyesore.

The school authorities, when faced with the cost of fixing up the building, felt it should be demolished. Not only was the exterior of the building sorely in need of repair, but the interior was in sad condition as well.

When the two-story school was first built, it was the most impressive building in Fresno, with the exception of the courthouse. It contained four large instruction rooms and two assembly rooms. Two small rooms served as the principal's office and the library. There was also a dressing room for the use of the lady teachers. Wood stoves provided heat in the winter. Students who were seated near the windows could look out and see cowboys, Indians, sheepherders and probably some sheep as well walking past on Fresno or O streets. By the fall of 1891, the newly formed Fresno High School held classes in the building until a growing number of students and increased funds led to the construction of a high school building on O Street.

As the years passed and the number of students grew, the large rooms were partitioned off to create more classrooms. Plaster began to fall off sections of the ceilings and walls. The floor was nearly worn through in places and the window sashes were sagging badly.

As the debate over what to do about this building became more heated, former pupils in the school began to remember the childhood education they received within its walls. Eventually, it was decided to repair the schoolhouse. It continued to serve the community for a number of years. The old schoolhouse has been gone now for many years, but one might say that it should be remembered because it caused Fresnans for the first time to think about the consequences of tearing down part of their historic architecture.

# The Fresno Bubbler

When one thinks of the town of Millerton in those days before the county seat was moved to Fresno Station, one thinks of a rag-tag tent city filled with all manner of colorful characters—gamblers, miners, and ladies of ill-repute mingled freely with the upstanding members of the town.

It might be surprising to note, then, that just three-quarters of a mile below this wide-open village someone tried to open a resort.

Since the 1840s, Americans had been pursuing leisure. They had begun to travel and "taking the cure" at natural hot springs or mud baths at a spa had become fashionable.

In 1873, five sulphur springs just south of Millerton were incorporated and, although history does not record the name of the entrepreneur, it is a matter of public record that the plan was to open a resort.

The springs, three of which bubbled out of solid rock, were given appropriate titles. The Indian Geyser, Diana's Bower, Fresno Bubbler, Invalid's Delight and Cupid's Bower all evoke romance or healing.

By the 1880s, the resort had failed, probably due to the decline of Millerton as Fresno emerged as a major city. During the decade of World War I an attempt was made to revive the idea of a resort. That attempt failed as well. In the mid-1940's, the completion of Friant Dam and the creation of Millerton Lake covered the site of the potential resort.

Today, stories of the sulphur springs have passed into obscurity. One can't help wondering, however, if the "Fresno Bubbler" and its cohorts still bubble merrily beneath the waters of Millerton Lake.

# Picking Daisies

In the early days of Fresno, long before it became incorpo-rated, two brothers, A. T. and Clark Stevens, ran the Black Hawk Stables at the corner of Fresno and L streets. Among the services they offered was taking private parties to Yosemite in one of their stagecoaches. The trip was hazardous since the stage road was narrow and ill-defined. It was also long and tiring without the modern rest stop conveniences of today.

On one memorable spring morning a group of school teach-ers, maiden ladies of a certain age, chartered one of the stages. It was A.T.'s turn to drive. With the addition of a gentleman who also wanted to go along, they began their journey. The gentleman did not particularly wish to sit inside with the ladies so he opted to ride shotgun with Mr. Stevens.

The journey began. It was lovely and warm and the fields were filled with wildflowers as far as the eye could see. About thirty minutes out of Fresno, one of the ladies called to Mr. Stevens that she and her friends would very much like to stop and "pick some daisies." The stage ground to a halt and the ladies had a chance to wander at their leisure, enjoying the flowers and heeding the call of nature. With this accomplished, they boarded the stage and the journey continued. Another forty-five minutes went by and the call came yet again. The stage halted—the ladies wandered in the field—and the journey continued. This pattern continued for many hours. Mr. Stevens was getting worried that at this rate they would never reach Yosemite Valley.

Finally, at wit's end, he told the teachers that there would be no more stops until nightfall when they reached a site where there would be lodgings. All was quiet for some time. Mr. Stevens then heard the gentleman whisper in his ear, "Please stop the stage. I want to pick some daisies." A firm "No" was the answer. Pretty soon the plea was repeated. Again, it was greeted with a "No." Finally, a desperate plea, much above a whisper was heard. "Please, Mr. Stevens, let me pick some daisies. If you don't, I'm going to pick a daisy on the seat." The stage stopped immediately. Such was travel and the lack of conveniences in the early years of our county.

A. T. Stevens is the driver of this six-horse stagecoach parked in a grove of giant redwoods in Yosemite Valley c. 1885. *The Image Group from the Laval Historical Collection.*

# Love by Wire

It has been said that the course of true love more often than not does not run smoothly. This was the case for of Mr. W. N. Nolan of Traver, California, and Miss Dora Cashron of Alvarado, Texas.

In the mid-1880s, when both were living in Alvarado, they met and fell in love. Even though it was known throughout the community that Mr. Nolan was a young man of sterling character, the young lady's parents opposed the match. So strong was their opposition that they sent their daughter to stay with relatives in Florida.

Nolan desperately tried to reach her, but all attempts failed. Disheartened, he moved to Traver, a few miles south of Kingsburg. Soon after settling in Traver, he tried to contact her at her old home in Texas and met with success. They began to write letters. Finally, he sent her enough money to travel to Traver; but, once again, her parents said no.

Nolan confided his story to a minister who, in turn, contacted the local railroad station agent, who arranged for the couple to be married by telegraph.

On Sunday, August 19, 1888, Miss Dora Cashron, accompanied by Justice of the Peace R. M. Chapman, stood at the telegraph office in Alvarado, Texas. At the same hour W. N. Nolan and his minister, the Rev. Joshua Lewis, stood at the telegraph office in Traver, California.

The wedding ceremony began with the questions and answers being sent over the telegraph wires by the agents at both stations. In a few short minutes Rev. Lewis said to the groom, "I now pronounce you man and wife." In Alvarado, Texas, Mr. Chapman gave the same message to the bride.

As the telegraph wires bore all these messages of love and joy, another chapter was written in our tales of the valley.

# The Petrified Woman

About six months after the discovery of the "Cantua Man" in 1890 (the subject of an earlier tale), a team of prospectors dug up the remains of a "petrified" woman in a canyon near the Kings River. The leader of the team, Pres Bozeman, a well-known rancher, claimed the find as his since it was discovered on his property. Bozeman, who decided this was his one opportunity to make a fortune, convinced his neighbor, R. V. Doggett, to invest in his scheme. The two became equal partners and exhibited their treasure up and down the coast.

All was well until the two began to travel to the East. In Salt Lake City, it was discovered that the so-called remains were instead a clay model of one of Bozeman's daughters. The truth was then revealed—Bozeman had suffered serious financial reverses in his ranching operation and thought this would be a way to recoup his losses. Instead, he found himself under arrest. The charge was fraud. He was tried in Selma, but the charge was dropped because the accusations against him were not substantiated by the testimony.

Unfortunately, Bozeman had given his interest in the hoax to Doggett who had, in turn, swapped it for a piece of land owned by Max Dutter. The land turned out to be as worthless as the so-called "petrified woman."

Nevertheless, both parties became irate at having been sold a bill of goods and launched a series of lawsuits that went on and on and on. Fourteen years later the case was finally settled out of court on January 28, 1905. Both parties came out about even financially, the costs for the lawsuits balancing out.

The old saying that "a fool and his money are soon parted" failed to add the caution that if more than one fool is involved the loss of money could go on and on and on.

# A Photo Flash

A blinding flash of light and an explosion that shook the ground stirred up the denizens of downtown Fresno. It was a few minutes past 8:00 on Friday evening, January 14, 1905, when this momentous event occurred. People ran from their homes and formed an excited crowd outside the Green Building at 1205 J (Fulton) Street—the site of the blast. Whispers of a dynamite bomber circulated through the crowd.

A third of the police force was called into action. Policemen Forman, DeVoe, Stingley, Coyle and Earp rushed to the scene. Police Chief Morgan arrived and announced that everyone could relax—the police were at the ready and the mystery would be solved quickly.

The police found an open door at the back of Chance Bros. Grocery Store, housed on the main floor of the Green Building. They quickly conducted a thorough search of the building. On the second floor was the studio of Maxwell & Mudge, photographers. A policeman rushed up the stairs to alert them about the problem only to find the door locked. The crowd on the street could see smoke pouring from the photo studio. The policeman knocked louder than ever. Finally, Mr. Maxwell opened the door.

"What are you fellows doing in there?" the policeman shouted. "Taking a picture of the Cumberland Presbyterian Church Choir," answered Maxwell. "Oops," replied the policeman, who then left to find the Chance brothers to tell them they should keep their door locked against intruders.

Evidently, those who witnessed the flash and explosion inside the studio found it much less frightening than did the witnesses outside. The reporter for the *Fresno Morning Republican* wrote the next morning that "when a church choir and an effusion of brimstone are found together, excitement is sure to follow."

# To Dance or Not to Dance

Every so often a fascinating bit of trivia fairly leaps off the pages of old issues of the *Fresno Morning Republican.* This was the case with some historic memories contained in a letter to the editor written by one A. W. Frederick of Anchor, Oregon, on January 31, 1923.

It seems that in the year 1888 a school board election was pending in the Sentinel School District in the foothills near Academy. The main issue before the voters was whether young people should be allowed to dance in the schoolhouse. Tempers flared as the subject was debated at dinner tables and at public gatherings. Solomon Lehman, a proponent of dancing, was sure that he would win the election because most of the men in this small district agreed with his point of view.

However, Joseph West disagreed with him and rallied the women in the district to cast their ballots. In these days before women were allowed to vote nationally, this was a progressive idea, indeed.

Mrs. Lucretia Morgan and Mrs. Belle McDonald came to the polls and cast their ballots, but were challenged by Solomon Lehman. "Since when do women have the right to vote," Lehman asked Joseph West. "They have the right to vote," West insisted.

In the end, the ladies' votes were counted along with the men's and the anti-dance trustee won.

According to A. W. Frederick, this was "the first exercise of woman suffrage at such a political election in California—friends of woman suffrage should give these women a medal."

# The Chicago Stump

A story with a strange twist began with a tree, a doubting public and a world's fair.

In the last half of the nineteenth century, stories began to be told of the gigantic redwood trees that were reputed to have been growing at the time of Christ's birth. Many Americans refused to believe the stories, thinking that they were tall tales told by Californians—perhaps the ravings of miners who had been drinking too much.

If the public did not believe, then perhaps they would pay to see these giants of the forest. Promoters eager to make money saw their chance. In 1853, the first of these trees was felled, breaking into pieces as it hit the ground. The bark was stripped and reformed into the semblance of a stump. It became a popular attraction in San Francisco and New York.

By 1893, the procedure had become more fine tuned. A photographer was present to record the cutting and slicing of a huge portion of one tree, the lumber of which was shipped to Chicago, reassembled and exhibited at the World's Columbian Exposition. The $15,000 fee for the cutting and delivery of the tree was paid for by the United States Department of the Interior.

After the exposition, the tree was moved to Washington, D.C., where it was exhibited for a number of years. Finally, the wood began to deteriorate. It was no longer possible to exhibit the tree. It was dumped into a marsh.

Some years later the marsh was drained because a new building to house the executives of the armed forces was going to be built on the land that the marsh occupied. The new structure, called the Pentagon, was constructed on top of the remnants of the giant redwood tree. The building that symbolizes the military might of the greatest superpower in the world has in its foundation the ruins of the greatest tree on earth—one that was thought of as a "California hoax."

What happened to the stump of this great tree? Called the "Chicago Stump," it still stands near Converse Basin in the mountains east of Fresno.

Daniel Rhoads, a member of the team that rescued the Donner Party. In 1857, he drove his cattle across the Coast Range Mountains and settled on land along the lower Kings River. He spent his last years in Lemoore.
*Courtesy of the Kings County Museum at Burris Park.*

One of the earliest pioneers of the great Central Valley was affectionately called "Uncle Dan" by the citizens of Lemoore, where he spent the last years of his life. He spent his retirement years in this community living on Evergreen Farm, property that he enhanced and beautified.

Born in Illinois in 1821, Daniel Rhoads lived in the Midwest until shortly after his marriage to Amanda Esrey in 1843.

Having read the accounts of John C. Fremont's first expedition to California, he was determined to travel west. In April of 1846, he and his wife, his father and other members of his family began the arduous journey with an ox-team and made their way to Sutter's Fort. He settled a mile away and became involved in cattle raising.

The following January, an Indian runner brought the news of the plight of the Donner Party. Rhoads immediately went to the fort to volunteer his help. For four days the men, women and children at the fort dried beef over fires and cracked wheat that was then run through sieves, which was the only way they had to mill wheat, to provide food for the Donner Party.

The rescue team, with their pack animals, set out. Fifteen men joined Rhoads. They had a difficult journey. There was no road, the streams were full and the way was fraught with canyons and steep mountain ridges. When they reached the snow line, two of the party remained behind with the pack train. The other fourteen men donned snowshoes and, with seventy-five-pound packs of supplies on their backs, trudged the remaining eighty miles on foot. So deep was the snow and so treacherous the way that seven of the men turned back. Rhoads and six of the men continued on their way, determined to reach the starving Donner Party.

For thirteen days they trudged through bone-chilling snow until the camp of the Donner survivors was reached. The area was so desolate they were afraid that no one was alive. Then someone saw a wisp of smoke coming out of the snow sixty yards ahead of them. One of the men yelled, "Hello." A woman appeared with a second woman following her. Seeing the men approaching, she looked at them and said, "Oh! Are you men from California or from Heaven!" They entered the hut to find the others too weak to get up.

Thirty members of the Donner Party had died. Now the survivors were to be taken to Sacramento by Rhoads and the rescue team. And the return trip promised to be harrowing as well.

They started out with just one day's supply of food—the remainder had been secreted in trees along the road they had made. They were horrified to discover that wolves had eaten their supplies. The only edible thing they had was the rawhide strips of their snowshoes that they roasted until they were crisp.

They finally reached Sacramento three days later. Daniel Rhoads and the other members of the rescue effort never forgot the horrible plight of the Donner Party. The members of that ill-fated group never forgot the sight of those seven men who came into their snow hut looking, to them, like angels from Heaven.

# *Scholarship & Service*

In the fall of 1925, the campus of Fresno State College was abuzz with plans for a new organization. Dr. Frank W. Thomas, president of the college; Miss Maude Schaeffer, dean of women; and Margaret McWhorter, president of the Associated Women Students, were in charge of working out the details for this new group. Membership would be based on academic achievement and outstanding participation in school activities. It was going to be the most exclusive organization on campus, with membership limited to twelve, and would be the most coveted honor of a woman's college career. Thus was Tokalon, the Fresno State College honor society for women, born.

On February 4, 1926, twelve women were initiated in a candlelight ceremony. A constitution was drafted, a pin was designed, and the organization was truly launched. Some of the early projects of the group were College Day, groundbreaking ceremonies for Ratcliffe Stadium, College Open House and College Night, which included a play written and directed each year by Tokalon members. This event was held in the east court of the Old Administration Building. Members also served in an "Ask Me" booth at registration, helped coordinate Women's Week, ushered at commencement and assisted at the president's annual reception. As the enrollment of the college grew, it was necessary to increase the membership from twelve to twenty-four.

In 1937, the Tokalon Alumnae was formed. In 1972, this group incorporated to become a non-profit organization. In 1974, Tokalon merged with Blue Key, the honor society for men.

Tokalon Alumnae's most memorable achievement has been its scholarship for women students. Today, Tokalon's Ina Gregg Thomas Memorial Scholarship benefits seven women each year. Six $1,000 scholarships and one $1,500 scholarship are given to women who meet the requirements, based on scholarship, activities and financial need. Named for the wife of Dr. Frank Thomas, who was such an inspiration to Tokalon members, this tribute was a "pledge of love, respect, tender appreciation, and an acknowledgment of her immeasurable service" to them.

Over the years the meaning of Tokalon, which is "the highest, the finest, and the most beautiful," has been borne out not only in the quality of its membership, but in the importance of the scholarships that it endows.

# A Visit from the General

On October 1, 1878, there was great excitement in the Central Valley. The ex-President of the United States, Ulysses S. Grant, his wife, son and several friends were going to visit Madera on their way to Yosemite Valley. Since Grant was due to arrive early in the morning, the party of people from Fresno who wanted to meet him left the day before and stayed at the Yosemite Hotel in Madera, across the street from the depot.

Grant arrived on the night passenger train from San Francisco. As was the tradition then, the sleeping coach with the passengers bound for Yosemite Valley was left at the Madera station. The rest of the train continued south. The travelers in the sleeping coach were not to be disturbed until morning. Since a chorus of anvils heralded the train's appearance at midnight, it is hard to believe that they slept peacefully.

Early in the morning, another chorus of anvils, sometimes used to announce the arrival of a famous person, especially a war hero, woke the passengers. As they walked across the street from the station to the hotel, they were greeted by cheers from the huge crowd that had gathered. People had come from all over the Central Valley and the foothill communities to see President Grant, who was heralded as the commander of the Union forces who had won the War Between the States. As Grant and his party entered the dining room of the hotel there were cheers from all the other diners. Grant shook hands with everyone, but did not give a speech.

After breakfast Grant and his friends boarded a stagecoach for the long trip to Yosemite Valley. The people who had driven up from Fresno gathered around the stage and visited with Grant, who was in a very good mood and enjoyed visiting with everyone, including a few who told him they had fought in the Confederate Army. With six horses pulling the stagecoach, the party left.

There from Fresno were Dr. Chester Rowell, Mr. and Mrs. Otto Froelich, Mr. and Mrs. Bernard Marks, Mr. and Mrs. John Shanklin, Mr. Jim White of White's Bridge, Mr. Louis Einstein, Mr. Frank Dusy, Mr. Clark Stevens, and Mr. and Mrs. A. M. Clark. For them, the trip had been well worth it. They had met the famous man and gained memories that would last a lifetime.

The original T. L. Heaton Elementary School building, designed by the architectural firm of Swartz and Ryland, was constructed in 1927 and demolished in 1971 after it was decided that it did not meet earthquake safety standards. This was the reason Fresno lost many of its historic buildings. Today buildings such as this can be retrofitted and brought up to code.
*Photo by Lynn Gordacan, former Heaton School student; presented to Beverly Smith, Principal on May 4, 1971. Courtesy of Nancy Hintzel, Principal of Heaton School.*

On San Pablo Avenue a cluster of one-story architecturally nondescript buildings marks the present-day home
of the T. L. Heaton Elementary School. Its play yard fills the rest
of the fenced site from McKinley to Home avenues. On the
McKinley side of the property a lovely brick structure once stood
which was the home base for the students of this school.

In those halcyon days of the late 1940s and 1950s, this building was the domain of Hattie May Hammat, principal extraordinaire, and her hand-picked group of teachers. Serious education
was conducted within these walls—a no-nonsense curriculum
based on the three R's with few frills and no bells and whistles.
Multiplication was drilled into the students as the teacher, with
ruler in hand, went up and down the rows as the students took
turns reciting, "Two times one is two, two times two is four," and
so on. Discipline was as strict as the curriculum. It was serious
business to receive an education.

But there was fun, too. In the late days of spring the temperature often soared. The brick building did not have air-conditioning, but it had tall windows that opened wide and caught any
north breeze that came along. The transom windows on the opposite side of each room provided a direction for the breeze to go.
On the days when it was too hot to take heavy physical exercise,
a special treat was planned. An all-school jacks contest was held.
Every student brought a towel and a bag of jacks. During recess
and after lunch the wide corridors were filled with students sitting on their towels on the cool concrete floors playing jacks. Scores
were kept, play-offs were held, and the excitement grew as the
contest continued.

Some of the students preferred playing marbles. They had their
own arena in the sand piles built for this purpose under the large
trees that shaded the south side of the building.

Occasionally, there were days when kickball and softball were
played in the hot, late spring sun. When it was time to come back
to the classroom, each student rushed to get a heavy paper towel
that was dampened with cold Fresno water and wrung out and
folded into a long rectangle. Each student sat at his desk, put his

head down and put the wet paper towel on his forehead or the back of his neck and closed his eyes and rested. On these hot afternoons, the teacher read wonderful stories while the students let their bodies cool down.

The beautiful old brick building that was Heaton School harbored memories of all kinds. For those who were lucky enough to study within its walls, it still holds a special place in their hearts.

# The Skunk in the Cloakroom

For those Fresnans who had the opportunity to attend elementary school in those grand old brick buildings that have been the victim of the wrecker's ball, memories of certain architectural features are held dear. The wooden floors that were swept clean each afternoon; the blackboards which held court on two walls of the classroom; the old wood and cast iron desks that never had quite enough room underneath for books; the inkwells which stood empty, but had been used by many young boys who dunked the pigtails of the girls who sat in front of them into the dark blue liquid; and the cloakroom, which was a separate room at the front of the classroom to which one gained entrance through the two doors on either side of the front blackboard. It was into this cloakroom that you went first thing in the morning to hang up your coat before the business of learning began. There was also a bench to sit on while you took off your galoshes and a hook on which to hang up your umbrella on a rainy day.

For Miss Vesta Hall's fifth grade class at Heaton Elementary School in the late 1940s, the cloakroom offered surprises as well. One of the students, Maggie Smith, loved animals and had many pets. Those who knew Maggie well were acquainted with her menagerie. Her latest pet, a skunk, was named Flower. Flower was a delightful creature and a great favorite among Maggie's friends. Flower loved to be held and carried about. Being a nocturnal creature, Flower roamed the house at will all night long and slept during most of the daylight hours. When Maggie's friends came over to play, Flower would usually wake up and play, too. This worked out quite well for everyone. The fact that Flower had been deodorized was appreciated by the parents of Maggie's friends.

One day Maggie took Flower to school and tucked her in a box in the cloakroom. Maggie forgot to tell Miss Hall and, since Flower was sleeping, it didn't seem to be necessary. Miss Hall was standing at the front of the room conducting a math lesson. Everyone was quiet and attentive. The cloakroom door inched open. First a little pink nose could be seen, followed by a long, sleek, bristly, black body with a white stripe down its back. Then the bushy tail in all its glory made its appearance. By now, all eyes were on Flower. Miss Hall, who knew neither about Flower nor her pleasing fragrance, took one look and froze. The ruler and math book dropped to the floor. Miss Hall turned ashen. Maggie jumped to her feet, grabbed the skunk, rushed out of the room, and ran all the way home. Miss Hall was not amused, but her fifth grade class never forgot the sight of Flower's debut at Heaton School.

B y 1870, the town of Millerton had begun its decline. Actually, the town had never really grown or prospered. A
massive flood on Christmas Eve, 1867, had destroyed a good part
of the town. It certainly had a demoralizing influence on the people
who lived there, who never really recovered from that terrible experience. Ira McCray, hotel owner and prominent businessman,
suffered more than anyone. He had been experiencing reverses in
his business. The flood was the last straw. He left Millerton a broken and destitute man. Sadly, he ended his days in the Fresno
County Hospital, cared for by the generosity of Dr. Lewis Leach.

Another event caused another death knell to the town. In
preparation for the 1870 celebration of the Fourth of July, a large
shipment of fireworks had been ordered from Stockton. When they
arrived, they were stored in the saddlery shop of D. B. McCarthy.

McCarthy and three of his friends decided to get a jump start
on the celebration of our country's independence and spent a major
portion of the evening of July 3 drinking in one of the saloons. As
the evening drew to a close, they retired to McCarthy's shop to go
to bed. Some question arose regarding the quality of the fireworks,
which McCarthy chose to settle by lighting one of the Roman
candles. As he held the sputtering candle in his hand, he waved it
around so that the room would be bathed in light and all the other
fireworks could be seen by his three buddies. Unfortunately, the
shooting flames ignited the other celebratory candles and created
a pyrotechnic display that was unlike any other ever seen in Millerton. The peaceful summer night was further disturbed by the
conflagration that ensued as one building after another caught fire.
The Farmer's Exchange and S. W. Henry's hotel, livery stable and
blacksmith shop were destroyed. Henry had been a financial backer
of McCarthy, who now had caused his financial ruin.

By the time the county seat was moved to Fresno Station in
1874, Millerton had suffered several major floods and the fire. Its
residents were ready to move on and most of them did—to the
town of Fresno Station.

# Mr. West Coast Relays

In 1927, a new event to highlight Raisin Week was launched. The brainchild of J. Flint Hanner, this happening was called the West Coast Relays. His idea was to bring together teams from western colleges and universities and valley high schools and junior colleges for a two-day track and field competition. He hoped that if the younger people had a chance to compete in the same field as the outstanding athletes they would be inspired by the experience and become the stars of the future. The idea grew with each year's event. It was a tremendous success. Such great athletes as Rafer Johnson and Bob Mathias competed for the first time at the relays, getting their start and their first taste of success.

Who was Flint Hanner, the man behind the dream? He was born in Greensboro, North Carolina, on May 21, 1898. His family moved to California when he was in high school. He attended San Jose High School, where he competed in track, football and basketball. It was here that he was introduced to the javelin. He entered Stanford University in 1919, eventually earning not only his bachelor of arts degree, but a master of arts degree as well. He became an outstanding athlete. He not only was the national intercollegiate javelin champion for three years, but also was named to the All-America track team all three of those years. In 1921, he was the first recipient of the title of National Collegiate Athletic Association javelin champion.

After holding coaching jobs at two high schools in Northern California, Hanner was called to Fresno State College in 1925. During his career at Fresno State, the Bulldog track and field teams won twenty-seven championships in the Far Western and California Collegiate Athletic Association conferences. Many of his students set world records and are remembered as "greats" in their fields. His coaching duties also included basketball and football.

Hanner retired from coaching in 1960, but he continued to serve on the West Coast Relays Games Committee until his death in 1974. A legend in his own right, Hanner made contributions to track and field in the Central Valley which have left a legacy that will never be forgotten.

J. Flint Hanner, seated in an Auburn automobile, posed with his 1932 Fresno State College track team.

*The Image Group from the Laval Historical Collection.*

# Men & Women & Marriage

In our modern era of the late 1990s, the ratio of men to women weighs in favor of the women. This was not the case in early days of Millerton and Fresno. The number of men outnumbered the number of women by an enormous amount.

Pioneer men believed the Biblical teaching that it is not good for man to live alone. The women added themselves in that classification. Women of marriageable age in both Millerton and Fresno did not have to worry about finding a beau—there were many eligible men just waiting to court them. In fact, there were not enough women to meet the demand, and the women who were here could be selective when choosing a mate.

If a woman's husband died, she did not have to wait long to find someone to marry and provide for her. Certainly in the primitive conditions that existed in the early years of Fresno, this must have made life bearable for many a woman who was left alone. Second marriages were common and third marriages also occurred.

It is interesting that in February of 1881, R. W. Riggs, a local historian and philosopher, made the following statement regarding this subject: "There were only fourteen marriageable girls in Fresno city, but two hundred willing ones to take them off their parents' hands." Evidently, this situation lasted for several years.

A rather funny news item appeared in the *Expositor* on August 7, 1872. It said in effect that "ten or fifteen marriageable young ladies, either of comely or plain appearance, are wanted immediately, Millerton being then without a single one and at least twenty-five old bachelors are in search of ribs." The rather blatant reference to Adam was followed by the statement that "there will be no necessity of long courtships as they all mean biz."

All of this is a far cry from the situation that women of marriageable age face today. This might be one instance in which some of the fairer sex might long for the "good old days."

# Mr. Shaver & His Lake

When spring comes and the blossoms appear on the fruit trees and the wildflowers carpet the foothills and valley with their panoply of color, thoughts turn to the arrival of warm weather and all the joys it brings. For many valley residents, it is time to pack one's bag and head for the mountain lakes. The snow has melted and it's time to open one's cabin for the weekend escapes and the lazy weeks of summer. For many valley residents, the destination is Shaver Lake, that beautiful mountain paradise. Many enjoy its amenities, but how many know anything about the man for whom it is named.

Charles B. Shaver was born in Steuben County, New York, in 1855. His family moved to Michigan in 1864. It was there that he received his public school education. When he was nineteen, he went to work for the lumber company of Whitney and Stinchfield in Detroit. He was made a foreman, a position he maintained until 1882. He left their employ and accepted a position with A. B. Long and Son of Grand Rapids. His new job required him to assist in the building of a logging railway. He also had an opportunity to study how their mills and lumber plant operated.

In 1889, he accepted a job with the White Friant Lumber Company in Michigan. During his two years with this company, he constructed fourteen miles of logging railway and put in over a hundred million feet of logs. In 1891, he and Lewis P. Swift, another lumber man, left for California, settling in Fresno. They joined the Fresno Flume and Irrigation Company, headed by Frank Bullard. A portion of the company's operation focused on twelve thousand acres of timberland near Stevenson Creek and Meadow.

The plans were to build a flume down the mountain to present-day Clovis to transport logs to a mill already in operation and to build a dam across Stevenson Creek, creating a reservoir that would be called Shaver Lake, where cut logs could be stored.

Eventually, Shaver and Swift bought out their partners and continued to build and develop the company. In 1894, Shaver was named president of the Fresno Flume and Irrigation Company.

After the sudden death of L. P. Swift in 1901, Shaver sent for his brother-in-law, Harvey Swift, who was still living in Michigan. Shortly after he and his family arrived, Swift bought his half-brother, Lewis P. Swift's share in the company.

Shaver continued in the role of company president until his death on Christmas Day, 1907. His contributions to the lumber industry in Central California will long be remembered. And the beautiful mountain lake that bears his name will continue to be enjoyed by many generations of Fresno County residents.

# July 4, 1874

The first Fourth of July celebration in the new seat of Fresno County was held with all the color and exuberance fitting such a grand event. At noon and at sundown the residents of Fresno Station heard a stirring salute played on anvils. Thomas Pryce was the marshal of a short parade that wended its way through the small business district.

Exercises were held at the freight room of the Central Pacific Railroad station. The program featured J. W. Ferguson, editor of the *Expositor*, reading the Declaration of Independence. Joseph Meyers sang. Mrs. J. L. Smith read Drake's Address to the Flag, and a number of tableaux were presented by some of the young girls of Fresno. The Lewis Bros. troupe was in town, adding excitement to the proceedings.

In the afternoon the Calithumpians presented a mock parade at the depot. This was followed by more patriotic readings.

That evening, seventy couples attended a dance at Magnolia Hall, followed by a dinner prepared by Mrs. Lord and served at the Velguth building on I Street (now Broadway).

In the descriptions of the day's events, fireworks are not mentioned. Perhaps the ever-present danger of fire weighed heavily on the minds of Fresnans.

An article in the *Expositor* the next day praised the citizens of Fresno Station for conducting themselves with dignity, harmony, and all-around good feelings for their fellow man. The writer applauded the lack of harsh words and deeds that might have spoiled the day. The rather pretentious comments leave the impression that perhaps the normal scheme of things would be rioting in the streets and other expressions of ill will. One must remember that our community was at this point still a Wild West frontier town, with few social amenities—an unpolished diamond in the rough.

A ferry on the Kings River. Many of the early day ferries were whaleboats, but as soon as sawmills were established, this type ferry was constructed and put into operation.

*Courtesy of William B. Secrest Sr.*

# A Ferry across the River

From time to time, our tales of the valley have mentioned the ferries that were an important part of transportation in the earliest days of Fresno County. Exactly what were they?

The ferry was simply a flat skiff that could carry a stage, people and animals across a river, charging a toll for the service. The purpose of the ferry was to make crossing a river safer. Before the ferry, a traveler simply forded the river, meaning that he crossed at a point where the river was shallow enough to wade across. However, such a crossing could be dangerous if the water was icy cold and the current was swift. It also might be necessary for the traveler to journey a long distance out of his way until he found a shallow point in the river. On the San Joaquin River, the earliest fords were at Cassidy's Gravelly Ford and at a few other points below the town of Millerton.

The first licensed ferry began operating in August of 1856. It belonged to Millerton businessman Ira McCray. It was located adjacent to his hotel and made crossing the San Joaquin River possible for local residents and travelers. A month later, C. P. Converse began his ferry operation across the San Joaquin below Millerton at Converse Flat, later known as Jones Store. Three ferries opened on the Kings River a year later. James Smith and W. W. Hill began their operations on the upper Kings at Campbell's Crossing and Scottsburg (present-day Centerville) respectively. The ferry owners had to pay monthly license fees of five dollars and three dollars and were under bonds of three thousand dollars. At first the ferry crossings were operated sporadically, but by 1860, traffic had increased and the roads to the ferries were declared public highways, so regular schedules were implemented.

In August of 1869, a new rate list was set. Some of the rates were: one-horse wagon or buggy fifty cents; two-horse wagon or buggy $1.00; four-horse wagon or buggy, loaded $1.50; four-horse wagon or buggy, empty $1.00; twelve-horse wagon, loaded $3.50; twelve-horse wagon, empty $2.25; horseman fifty cents; footman twenty-five cents; loose cattle or horses, per head ten cents; hog's three cents; and sheep two cents. On one day in June of 1871, a

Millerton operator ferried 24,000 sheep across the river without losing a single one.

The ferries served an important function. Although they are almost forgotten, there is an interesting footnote to our story for Fresnans. The next time you decide to travel north and drive through Herndon to reach Highway 99, you are driving through the site that 130 years ago was called Sycamore. Then as you drive over the bridge that crosses the San Joaquin River, remember for a moment that at this spot there was a ferry that took travelers across the river. The method for crossing may be different, but the need to do so has not changed.

Among the letters gathered during Fresno's Centennial year by the Pioneer Families Committee was one written by Minnie Jo Aldrich. It is filled with nostalgic recollections of her girlhood in Fresno and stories her late husband had shared with her as well. He had told her many times about how he and his friends swam in the old mill ditch that ran down the middle of Fresno Street. Her most memorable recollection concerned M. Theo Kearney's mansion and a president of the United States.

It seems that in 1911, when Mrs. Aldrich was working as a secretary to Milo Rowell, one of the owners of Hobbs-Parsons Produce Company, President William Howard Taft and his aide, Major Archibald Butts, paid a visit to Fresno. Congressman Englebright, an uncle of Mrs. Aldrich, was a member of the party. Automobiles were just beginning to come into vogue and there were not too many in Fresno. However, George C. Roeding, at the wheel of his Thomas Flyer, drove President Taft, his aide and several others through the downtown business district and out Kearney Boulevard so the president could see Kearney Park and tour the mansion. A few other people loaned their cars so that all the president's party could be accommodated.

Mrs. Aldrich makes a point of saying that "there were no women in the group. We weren't so liberated then." Mr. Rowell did close the office so that his staff could go out to the park and see the president as he passed by. When the car in which her uncle was seated drove within earshot, she yelled and waved. He ordered the car stopped and opened the door so she could join him. As their entourage entered Kearney Park all the gates were closed so no one else could enter. She was the only woman in the group. When they arrived at Kearney Mansion her congressman uncle introduced her to President Taft and Major Butts. It was a proud moment in her life.

As she wrote this letter in 1985 at age ninety-seven, this memory burned brightly for her. In a postscript she added a note that recalled another event, one of the great tragedies of our century. It seems that a year later, in 1912, the president's aide, Major Archibald Butts, went down with the *Titanic*.

# A Lawyer Named Grady

By 1876, Walker Drane Grady was practicing law in Fresno. The methods that he used were sometimes called into question. He was described by those who knew him as "clever, fearless and arrogant."

In the early 1880s he built a meeting room called, as was the custom of the time, the Grady Opera House. Located on I Street (now Broadway), this structure was often the scene of theatrical productions as well as other public gatherings.

Grady's finances were not always on an even keel. He see-sawed month-to-month between wealth and insolvency. One of his creditors brought suit and won his case. Grady said he could not pay. A writ of execution was obtained by the man to whom Grady owed the money. The writ, with instructions that Grady's opera house be sold, was given to the sheriff. Grady announced that no sale would take place. But, of course, the sale was scheduled and everyone in town came. When they arrived, they were greeted by Grady who, seated on an orange crate in front of the door, was holding two shotguns on his knees. No one bid. There was no sale.

On another occasion Grady got into one of his infamous barroom brawls. He emerged from the event with the ear of his opponent held neatly between his teeth. In the jury trial that followed, he gave the following testimony in his defense: "Yes—there was a barroom fight. We grappled and rolled around on the floor and under a table. While under the table, the complaining witness projected his ear between my teeth, them he projected his knee up against my lower jaw, and in so doing my lower jaw was forced against my upper jaw, and as a consequence, the ear was severed. So, the complaining witness bit off his own ear." The jury deliberated briefly, then acquitted Grady of any wrongdoing.

# A Man Named Shaw

One of the busier streets in Fresno stretches from the foothills west to a bend in the San Joaquin River. It makes a brief appearance south of Firebaugh and then again between Miller Road and Oxford Avenue just before reaching Interstate Highway 5. It can truly be said that it stretches across a large part of Fresno County.

In the 1950s, Shaw Avenue was a two-lane road. Then, in 1955, the Fresno State College campus relocated to the corner of Cedar and Shaw avenues, pulling growth to the northeast. On December 2, 1966, the Fresno City Council voted 5 to 2 to approve the building of a regional shopping center on Shaw Avenue. The vote was a controversial one, coming so soon after the opening of the Fulton Mall. The developer of this new center, called Fashion Fair, promised to help bring new commercial interests to downtown. The promise was not kept.

With the increased traffic, Shaw Avenue became a major thoroughfare.

Have you ever wondered as you drive along this street how it got its name?

On April 26, 1878, William Shaw arrived in Fresno with his cousin, M. R. Madary. They immediately went about the business of settling in to their new surroundings. They invested in land in the new town. Seeing the necessity for homes for the many people arriving in Fresno, they went into the business of filling this need. Madary constructed a lumber mill that provided materials. Shaw became a building contractor.

In 1882, William Shaw married Threna Hedges. Threna's father, H. P. Hedges, served on the fire commission. (Hedges Avenue, which was the northern boundary of Zapp's Park, an early Fresno park, is named for him.)

In 1892 and in 1894, Shaw was elected constable of the Fresno township. In September of 1906, he was appointed chief of police and served in this post until September, 1911. Later, he was named to the police and fire commissions. He served his city well for many years. When development pushed north, Shaw Avenue was named in his memory.

# Livery Stables & Democracy

The livery stable played an important role in the early period of Fresno's existence. The livery stable was the last remnant of the stagecoach era. In many ways, it preserved some of the traditions of the inn in American culture. Although most often the livery stable was a rather crude structure with a hayloft above and horses below, its plainness belied its social importance.

Here men gathered to gossip and discuss politics. Those who were accepted into its inner circle of habitues felt a certain distinction. It was a center of democracy because everyone in town came to transact business and in so doing shared opinions on most of the major issues of the day. If a politician wanted to know how his constituency felt about a certain matter, the best place to find out was the livery stable.

In our modern society there is not another business to which it can be directly compared. The mechanic's garage compares only in the sense that cars and horses are both methods of transportation. The noise and fumes in a garage certainly don't invite conversation and socializing. In the livery stable the smell of old leather, the whinny of horses and the sound of hoofs pawing at the ground were pleasant and soothing, inviting lingering visits.

During Fresno's first decade, the stagecoach, with all the romance it evokes, was a major form of transportation for those traveling outside the reach of the railroad's lines. Horses were needed for both private and rented carriages and for delivery wagons. The importance of the livery stable cannot be overstated. When the automobile arrived on the scene and the livery stable passed into memory, a major part of the romance and color of the West went with it.

One of Fresno County's earliest towns has had five names in its long history. When a post office was opened there on December 3, 1856, it was called Scottsburg after William Y. Scott, the owner of a restaurant and saloon. In 1866, the name was changed to Kings River. Three years later, it became known as Centerville because it was located at a central point on the Kings River. In 1895, it became Kingriver and then, finally, in 1905, it became known again as Centerville. This time the name stuck and the name Centerville is still used today.

One of Centerville's citizens, J. B. Sweem, arrived in Fresno County in 1855, one year before the county was officially organized. He built and operated the first flour and grist mill in Fresno County. There is a local story that on one occasion the dam that supplied power for the mill's operation broke, flooding the land around it. As a result, a lot of grass seeds germinated and began to grow. When the water receded, other vegetation was beginning to grow also. This made Sweem realize that if he could bring water to his land, he could grow grain. He decided to build an irrigation ditch that would carry water from the Kings River to his property. Another ditch had been built near Centerville three years earlier, in 1866, by Anderson Akers and Spyars Singleton Hyde.

About 1870 Sweem's ditch was purchased by Moses Church and A. Y. Easterby for $1,800. It was the beginning of their enterprise that was later consolidated as the Fresno Canal and Irrigation Company.

The next time you drive out Highway 180 and go through the town of Centerville, remember that this is where the concept of irrigation began, the concept that formed the basis for our agricultural economy in Fresno County.

# John C. Hoxie

John C. Hoxie was born in Sandwich, Massachusetts, on March 15, 1848. In 1852, his parents decided to come west to California. They traveled by way of the Isthmus of Panama and settled first in Tuttletown, Tuolumne County. John's father built the first quartz mill in that area. Four years later, they moved to an Indian reservation where he taught carpentry. In 1858, the Hoxie family traveled by stagecoach to Millerton.

There were no schools in Millerton, but John Hoxie was taught at home by his mother. In 1860, the first school in Fresno County was formed in the dining room of the old hospital at Fort Miller, with Rebecca Baley as the teacher. John was in her class. By the time he was fifteen, John Hoxie had become a farmer, raising cattle and sheep. His holdings increased over time and he became prosperous. In 1873, he married Mary J. McKenzie, the daughter of a prominent Millerton family. The ceremony was held at Fort Miller, where Mary had been born.

In 1874, Hoxie followed most of the other Millerton residents and moved to Fresno. He bought a parcel of land and built a fine residence. Later, he constructed another home at the corner of L and Stanislaus streets where he lived until his death.

In the 1880s, Hoxie became interested in mining operations in the foothills. He and his partners, W. H. McKenzie and T. C. Hart, purchased the Mud Spring Mine. They developed and operated it and turned it into one of the finest mining ventures on the West Coast. Hoxie's knowledge of this subject grew over the years to such an extent that he was asked by the directors of the Panama Pacific International Exposition at San Francisco to create a collection of minerals and metals of Central California to be exhibited in the California building.

His wife, Mary, became the first teacher in the city of Fresno. John and Mary Hoxie were valued members of the Fresno community. They represent just one of the many families who made enormous contributions not only to Fresno, but had played an important role at Millerton in the earliest development of our county.

Any number of California towns, particularly mining towns, experienced sudden growth followed by virtual oblivion a few years later. But for this pattern to happen to a town where agriculture was the basis of the economy was unheard of. However, it did happen right here in the Central Valley. The town is called Traver.

By March of 1884, the construction of the main canal of the 76 Land and Water Company had been completed up to the Southern Pacific Railroad just south of where the rail line crossed the Kings River. The 76 Company owned land by the railroad that was laid out for a town site. It was named Traver in honor of Charles Traver, one of the directors of the company. Lots were auctioned and sold quickly. Within two months the new town boasted many stores, hotels, livery stables, a post office, a railroad depot and a Chinatown. A year later 400 people were living in Traver.

Farming in the area consisted of orchards, vineyards and alfalfa. Everything planted flourished. The town also boasted three large grain warehouses. Traver became the principal shipping station for grain. During the year 1886 and the first seven months of 1887, more grain was shipped from Traver than from anywhere else in the world any time. The area had grown to such an extent that people were talking about incorporating their town.

Then two things happened. First, on October 30, 1887, there was a fire—not just an average fire, but a huge conflagration. In the kitchen of the Semorile Hotel on Seventh Street, the cook let some grease boil over on a very hot stove. The resulting fire leveled a large part of the business section of town. Four other terrible fires occurred in the downtown area immediately after this one.

Then, another tragedy struck. The fertile ground, which had produced such vast and wonderful crops, produced something else. The irrigation water that had gone into the ground caused the water level to move up from ten feet to three feet and soon to one foot. The rising water brought up alkali that spread to such an extent that the land turned white. Nothing would grow. The boom was over. The decline set in. People left. Soon all that remained were a few buildings. Today, with the exception of the old Traver jail, even those buildings are gone.

# John W. Humphreys

As one takes the well-traveled road to Shaver Lake, there are a number of interesting place names along the way. One of these is Humphreys Station. Did you ever wonder for whom it is named?

John W. Humphreys was born in Athens, Alabama, on January 11, 1830. As a young man of twenty-two, he made his way to California, settling in Tuolumne County, where he engaged in mining. In 1860, he moved to Mariposa and went into the sawmill business. He married three years later and, in 1867, moved his mill to Pine Ridge, just six miles from Tollhouse. The area had few residents. Most of the population consisted of Native Americans, whom he hired to work in the woods and his mill. His wife and her sister were the first white women in the neighborhood.

No roads had been built, but Humphreys' workers cut timber and pulled the lumber up the hill using teams of oxen. He assisted in building the Tollhouse grade that rises 2,000 feet in two miles. Today, the road has been improved remarkably and offers not only a steep ascent, but spectacular views of the valley. In the late 1860s it was a nightmare climb, and descent was terrifying. Stagecoaches had to tie a log on the back to act as a brake when coming down the hill.

In 1874, Humphreys sold his mill, but two years later began operating three other mills in the area. In 1892, he retired to his ranch in Tollhouse. When he died on March 20, 1900, he was mourned as one of the venerable pioneers of the county.

John's brother, James, owned the saloon at Humphreys Station. It took the stagecoaches exactly one day to reach this spot from Fresno. Here the horses could rest and travelers could eat and obtain overnight lodgings.

Next time you drive on Tollhouse Road to visit the mountain lakes, take a moment when you pass Humphreys Station to remember J. W. Humphreys, the man who pioneered the building of the road on which you are driving, and his brother James, the man for whom Humphreys Station is named.

The last building to survive the boom period in the town of Traver. Today, it is part of the Burris Park Museum complex.
*Courtesy of the Kings County Museum at Burris Park.*

M any years after the residents of Traver had moved elsewhere because of the scourge of alkali in the Traver soil, the buildings fell into disrepair and, eventually, were torn down. By 1953, only the old Traver jail—some called it the "Calaboose"— stood as a remnant of the boom period of the town.

Before the jail was built in 1886, prisoners were housed in a railroad boxcar because the supervisors of Tulare County had never appropriated money for a jail facility. In December of that year, the newly elected constable, William E. Russell, collected money from local businessmen to finance a building and to help construct the building. Lumber was purchased from Emil Seligman; Cisero Spears, the local drayman, hauled the lumber to the building site; and Harry F. Winnes and Emery Barris did the actual construction work. The jail was ready for its first prisoner by the year's end.

The jail is an unusual building. Built in the "plank on plank" type of construction, it has no frame. It was made by "stacking 2 x 6 planks flat and securing the corners with spikes. Even the roof and doors are made of 2 x 6s. The resulting structure is 12' x 16' and has two cells, each with a small window." The only other known buildings of note in the Central Valley using this method of construction are the huge grain silo at Strathmore and a jail in Firebaugh.

The old jail, the lone building to survive from the boom period of Traver, stood in a state of disrepair for many years. The late Mrs. Maude Montgomery of Kings County purchased the jail and had it moved to Burris Park, north of Hanford. Here, it is a part of the Burris Park Museum complex and stands as a reminder of an important period in the history of Kings and Tulare counties. Sadly, it is in need of funds for restoration. Until that happens, it is preserved in a place where visitors can see it and, for a moment, learn another story in the tales of our valley.

# Lone Star

In 1882, before any school district was in existence, a one-room schoolhouse was built by volunteer labor on the northwest corner of Clovis and North avenues. Woodson Pool, Mellie Hughes and Jesse Weber, who were to attend school there, were asked by their elders to select a name. They said the little lone schoolhouse set in the middle of a vast grain field reminded them of a "Lone Star." The next year a larger two-room school was erected on the same site when the Lone Star School District was formed.

In 1898, the Santa Fe Railroad branch running east from Fresno was completed and a new, large two-story Lone Star school was built on Fowler Avenue near the railroad crossing. Soon a Lone Star Village grew up nearby with a railroad station, post office, store and blacksmith shop. The area generally bounded by Peach, Tulare, American and Dockery avenues became and is still known as the Lone Star area.

In 1899, the Lone Star Hall was built with mostly volunteer labor. This was the social center for a large part of southeast Fresno. Weddings, dances, "literary" meetings and various other community events were held in the hall for many years.

In 1914 the school was moved across Fowler Avenue to its present location and the two-story building was demolished.

In 1915, John S. Wash became principal of the Lone Star School, a position he held until 1938. His teaching methods were a mixture of old-fashioned 3R's and progressive ideas. He believed that children should learn at their own speed, allowing the more capable students to forge ahead as quickly as their abilities allowed. Special attention was given the slower students. He did not believe in report cards. He taught with strict discipline and humor. For many years he conducted a summer school for teachers at Lone Star. He never married and lived in a small cabin across the street from the school. His life was his teaching.

In 1961, a new school was built in the Sunnyside area of the Lone Star School District. The trustees, most of whom had been his students, decided to name the new facility in honor of John S. Wash, an effective, much-loved educator.

# A Parkway for the River

The germ of an idea was planted in 1918 when Charles Henry Cheney recommended in his *Progress of a City Plan For Fresno* that the governing body of the city of Fresno buy the land along the banks of the San Joaquin River. It was, he reasoned, necessary to purchase this land to create a parkway, a green belt as it were, for all the people of this community and their descendants. It was a visionary idea that would utilize the one major scenic resource of the Fresno area and preserve it for generations to come. As with so many plans, this one was shelved.

It took another time and a pressing issue to bring the vision to light again. In 1985, three women, Peg Smith, Mary Savala and Clarey Creagor, were concerned about the possibility of development in the river bottom of the San Joaquin River. Each of them had called Jan Mitchell, a planner with the city of Fresno's Development Department, who gave them each other's names. They met in Peg's living room to discuss what could be done. Over steaming cups of coffee that day, the concept of a parkway along the San Joaquin River began to develop. Soon after this conversation the River Committee was formed.

An editorial column in the *Fresno Bee* by Roger Tatarian brought the vision of a parkway to another person. Coke Hallowell read the column, cut it out, and read it over and over. Long an advocate of protecting and preserving the environment, she put her volunteer expertise to work. The San Joaquin River Parkway and Conservation Trust was born as a result of the vision and support of many.

Today, the parkway is well on its way. A patchwork quilt in the making, parcels of land have been purchased, each an important part of the envisioned plan. When all the pieces of land are finally together, the quilt will be complete and the Fresno community will have twenty-two miles of paths—equestrian, bike and hiking—for this and future generations to enjoy.

Charles Henry Cheney would be delighted.

# The Lewis S. Eaton Trail

As the vision for the San Joaquin River Parkway becomes a reality, each new piece that opens to the public is another cause for celebration. The gateway to the parkway is the Lewis S. Eaton Trail, named for financier and philanthropist Lewis S. Eaton. It begins at the corner of Audubon Drive and Friant Road. A large marker, etched with the names of the Friends of Lewis Eaton, honors those who made the donations that launched this project. This is the beginning of the trail. The first mile stretches through Woodward Park, making for the hiker a transition from an urban to a nature environment.

At the end of the first mile, the hiker reaches the American Express Overlook at the bluffs high above river bottom land. At the overlook, the hiker can learn about the wildlife and ecology of the river. Also, in the pavement can be seen the names of the businesses and people who contributed to this project.

On Saturday, May 31, 1997, the groundbreaking took place for an additional three miles of trails for hikers, cyclists and equestrians along the Lewis S. Eaton Trail.

Other pieces of the parkway have been acquired to date. The Willow Unit and the Milburn Unit, both state ecological reserves, stretch through sections of the river. Camp Pashayan, another section of the parkway near Highway 99, is under the auspices of the State of California Wildlife Conservation Board. At this site, some nine thousand children come to the river every year on docent-conducted field trips. With blue nets held high, students flock to the river bank to dip their nets into the water to discover and study the creatures that live in this environment. They are taught to carefully return the wildlife to the river. An art project rounds out their lesson. Teacher education workshops are available to prepare teachers for the experience they will share with their students. Camp Pashayan is open to the public on weekends. It is noteworthy that many areas purchased by the parkway trust are former sand and gravel mining sites that have either been reclaimed by nature or have been restored with native plantings as wetlands and wildlife habitat.

When the San Joaquin River Parkway is completed it will

stretch twenty-two miles from Friant Dam to Highway 99. Everyone in the Fresno community will have the opportunity to savor all the treasures this natural habitat has to offer, including beautiful vistas of the river and the Sierra, rookeries filled with nesting great blue herons and white egrets on the ecological reserve of Rank Island, and all the incredible native species of plants and trees that fill the land along the river.

# A House with a View

A drive along Friant Road heading toward the foothills brings the traveler into a section of Fresno County that is a major scenic resource. As the road curves and the Sierra come into view, the peace and beauty of this setting are almost tangible. The road curves again and the traveler turns left onto Old Friant Road, dipping down and emerging on land that is just a little above the river bottom. Another couple of turns and a row of palm trees lets the traveler know that he is approaching the Riverview Ranch. A left turn into the drive and he is face-to-face with the historic Williams/Phillips Home, a structure in which the patina of time is etched into every board and window.

Built in 1890, this was the home of nurseryman W. M. Williams. On entering the house through a screened porch, the traveler finds that he is standing in a large entry hall with stairs at the back going to the second floor. The design of the house is called an early California "four square." Literally, that means that on the second floor there are four bedrooms, each occupying a corner location. Over the years other rooms were added. The kitchen was a separate building behind the back porch. It is gone, but the original smokehouse remains.

The house and land were purchased by William Walker Phillips in 1893. He continued to live in Fresno, and a foreman ran the farming operation that included plums, grapes, and a herd of champion dairy cows. Around 1915, his son, John Pressley Phillips, Sr., moved out to the ranch. In 1918, he married and brought his wife, Ruth, to live there. Their first child, Martha, was born in the house. In the early to mid-1920s, the farm was sold.

In 1986, CalMat Company, a sand and gravel mining operation, purchased the house and surrounding land that has been a source for sand and gravel building materials for over forty years. When Russ Austin, CalMat's district manager, saw the house he immediately realized that this was a historic home and saw the potential it had. CalMat began to talk about restoring the house for use as offices and community gatherings.

Parkway planners and the San Joaquin River Parkway and Conservation Trust, the local land trust planning the parkway, also saw the house and its possibilities. It could house an interpretive center and a stopping point for hikers on the parkway. There are also plans for an education center and for a nursery for propagating native plants for river restoration.

The agreement under consideration between the two groups, as of this writing, is a gift/purchase for the parkway of a twenty-acre parcel, including the house and barn, from CalMat. The house and barn will remain on their four-acre site. Sixteen acres will be mined by CalMat and then reclaimed as wetlands and wildlife habitat.

One day soon, the traveler who turns on Old Friant Road will not only view the historic Riverview Ranch, but also will see schoolchildren, teachers, tourists and those who love the scenic beauty of the San Joaquin River hiking up to the Williams/Phillips House, where an interpretive center will give them an even greater appreciation for all they have seen.

# The Man Who Lives on Missouri Hill

One road through our valley takes the traveler south and east of Fresno into the countryside. As one farm after another dots the slightly rolling terrain, houses can be spotted amid orchards and vineyards. On the west side of Temperance Avenue near Lone Star a driveway goes up a hill, curving as it reaches the summit. The traveler has arrived on "Missouri Hill." A cozy home with a porch stretching across its width invites the traveler to rest and enjoy an unparalleled setting. The Sierra to the east, the sweeping vista of vineyards to the north, and, off in the distance, downtown Fresno to the northwest create a lush visual landscape that causes the traveler to stare in wonder.

Although a local native, the master of this domain is a true "southern gentleman." His courtly manners, gentle smile and quiet charm are as natural a part of his character as his keen intelligence. He is a graduate of Boalt Hall, one of California's most prestigious law schools, and practiced law for a number of years before becoming Fresno County's first county counsel. He held this position for twenty-eight years. He was a member of the bar of the United States Supreme Court and the American Judicature Society. After retiring, he served as interim county counsel for Mariposa County.

It is for his interest in state and local history that he has left another enduring legacy. Past president of the Fresno County Historical Society, past Noble Grand Humbug of the Jim Savage Chapter E Clampus Vitus, a founder and member of the Garden of the Sun Corral of Westerners International, and a founder and member of the San Joaquin Valley Civil War Round Table, he is a co-author of *Fresno County in the 20th Century*, was an instructor in San Joaquin Valley history for the extension division of the University of California at Santa Cruz, and has written many articles on local history for numerous publications. He is the author of a book of poetry titled *This Is My Valley*. He is now and for many years has been a member of the Fresno County Historical Landmarks and Records Advisory Commission. Hundreds of schoolchildren know him for his portrayal of Jefferson Davis each year at Kearney Park during the Civil War Revisited.

He is a descendant of two of Fresno County's early pioneer families. When his family purchased their property in 1891, they had just arrived from Missouri with its hilly terrain. Faced with a fairly flat landscape in their new surroundings, they bought the one hill they could see. One hundred and six years later, he and his family still live on "Missouri Hill," farming the land and savoring its history.

A legend of our valley in the truest sense is Robert Martin Wash.

# James Smith & Smith's Ferry

Born in Pennsylvania in 1821, James Smith received an excellent education. He taught school in Ohio, married and left for California's gold fields in 1848. He was the first to take up a claim at the site of present-day Columbia. His mining operations were successful, and he brought his family out from Ohio.

In 1855, he established a ferry on the Kings River just southwest of present-day Reedley, on the Stockton to Los Angeles stage road. Since he needed a place for his family to live, he built a two-story hotel on the hill above the ferry that also provided lodgings for travelers. Using teams of oxen, he hauled lumber from the Thomas mill in the Sierra to the site where the construction work was taking place. The cost of building the hotel and ferry totaled $5,600.

One interesting feature of the hotel was that it lacked a saloon. The Smiths had four children. Since they did not want their children to come under the evil influence that a saloon could bring, they just did not put one in their hotel.

The business continued to operate for many years. When Smith died in 1862, his widow ran the business. When she remarried several years later, her new husband and, later, other owners kept the ferry going until 1874, when the railroad was in full operation and the stagecoach was not operating as frequently.

For those of us in this present-day era when freeways and roadways allow us access to every nook and cranny of our state, it might be of interest to know how stage roads were laid out. When James Smith decided to mark a road from his ferry to Jim White's Casa Blanca on the Fresno Slough, he had his teamster, "Big Jake," and his men cut a lot of willow trees. Big Jake staked these in a straight line across the plain, each one a quarter mile from the last. They were set in the ground in such a way that they could be seen, even when the winter fog set in. As the stagecoachs made their way across the valley from marker to marker, the road became well-traveled and well-rutted.

Today, the mountain above the site of Smith's Ferry is named Smith's Mountain for the well-respected James Smith, who not only was the first settler of the Reedley area, but who also served two terms in the California legislature.

As one drives through sections of Fresno, it is interesting to note the variety of names that are given to different areas of our city. In other tales, the origins of the Tower District and Old Fig Garden have been discussed. Do you know how the southeast part of Fresno, known as Sunnyside, got its name?

In 1868, the German Syndicate, a group of San Francisco capitalists, acquired about eighty thousand acres of land east of present-day Fresno. The parcel stretched in an irregular fashion from just south of what is today Clovis to the future town of Easton. The purchase price was less than two dollars an acre. When the syndicate divided its holdings among its members, Frederick Roeding acquired a parcel that was bounded by, in present-day terms, Kings Canyon, Clovis Avenue, the railroad, and Fowler Avenue.

In 1888, Roeding sold eighty acres of this land to A. A. Butler. In 1890, he sold the remaining land to William N. Oothout. Mr. Oothout planted grapes and peaches on this land that he named "The Sunnyside Vineyard." As time passed, another ranch took the name Sunnyside and other enterprises did as well. It is interesting that Mr. Oothout built a large, two-story colonial style home in the middle of his ranch. He planted a tree-lined driveway that led up to the house. Today, this drive is a portion of Butler Avenue.

In 1911, a group of local investors, including George and Frederick Roeding, C. C. Teague and Frank Romain, purchased the portion of the Sunnyside Vineyard just south of Butler Avenue. Their idea was to build a golf course, using the historic Oothout home as the clubhouse. The Sunnyside Golf and Country Club came into existence, perpetuating the name of the old ranch. In 1935, a merger with the University-Sequoia Club gave the club a new name, the University-Sequoia-Sunnyside Country Club. On November 9, 1941, a ball was held in the clubhouse. A fire started in the kitchen and soon engulfed the entire structure, burning it to the ground. A modern building now stands in its place.

Today, the name Sunnyside denotes a large portion of southeast Fresno. It brings to mind stately trees, lovely homes and green vineyards. Next time you drive through this section of Fresno, think for a moment of Mr. Oothout and the first Sunnyside Vineyard.

The historic
Oothout home
which became the
clubhouse for the
newly formed
Sunnyside Country
Club in 1911.
*Fresno County Free
Library.*

William Hazelton—the Mariposa gambler and soon to be cattle king. From a daguerreotype made in the 1950s. Hazelton Family Collection.
*Courtesy of William B. Secrest Sr.*

On September 7, 1825, William Hazelton was born in Albany County, New York. As a young man he worked in a mercantile establishment. He enlisted in the army in 1845. He was discharged about the time the Mexican War began. He went to Mexico where he served as a teamster in the army commissary department until the war was over. He returned to New York, but he was not content to stay. The west offered adventure and promise. He left New York, traveled to Texas and on to California, spending the winter in San Diego.

It was 1849. The Gold Rush was in full swing. Hazelton headed for the northern mines. He managed to make a small living, but when he needed extra money he found the gambling tables more lucrative. One night at a saloon he and a friend, John Patterson, got into an all night faro game. They hit a winning streak and pocketed $20,000. The next morning they agreed never to gamble again. About this time they decided to head south to the upper Kings River area of what was then Mariposa County. They filed on a quarter section of government land. With the creation of Fresno County in 1856, they found themselves land owners in the new county. Engaged in stock raising and agriculture, they made a good living.

Scottsburg, later to be called Centerville, was the closest town. Hazelton headed to Mexico to buy a herd of longhorn steers. On his return, Patterson sold out his interest in their land to Hazelton. Over the years Hazelton added to his land holdings and became the largest land owner in the area. In 1857, he married Mary Akers, a local girl. This union produced ten children.

In 1861, on one of his cattle buying trips, Hazelton brought back some oranges as a treat for his wife. Mary planted the seeds that produced the first orange grove in Fresno County.

During the Civil War years, Hazelton stood firm on the side of the Union despite the preponderance of neighbors with Southern sympathies. This earned him the nickname Yank.

William "Yank" Hazelton lived to the age of eighty-one and is considered one of the foremost pioneers in the development of Fresno County. Today, Yank's great-great-grandson, Douglas Hazelton, lives in the old home place on the Hazelton Ranch. On September 30, 1995, the members of the Jim Savage Chapter E Clampus Vitus journeyed to the Hazelton Ranch and dedicated a monument to Yank Hazelton, a legendary man.

# Can the Canal Builder
## and the Rancher Be Friends?

When the first canals were being dug to divert water from the Kings River in the late 1860s, it seemed like a miracle that the farmer could now have a dependable water source for crops. Moses Church and A. Y. Easterby were proud of their achievement—this was just the thing for Fresno County. There was one huge problem, however.

Up to this time, cattle ranchers had the protection of the Open Range Law, which allowed them to let their cattle run wherever they liked. Since the 1850s, ranchers like Yank Hazelton had free reign over the land. Suddenly someone was fostering irrigation and growing wheat. It was easy to see that if land was going to be used for crops, it would mean that range land would be diverted to other purposes and would be fenced as well. Legislation to protect this would surely follow and the projected railroad, with an eye on its economic interests that included plans to ship crops out of the valley, would be a formidable foe to the ranchers' interests.

Church had built a canal literally in Hazelton's back yard. Hazelton pondered what to do next. It was only natural that he would want to protect the empire he had spent years building. Violence might not be the answer, but intimidation was worth a try.

Church was overseeing work on his ditch when a group of Hazelton's horsemen appeared. They threatened to kill him if he did not leave the county. Church did not budge. A few days later another group, this time led by Hazelton himself, rode up. Telling Church that he had been duly warned, this time Hazelton demanded he leave immediately. Church said he needed time. Hazelton turned to his men and asked, "Boys—what shall we do with him?" One of his men grinned and suggested that if Church did not leave, he would be happy to build him a coffin. Church again said he needed more time. Hazelton told him he had until nine o'clock the next morning. The next morning Church rode off to look for a new location. When he returned, his house and barn had been torn down.

Church moved, but started his canal work once again. More trouble was to follow before the issue was settled. Church, however, was determined to stay in the area and complete his work.

William
Hazelton, the
cattle king.
*Hazelton Family
Collection. Cour-
tesy of William B.
Secrest Sr.*

Mary Akers
Hazelton, the
wife of William
Hazelton.
*Hazelton Family
Collection. Cour-
tesy of William B.
Secrest Sr.*

When we last left Moses Church, he was dealing with threats from cattle rancher William "Yank" Hazelton. The dispute centered on Church and Easterby's canals that were being built near Hazelton's range land. The question—can agricultural land and range land for cattle co-exist?

If Church thought that the threats were difficult to live with what would he have done if he had known that the worst was yet to come? Two plots on his life were secretly revealed to him by two members of the conspiracy, neither knowing that the other had divulged the plans. Two more surprise confrontations of a more serious nature would follow.

The first plot involved a planned encounter in Centerville at Jacob and Silverman's store. Knowing that Church would be in to pick up his mail, Bill Glenn would be waiting. He would spit tobacco juice in Church's eye. If Church got upset, he would shoot him and claim self-defense. Church thought this was a bluff. However, the next time he picked up his mail, he saw Glenn in the store. He left through a back door and rode away.

The second plot involved Bill Caldwell and Bill Glenn. They were to drive their buggy to Church's house, call to him to come out, and insult him. When they arrived, Church sent his wife and daughter out. The ranchers did not know what to do. While the women visited with them, Church came out and inquired what they wanted. Caldwell accused him of horse stealing. Church made a joke of it and the men rode away.

Soon after this encounter A. Y. Easterby and Church walked into the Centerville store to pick up their mail. Caldwell accused Easterby of stealing cattle which Easterby angrily denied. Caldwell knocked Easterby into a stack of canned goods, then turned to Church, hitting him in the jaw. Church saw a gun in Caldwell's hand and started to flee. Tom Bates grabbed Church, but he escaped.

The final confrontation took place later that month. Once again Church entered the store to get his mail. As Church walked through the store, George Smith threw sand in his eyes and knocked him to the floor. Church got up and started to fight Smith, forcing him back. Paul Stover kicked Church in the jaw. Bill Glenn started to kick Church in the head. Church grabbed the man's foot and flipped him to the floor. Church ran out onto the street only to be confronted by a gang of cowboys. He told them that if they wanted to kill him or whip him, this was their chance. They walked toward him, then turned and went into the saloon.

Church headed for the home of his friend, F. E. DeWolf, who gave Church a gun to carry for safety. It was the first time Church had carried one, but he decided he must. He headed back to his work crews and warned them that there would probably be another fight. Soon the stockmen arrived. They called for Church, who had hidden himself in a ditch. Church's foreman and work crews faced the group down. They said they were all armed and would defend their boss with their guns. The stockmen departed. The irrigation work continued.

According to Hazelton's granddaughter, Sophia Hazelton Gerner, Hazelton invited Church to his home. They talked through their differences and then ate together around Hazelton's table. Both men, in spite of their differences, made important and lasting contributions to the history of our valley.

# A Taste of Northern Italy

One of Fresno's strengths is the family owned businesses that are tucked away in various parts of town. With long histories in the community, they give our city a special quality.

One such business is located on Olive Avenue in the heart of the Tower District. The red, green and white striped awning out front gives the visitor the first hint of what awaits inside. As you step through the door, all the food aromas of northern Italy mingle together and assail your nostrils in an instant. Your eye first sees the pasta in neatly arranged stacks, then the shelves of specialty canned goods and olive oils. To the left a long deli counter extends to the door at the back of the store. Several people are busy making sandwiches and helping customers. The hooks on the wall hold roped balls of parmesan cheese and long chains of dry salami and garlic. You are inside Piemonte's Italian Delicatessen—for sixty-seven years a favorite food stop for Fresnans.

At the heart of the operation is Olga Porasso. Eighty-five years old and full of sparkle and energy, she still handles the bookkeeping and never misses a day at work. In 1930, her husband, Gino Porasso, who had run a sausage factory in Madera, formed a partnership with the owner of Piemonte's, a butcher shop on C Street in West Fresno. The partnership broke up, but Gino continued to run the business with Olga at his side. They gradually expanded the business and, in 1966, moved to the Tower District to the same location on Olive Avenue where they are today. Their two sons, Joe and Larry, grew up helping in the store and today run the business.

The homemade spaghetti sauce, thick and meaty with a touch of white wine, made fresh daily, reflects the cuisine of northern Italy. According to Joe, fresh, homegrown Italian thyme gives the sauce its special flavor.

Joe makes three kinds of sausage from an old family recipe. Five hundred to six hundred pounds of sausage are sold each week. At noon the store bustles as four hundred sandwiches a day are made for hungry patrons.

Those who come to the Tower District to satisfy their taste for Italian food know that the Porasso family will be providing the same quality that they have for the last sixty-seven years.

# The Burris Family

David Burris, pioneer cattle rancher in Tulare and Kings counties and his wife Julia Wilburn Burris. *Courtesy of the Kings County Museum at Burris Park.*

In 1849, David Burris left Missouri and traveled to California. The Gold Rush was in full flower and he stayed for three years, then returned to Missouri. He was there a short time and then joined an emigrant train driving a hundred head of cattle to California. He settled in Napa County and married Julia Wilburn.

In 1859, he moved to Tulare County, where built an adobe house for his family and established a cattle ranch. The new location proved to be unhealthful. Not only were they frequently ill, but the threat of malaria was also an ever-present danger. They left and resettled in Sonoma in 1869. This proved to be a healthier situation. David Burris became an active member of the business community and was instrumental in starting three banks.

In 1884, they decided to move back to Tulare County and resume their ranching operation. Burris built a two-story, fourteen-room frame house with a tank house for his ten children. Burris continued to acquire land and the ranch grew to 5,000 acres.

There were fifty-seven acres of Burris' holdings that lay in the horseshoe bend of the Kings River. The land had never been developed. Four of Burris' sons, Edward Everett, Henry Clay, Joshua Sinclair and Franklin Marion, donated this land to Kings County in memory of their parents.

On June 27, 1924, Burris Park was opened to the public. Great oak trees, barbecue pits, a well, dancing platform, swings and a seesaw were there for the enjoyment of the public. Today the park also is home to the Kings County Museum. The park is a reminder of David Burris and his family and their contributions to Kings and Tulare counties.

# The Brooks-Foster Wagon

Across the road from the Kings County Museum in Burris Park is the Annex Building that contains an abundance of antique passenger conveyances. An 1860s stagecoach, complete with a tall hand and foot brake; a wooden surrey; a Rushford farm wagon; an iron water wagon; and a hay wagon evoke an era when daily travel and chores were not accomplished with the ease of today.

The highlight of the exhibit, without a doubt, is the Brooks-Foster Wagon. The wagon, a freight wagon, was manufactured by the Schuttler Wagon Works of Chicago. At the time this particular wagon was known as the cadillac of the wagon trade. John Clark Foster purchased the wagon and brought it from Arkansas to California in 1853. It carried all his family's worldly goods. The Fosters settled in Placerville. It was here that they met Judge Thornberry Brooks, who was not a real judge; he had been given the name Judge at birth. He married Foster's daughter, Frances.

Brooks left his native Georgia in 1850 for the Gold Rush. He traveled to California by way of New Orleans, where he boarded a steamer bound for Panama. He walked across the Isthmus and boarded another steamship that took him to San Francisco. He bought a part interest in a sawmill in Placerville.

In 1866, the Fosters and the Brookses moved to the lower Kings River. Again the wagon was put into service to bring both families' belongings. Brooks settled on the north side of the Kings River. He cleared the land and, for the next five years, worked the soil. Then, to his horror, he discovered that he could never own the land because it was part of the Laguna de Tache land grant. He moved his family across the river and started over, eventually becoming a successful rancher.

A few years ago, a replica of this huge wagon was built by Wagons West International of Malin, Oregon. It is used in parades in Kings County. Future plans include sending it to schools.

If you watch a parade in Kings County, you may see this reproduction. To see the original, and it's well worth it, a visit to the Kings County Museum at Burris Park will satisfy your wish.

The
Brooks-Foster
Wagon in a
Hanford parade in
1928.
*Courtesy of the Kings*
*County Museum at*
*Burris Park.*

# A Museum in a Park

Nestled among the great oak trees in a horseshoe bend of the Kings River south of Kingsburg is the charming Kings County Museum. Hidden in this section of Kings County, off the beaten path, it is well worth a special visit.

The first Kings County Museum was located in the basement of the Hanford Auditorium. In 1928, the Hanford Exchange Club raised $5,000 to buy the Dr. Frank Griffiths collection that formed the basis for the museum exhibits. In the mid-1950s, the space in the auditorium was needed for other uses. County Supervisor C. R. Swanson and his wife offered to build a new building for the museum if land could be provided by the county. Burris Park, which offered a lot of space and a lovely setting, was the chosen site. In 1955, the Kings County Museum at Burris Park opened.

Next to the museum building can be seen all sorts of original farm implements. One outstanding piece is a six- by seven-foot tall box-like structure that is a raisin cleaner and stemmer from the late 1880s. A spring wagon, which the museum hopes to restore, also can be seen.

Eclectic beyond description, cases extending throughout the building are filled with all manner of pioneer treasures. Photographs, powder horns, guns, butter churns, a Chinese wedding dress, kitchen implements, and buffalo skins are only a few of the items on display. A model of a machine that separates gold from crushed quartz is an interesting period oddity. An 1887 bamboo noodle pole, used for making noodles in the first noodle house in Armona, is seven feet long. A rifle used by a member of the Donner Party and anchors from boats that used to ply Tulare Lake are fascinating to see. So are the buoys from the Kingston Ferry.

The Tulare Lake Indian relics are worth the trip alone. Beautifully formed charm stones, beads, arrowheads and baskets round out this collection.

In one of the rooms, the curator of the museum has mounted a fascinating collection of antique sewing machines. Each one dates from before 1900. They give a few glimpses of life during that period. One was paid for with a cow and a calf. The machine cover on another has a bullet hole in it. It seems the husband aimed a gun at his wife and missed, hitting the machine instead.

In the early 1990s, the members of the Fresno County Historic Landmarks and Records Commission decided that it was important to identify and recognize farms in Fresno County that have been in existence for a hundred years or more. Criteria were set up to determine the definition of a centennial farm.

It was decided that a centennial farm was one which "has been owned by a member or members of the same family, related by blood or marriage, for substantially all of the hundred-year period prior to application. The property shall have been devoted to agricultural use for such hundred-year period and the present owner or owners are related by blood or marriage to the owner of the property a hundred years ago and engage in managing the farm."

It also was determined that if the owner of the farm is a corporation, "the majority stock of such corporation must be owned by the person or persons related by blood or marriage to the owner of the property a hundred years ago."

The first application for centennial farm status was submitted to the commission and approved by the board of supervisors on February 15, 1994. Located in Riverdale, the Harlan Ranch was purchased by Elisha Harlan for $500 on May 22, 1874. It comprises 220 acres.

Six other farms have been listed since that time. The Charles B. Drake Ranch in Squaw Valley was homesteaded between 1870 and 1872. The ownership document was signed by President Rutherford B. Hayes in 1876. The Richard W. and Barbara J. Milton Farm in Reedley was purchased by the family in 1891 with $3,400 in gold coin.

The Schultz Ranch, Inc. in Burrel, the Missouri Hill Ranch in Fresno, the Reese Davis Ranch in Selma and the Levis Ranch in Selma also have been deemed worthy of centennial farm status.

Each ranch and family has a unique story to tell. The fact that the same families are still working the farms their ancestor purchased and labored to make productive attests to very deep and special commitments to the land and agricultural lifestyle of our great Central Valley.

# Happy Jack & The Hangman's Knot

Jack Allen Hawn, known as "Happy Jack" to his friends, was born in a little house on H Street just across from Hobbs Parsons produce company. The family moved to a parcel of land along the San Joaquin River when he was a small boy. He attended the Herndon School but quit after the fourth grade because he was needed to work on the ranch. His father gave him a buckskin mare named Sally and put him in charge of herding two hundred horses. Every day he rose before dawn, drove the horses over the hog wallow land and brought them back to the ranch after dark.

When he was older Jack became one of the original twenty-mule team drivers who hauled borax over the mountain roads to Bakersfield from the mines in Death Valley. He later drove a twenty-four-mule team with five wagons.

By 1908, Jack was touring the country with a show called Jack's Wild West Riders. The show featured twenty-five bucking horses. Occasionally, he landed a bit part in western movies.

Of all his recollections as he looked back on his long life, one stood out above the rest. On an October day in 1893, he came to Fresno with his father. They saw that a crowd was gathering in Courthouse Park and went to see what was going on. Two policemen came up to the group and asked if anyone knew how to tie a hangman's knot. Jack had learned how to do this from an old cowhand, so he offered to tie the knot for them. It was after he tied the knot that he found out why there was so much excitement in the air. There was going to be a public execution. Everyone was talking about it. Dr. Frank Vincent was going to be hanged for the murder of his wife.

Jack and two other boys climbed a tree and watched the execution from that vantage point. Happy Jack Hawn lived a long, full life, but he never forgot that it was his hangman's knot that choked Dr. Vincent on that fine October day in Courthouse Park.

# Judge Samuel A. Holmes

The constitutional convention of 1849 created the constitution by which the state of California had been operating since attaining statehood. The men who drafted the document were primarily interested in gold mining. As the state grew in population, other forms of commerce developed. Agriculture, for instance, was becoming a very important business.

Also, the court system was very complicated. Trial courts had been created for many different purposes. The state government, when faced with a judicial problem, had dealt with it by creating a new type of court. The time was ripe for a review of this state of affairs. Another constitutional convention was called in 1879.

Fresno County's representative to that convention was Samuel Ash Holmes. A Southerner by birth, Holmes had served in the Confederate Army during the Civil War. After the war, he brought his wife to California, settling in the Alabama settlement near Madera, which was still part of Fresno County at that time. A man of great personal integrity, Holmes had been admitted to the bar in North Carolina, had a private law practice and had served in the state legislature. He also had farmed a large plantation. In California, he engaged in farming again.

Now he was called to serve his county by helping to draft a new state constitution. The convention in Sacramento that had been slated to last 100 days dragged on for 157 days. One of the changes was to the court system. It was streamlined dramatically.

Newton Booth, the governor of California, appointed Holmes to the new office of superior court judge. He was to fill the position until an election was held in 1880. When the election was held, Holmes became the first Fresno Superior Court judge voted into the office.

During his tenure on the bench, he became known for his strong belief that to deter potential offenders, it was necessary to strongly enforce the law. One of the cases before his court was a young man who stole a horse and sold it for thirty-two dollars. He was sentenced to two years in Folsom Prison. A more noteworthy case to come before his court was the trial of Dr. Vincent, accused of murdering his wife. The trial lasted eleven days. The doctor was found guilty and was executed on October 27, 1893, at the only legal hanging in Fresno County.

At the end of his term in 1884, Holmes returned to private practice. Six years later, he was re-elected to the office. He served in that position until his death in 1894.

# Mr. Historic Preservation

No one in Fresno loved field trips as much as the late Russell C. Fey. All one had to do was suggest that there was some historic architecture worth looking at or an interesting bungalow district to discover and he would volunteer to lead the way. Not only would he lead the group, but his incredible store of knowledge would come into play in a way that excited the interest of everyone around him. A man of passionate interests and an infectious zest for life—that was Russ Fey.

Fey was born in Lincoln, Nebraska. His family moved to the Philippine Islands when he was three to serve as missionary teachers. The family returned to the United States three years later. During the next several years, the family moved a number of times.

Fey served in the U.S. Army during World War II. He graduated from Hiram College in Ohio with a bachelor of arts in sociology. He later received a master of arts degree in city planning from the University of California at Berkeley. His career in planning began in Berkeley, and continued in Modesto, where he served in the planning department for twelve years, the last seven as city planning director. In 1969, he began a teaching career in the department of urban planning at California State University, Fresno. He was awarded emeritus status in 1995. During this period he received a master of arts degree in historic resources management.

He was a gifted photographer, and his work was often shown in the Spectrum Gallery, of which he was a member. He often put his talent to use to promote his love of historic buildings. The majority of the photographs in the book *Heritage Fresno: Homes and People* are his work.

He strongly believed that historic preservation was an important factor in the planning process. He served on Fresno's City Planning Commission, the board of the California Preservation Foundation, as chair of the Preservation Committee of the Fresno Historical Society, and on the design review committee for Fresno's Mainstreet Program. Perhaps one of his most lasting contributions is his successful effort to have the city of Fresno reinstate the Historic Preservation Commission. Fittingly, he served as its first chairman. He continued to serve on the commission until his death in April of 1996.

A tireless speaker on preservation and planning issues, Fey traveled all over the Central Valley speaking to groups about his two favorite subjects. With his wife, Pat, at his side, he could be seen wherever there was a gathering to discuss preservation—both tireless workers in the cause of preserving our historic architecture.

With Russ Fey's death, Fresno lost one of its biggest boosters and the cause of preservation lost one of its most articulate and knowledgeable spokesmen. He is sorely missed.

The home of George C. Roeding was located three miles east of Fresno between Belmont and Ventura. It was a three-story showplace.
*The Image Group from the Laval Historical Collection.*

In other tales of the valley we have talked about the Roeding family and Roeding Park. There is another story about this remarkable family to tell as well. George Christian Roeding, son of Frederick C. Roeding, graduated from high school in San Francisco in 1885. He moved to his father's ranch in Fresno, called Roeding Place.

Unlike his father, who was more interested in business, young George almost at once became fascinated with growing things. In spite of his father's discouragement and urging to continue his education, George immersed himself in the ranch. He soon made it pay and in about three years took over complete management. He beautified the grounds around the house with special landscaping. He had great initiative and was especially interested in experimenting with new varieties of plants. Soon the Fancher Creek Nurseries were a major contributor to the greening of our valley.

After his father returned to San Francisco, George Roeding became the owner of Roeding Place and Fancher Creek Nurseries. He became recognized as the greatest exponent of economic and ornamental horticulture in Western America.

Almost from the beginning Roeding had a special interest in figs and planted a considerable acreage of them. At that time, the black mission and white Adriatic were the only commercial varieties planted here. Both were greatly inferior to the imported Smyrna. Roeding planted some Smyrna figs, but the fruit failed to mature. After much study George determined that for the fruit to mature it had to be pollenized by the Capri fig. The only way to accomplish this was with a tiny wasp called blastaphaga. None of these moths was available in Fresno. After much difficulty he was able to obtain a few wasps from Asia Minor. He placed these into his Capri figs where they thrived and multiplied.

In 1899, George began to pollenize his Smyrna figs with these wasps, and so, here on Roeding Place originated the delicious Calimyrna fig.

This major contribution to the development of fig production in the Central Valley was fully realized in 1910 when J. C. Forkner, using the method of pollenization discovered by Roeding and taught to him by Melcon Markarian, began large scale production of the Calimyrna fig.

When some of Frederick Roeding's original land holdings were donated to the city of Fresno for a park, George Roeding, as park commissioner, oversaw the implementation of the landscape plan designed by Johannes Reimers. In so doing, he made a vast contribution to the beautification of Fresno for future generations.

Next time you visit Roeding Park or eat a delicious Calimyrna fig, think of George Roeding and the unique contributions he made to our valley.

The Fresno County Courthouse stood all alone when it was completed in 1875 at a cost of $56,370.
*The Image Group from the Laval Historical Collection.*

On Thursday afternoon, October 8, 1874, the cornerstone for the Fresno County Courthouse was laid. Cornerstone Day was a cause for celebration in the new county seat of Fresno. People arrived from Merced, Modesto, Lathrop, Stockton and Visalia, and from every corner of Fresno County.

Even the weather seemed to let everyone know this was going to be a perfect day. There were just enough clouds in the sky to prevent the sun from being too hot and the gentle rain that fell in late morning refreshed the atmosphere.

The ceremonies were to be carried out by the Masonic fraternities. Issac S. Titus, M.W.G.M., attended. The Merced lodges, Free and Accepted Masons, and Independent Order of Odd Fellows joined with county officials and citizens in a parade. The Woodman's brass band from Stockton led the way.

At the cornerstone laying, a choir comprised of Mrs. W. W. Phillips, John Hoxie, William Lambert, Mr. Faymonville, A. W. Burrell and S. W. Geis sang songs befitting the occasion. Claudius G. Sayle, district attorney, asked the grand lodge to lay the cornerstone for the building that "is expected to stand the heats of summer and the storms of winter for a period of a thousand years or more."

The Masonic ritual followed. Then Judge Elisha Cotton Winchell delivered an oration. A casket containing nineteen items was placed in the cornerstone. Some of the items were an 1874 twenty-dollar gold piece, a copy of the Fort Barbour treaty of peace of 1851, a copy of the 1851 muster roll of the Mariposa Battalion of Major James D. Savage, assorted historical documents and a Bible contributed by Dr. Lewis Leach. The latter item was a notable gift since, according to tradition, it was the only Bible in town available for this purpose.

In the evening a ball was held at Magnolia Hall. Over a hundred and fifty couples danced until about 1:30 in the morning. Everyone agreed it was a successful day.

The courthouse was completed, added to and served as the focus for the Fresno community for many years. Beloved by most of the citizenry, but not enough by the supervisors, who voted in 1964 to tear it down and build a new building, the historic building was destroyed in 1966 by the demolition experts.

However, this was in the future. On a fine October afternoon in 1874, the citizens of Fresno County celebrated a new beginning and a new courthouse.

# The Ultimate French Dip Sandwich

In the late 1940s and through the 1950s, Fresnans who wanted a truly memorable French dip sandwich knew there was only one place to go—The Pub in downtown Fresno, owned by Sidney Janofsky.

Sid Janofsky was a fascinating character. Born in Chicago in 1909, he moved to Los Angeles when he was eight years old. When he was thirteen, he ran away from home, hitching a ride on a freight train bound for San Francisco. To survive, he sold newspapers on Geary Street and slept in the mail room of the *San Francisco Chronicle*. The street corners were controlled by rowdy, tough guys so Janofsky began selling his papers on streetcars. One night he witnessed the murder of his supervisor, Dago Louie. He decided to leave and, once again, caught a freight train.

He got off in Oroville, but eventually ended up working for a spell as a squirrel poisoner on the Miller & Lux Canal Farm in Los Banos. He followed this with a turn as a range cowboy at the Hog Camp Ranch near Firebaugh, and, later, trailed herds from Oakdale to Hornitos for the Crocker Hoffman Land and Water Co. After driving trucks for a couple of years, he moved to Los Angeles and began selling French dip sandwiches. The secret of his sandwich, he said, was that he used the best beef brisket he could find.

In 1948, he moved to Fresno and opened The Pub at 1918 Mariposa Street, the location of the former Omar Khayyam's Restaurant. A couple of years later, he moved his successful business to 1117 Broadway. During the '50s, this was a favorite spot for some of Fresno's most memorable people. On a typical day, in a large booth in the back of the restaurant, one would see the likes of William Saroyan, his uncle Aram, Eddy Arkelian, Voss Gunner and Mayor Gordon Dunn, solving the world's problems and eating Janofsky's French dip sandwiches. Saroyan was there so much that Janofsky put a sign over his booth that read, "Saroyan's Nook." The Pub was open twenty-four hours a day. The lunch hour crowd was so huge that the line would be all the way down Broadway to Mariposa Street.

In the early '60s redevelopment wiped out the entire block on Broadway so Janofsky moved his pub to the corner of Olive Avenue and Fulton Street in the Tower District. In 1976, he and his wife, Shirley, moved back to San Francisco, but in June of 1989 returned to Fresno to be near their children and grandchildren. He died on June 5, 1992. His Tower District restaurant was popular, but it was his years on Broadway that were the most memorable. To this day, there are those who remember the famous French dip sandwiches and the lively conversations in Janofsky's pub on Broadway.

Northfield was built in 1912 by local architects Swartz and Swartz. It featured large porches on the first floor and sleeping porches on the second floor.
*The Image Group from the Laval Historical Collection.*

Several years ago, before a developer cleared the property, the northwest corner of Bullard Avenue and Van Ness Extension was shrouded in foliage. Lush vintage hawthorn roses dipping to the ground spilled over the high fences. A low wall built of hardpan faced Van Ness Extension. A break in the wall allowed entry into a driveway that curved under a ceiling of branches. As you drove onto the property, a two-story shingle, craftsman-style home came into view. Parking in the porte-cochere, you climbed the steps to the large porch. Entering the house, you were greeted by the chatelaine of Northfield, Lewella Swift Forkner.

Lewella Swift was born in Michigan on March 4, 1890, and came to Fresno two years later. Her father, Lewis P. Swift, brought his family to Fresno when he joined the Fresno Flume and Irrigation Company as head of construction and operations. Lewella went to Lowell Elementary School and attended high school at Huntington Hall in Los Angeles.

She returned to Fresno and met real estate developer Jesse Clayton Forkner. They married in 1912. She devoted her life to raising her family of three sons and one daughter and to supporting her husband's endeavors. They lived at Northfield for eight years while Mr. Forkner began to develop the 12,000-acre Fig Garden District. They then moved to the Forkner-Giffen Tract, today known as Old Fig Garden. During this time, she helped her husband by entertaining prospective buyers. They later moved back to Northfield—her home until her death in 1991.

Lewella Forkner was active in community affairs, serving as president of the Training School and Fresno High parent teacher associations. She was an active member of the YWCA and was honored by that group several times. At age ninety, she joined Forkner School's PTA, attended its annual luncheons, and was visited by the students, after the school was named for her late husband. For her, it was as though a new life had opened up for her.

For those who knew her well, opportunities to chat with her over tea in the living room at Northfield or a cup of coffee by the wood stove in the kitchen were moments to savor. It was here she shone. A witty, intelligent conversationalist and an authority on local history, having lived so much of it, the conversational well never ran dry. Her opening words to visitors were usually, "Please sit down and tell me all the latest news." She was interested in everything to do with her city and the world. She was also an avid reader and loved to share her latest literary find.

In 1985, during the city's centennial, Lewella Swift Forkner was honored as one of the Fabulous Fresnans. The mayor proclaimed September 10, 1985, as "Fabulous Fresnan Lewella Forkner Day." This was very fitting for this great lady, who will be remembered as a true legend of our valley

# The Fresno Plaque

Every once in a while each citizen of Fresno should visit Courthouse Park. Not only is it our historic town center, but it is filled with memorials and sculptures that tell stories about our community. One memorial plaque stands out above all others and is one that every Fresnan should read.

Located on the M Street side of the park, the bronze plaque can be found just after one walks through the breezeway under the courthouse. Originally it was placed in front of the historic courthouse which was demolished in 1966. It was prepared, erected and donated by the Fresno County Historical Society. The large piece of granite to which the plaque is anchored came from a quarry near Raymong, northwest of Madera. The Fortier Trucking Company volunteered to bring the granite to Fresno.

On June 27, 1954, at the dedication ceremony for the plaque, Mayor Frank Homan, who was president of the Historical Society, said that "the purpose of the plaque is threefold: to acquaint the people of Fresno with our past history, to record for posterity how Fresno County came into being, and to pay tribute to the pioneers and their descendants."

The plaque's three hundred-word inscription tells the story of the meaning of the word "Fresno," the founding of Fresno with the coming of the railroad, the moving of the county seat to Fresno and the building and expanding of the courthouse. Written by Robert M. Wash, who was then county counsel, it tells the story with moving eloquence and also paints a wonderful word picture of how this area looked before it was settled.

The next time you are visiting Courthouse Park, pause for a moment and take time to read the words that are inscribed there. Try to tune out the sounds of the city and try to picture in your mind's eye what it was like in the beginning before the little town of Fresno Station was settled. Follow the story and savor what the words have to say. Perhaps you will walk away with a little deeper appreciation of your city. It only takes a couple of minutes and you will be glad you spent the time.

# Notes

THE LEGACY OF "POP" LAVAL
Jerome D. Laval, *As 'Pop' Saw It*, Graphic Technology Co., Vol. I, pg. 5.
THE EDITOR & THE WILD HOGS
Charles W. Clough and William B. Secrest Jr., *Fresno County - The Pioneer Years,* pg. 89.
CHURCHES, CANALS & CATTLE
Interview with George Healey Tondel.
COURTS & COURTHOUSES
Clough and Secrest, *Fresno County - The Pioneer Years,* pg. 123.
Wallace W. Elliot, *History of Fresno County, California*, pg. 93.
THE DAY THE TEMPLE ALTAR WAS SAVED
Clough and Secrest, *Fresno County - The Pioneer Years,* pg. 140.
THE RAISIN - THE PROFITABLE MISTAKE
Clough and Secrest, *Fresno County - The Pioneer Years,* pg. 147.
THE ARCHITECT & HIS PIT BULL
*Fresno Morning Republican*, October 30, 1904.
John W. Caughey, *California*, pg. 422.
MOVIES & A CANNY SCOT
Edwin M. Eaton, *Vintage Fresno*, pp. 93, 94.
Charles W. Clough, et al., *Fresno County in the 20th Century*, pg. 375.
FRESNO STATION
*Fresno Past & Present*, Vol. 27. No. 3, pp. 19-22.
Soldier's homecoming witnessed by author on Christmas Eve, 1968.
BASEBALL HEROES
Clough, et al., *Fresno County in the 20th Century*, pp. 462, 463.
THE STREET NAMED FOR AN ENGLISH JURIST
*Fresno Past & Present*, Vol. 12, No. 2, pg. 3.
Interview with Susan Stiltz, Executive Director, Tree Fresno.
BLACKMAIL & MURDER IN 1890
Clough and Secrest, *Fresno County - The Pioneer Years,* pg. 241.
A FOOTBALL HERO
Robert Wash. Pioneer Families Dinner Speech. Fresno City Centennial. November 14, 1985.
As told to the author by Eugenie Kinsley McKay and Catherine McKay Morison.
THE PEOPLE'S RAILROAD
Clough and Secrest, *Fresno County - The Pioneer Years,* pg. 334.
Diane Seeger, Santa Fe Depot, National Register Nomination, May 28, 1976.
THOSE CRAZY FLYING MACHINES
Clough, et al., *Fresno County in the 20th Century*, pg. 264.
SEVENTY-SIX TROMBONES
Clough, et al., *Fresno County in the 20th Century*, pp. 381, 382.
HISTORIANS & PIONEERS
Clough, et al., *Fresno County in the 20th Century,* pp. 485, 486.
EARTHQUAKE RELIEF
*Fresno Morning Republican*, April 19, 1906.
FESTIVALS, FETES & RAISINS
Clough, et al., *Fresno County in the 20th Century,* pp. 176, 179, 470.
Michael R. Waiczis and William B. Secrest Jr., *A Portrait of Fresno 1885-1985*, pg. 49.
RACQUETS & WHALEBONES
*The Fresno Bee*, October 27, 1935.
ONE-HANDED ENGINEER & DAM BUILDER
William B. Secrest Sr., "A Man Named Ingvart," *Fresno Past & Present,* Vol. 33, No. 2, pg. 10.
*The Fresno Bee,* September 27, 1950. Teilman obituary.
A SPECIAL FRIENDSHIP
Tuck Family Papers, Fresno City and County Historical Society Archives.
Clough and Secrest, *Fresno County - The Pioneer Years*, pg. 87.
THE KEARNEY-ROWELL "JOSH" DILEMMA
Schyler Rehart, "The Famous Feud: M. Theo. Kearney and Chester H. Rowell," *Fresno Past & Present,* Vol. 30, No. 3., pp. 10, 11.

# Notes

THE JONES MILL
  Clough and Secrest, *Fresno County - The Pioneer Years*, pg. 128.
  Jones Family Papers, Fresno Historical Society Archives.
A GERMAN BEER GARDEN FOR FRESNO
  Schwarz Family Papers, Fresno Historical Society Archives.
THE FATHER OF REEDLEY
  Clough and Secrest, *Fresno County - The Pioneer Years,* pg. 290.
BIG HATS & BUCKING BRONCOS
  Claire Baird Zylka, Ken Greenberg, and Jessie Myers Thun, *Images of an Age, Clovis,* pp. 43, 44.
  Clough, et al., *Fresno County in the 20th Century,* pg. 107.
PREPARING "TYPEWRITERS"
  Deborah Boyett, Boyetter Advertising, *4C's Celebrates Centennial,* News Release, pp. 1-4.
SHIPPS, TRAINS, WAGONS & SHEEP
  Clough and Secrest, *Fresno County - The Pioneer Years,* pg. 94.
  Shipp Family Papers, Fresno Historical Society Archives.
THE HOUSE ON FULTON STREET
  American Association of University Women, *Heritage Fresno Homes and People,* pg. 45.
HISTORY ON BULLDOG LANE
  Interview with Sheldon Solo.
  Interview with John Edward Powell.
SIGMA NU ON THE MOVE
  *Insight*, California State University, Fresno, Vol. XXI, No. 23, Wednesday, May 10, 1989, pg. 4
  Interview with Roger Taylor
OF KNOTHOLES & COURTHOUSES
  Tour of the Fresno County Free Library Archives.
  Interview with Linda Sitterding.
THE P STREET NEIGHBORHOOD
  Interview with Mary Helen McKay.
SERVICE ABOVE SELF
  Interview with staff during visit to the Rotary Office.
  Clough, et al., *Fresno County in the 20th Century,* pg. 457.
FRESNO'S HOLLYWOOD "HUNK"
  Ben Walker Collection, Fresno Historical Society Archives.
HOT SALADS & HISTORY
  Interview with Donna Drith.
THE MAGICAL GRAPE
  Interview with Sharon Huber.
THE BIG FIG GARDEN FLOOD
  Interview with Doug Harrison, District Manager, Fresno Metropolitan Flood Control District.
  *The Fresno Bee*, January, 1997, Fresno Metropolitan Flood Control District Supplement.
FRESNO'S RAGTIME RHYTHMS
  Stephen Kent Goodman, "Fresno's Forgotten Ragtime Composers," *West Coast Rag*, Vol. 3, No. 3, pp. 1, 18, February, 1991.
TRIBUTES ON A SPRING AFTERNOON
  *Fresno Morning Republican*, May 25, 1912, pg. 1.
  *Fresno Morning Republican*, May 26, 1912, pp. 1, 2.
  *Fresno Morning Republican*, May 27, 1912, pp. 1, 2.
"THE GROVE"
  Interview with Mary Helen McKay.
  As told to the author by Eugenie Kinsley McKay.
A PHOTOGRAPHER FOR THE SIERRA
  The Ansel Adams Gallery, Yosemite National Park, Biographical information.
  *The Fresno Bee*, June 22, 1969.
  *The Fresno Bee*, October 13, 1974.
  *The Fresno Bee*, August 21, 1977.

# Notes

A LOG CABIN IN THE WOODS
William Tweed, Gamlin Cabin, National Register Nomination, March 9, 1976, Fresno Historical Society Archives.

"FRESNO"
Bob Wisehart, "Finally A Soap With a Sense of Humor," *The Fresno Bee,* TV Week Section, pp. 3, 5.

PREMIERE PARTIES & PRODUCE
Kathey Clarey and Doug Hoagland, "Fresno laughs along with 'Fresno,'" *The Fresno Bee,* November 17, 1986, pp. A1, A10.

"RAISIN CANE"
Jim Steinberg, "'Fresno' saga of 'greed, lust' takes to the streets," *The Fresno Bee,* July 16, 1986, pp. A1, A10.

YOSEMITE'S ENCHANTED CHRISTMAS
Edwin Kiester Jr., *Modern Maturity*, pp. 30-34, 88-91.

THE ROMAIN HOME
Dr. Ephraim K. Smith and William E. Patnaude, Romain Home, National Register Nomination, October 8, 1980.

A NEWSPAPER & A MUSEUM
John Edward Powell, The Fresno Bee Building, National Register Nomination, March 29, 1982, Fresno Historical Society Archives.

A SCROLLED CORNICE BRACKET
John Edward Powell, *Archifragment: Ode To a Fallen Bracket,* November, 1991.

FRESNO'S IVY LEAGUE STREETS
Interview with Ken Hohmann.

FRESNO'S FIRST AIRMAIL SERVICE
Clough, et al., *Fresno County in the 20th Century,* pp. 266-268.

TAKING CULTURE SERIOUSLY
Clough and Secrest, *Fresno County - The Pioneer Years,* pg. 323.
Fresno Historical Society, *Imperial Fresno,* pg. 77.

THE SHORT HOME
Eaton, *Vintage Fresno,* pp. 102-104.

KINGS RIVER SWITCH
Clough and Secrest, *Fresno County - The Pioneer Years*, pp. 165-168.
Cindy Olsson, "Kingsburg: From 'Tough Place' to 'City of Churches,'" *Fresno Past & Present,* Reprinted from the *Kingsburg Record,* Vol. 30, No. 3, pp. 1-3.

THE GREAT CAMP PINEDALE OFFENSIVE
Ben Walker Collection, Fresno Historical Society Archives.

THE VALLEY'S SWEDISH VILLAGE
Pauline Mathes, *Bit of Sweden In the Desert,* pp. 49-51.

AN OLD-FASHIONED PHARMACY
Interview with Jim Winton.

A 20TH CENTURY FUR TRAPPER
William Tweed, Shorty Lovelace Historic District, National Register Nomination, August 29, 1977.

RAISINS, RAISINS & MORE RAISINS
Sun-Maid Growers of California, *The Sun-Maid Story.*
Sun-Maid Growers of California, *History of the Sun-Maid Organization and Its Antecedents.*

FASHIONS & FOIBLES
Interview with Mary Helen McKay

THE VILLAGE IN THE FIG GARDENS
*Villager,* 30th Anniversary of Fig Garden Village Edition.
Fig Garden Village 30th Anniversary Commemorative Poster.

THE SAMPLE SANITARIUM
As told to the author by Catherine McKay Morison.
The author's birthplace. Written on her birthday from the vantage point of her car parked down the street from the building.

# Notes

THE HOME OF CLOVIS COLE
   Clough and Secrest, *Fresno County - The Pioneer Years*, pg. 237.
   Clough, et al., *Fresno County in the 20th Century*, pg. 39.
THE FRESNO ADVENTIST ACADEMY
   Debora Boyette, "FresnoAdventist Academy Centennial 1897-1997" News release, July 28, 1997.
   Clough and Secrest, *Fresno County - The Pioneer Years*, pg.325
CAMERAS & COFFEE
   George Hostetter, "Horn Photo, Kodak adding to Fig Garden's Picture," *The Fresno Bee,* July 16, 1997.
   Interview with John Horn, August 13, 1997.
   Interview with Shelly Grosz, August 13, 1997.
FRESNO'S SPECIAL LEGACY
   Interview with Rabbi David L. Greenberg.
THE CHAMPION & THE COURTS
   *The Fresno Bee*, March 26, 1926.
THE MESSENGER OF THE GODS
   Mrs. E.A. Hamilton, donor, photo and information, Fresno Historical Society Archives.
THE CHAMP WINS AGAIN
   *The Fresno Bee*, June 15, 1926.
A CLOSE SHAVE
   Interview with Bill Ennis.
DE VAUX & DEMPSEY
   *The Fresno Bee,* May 21, 1928.
   *The Fresno Bee,* May 24, 1928.
   *The Fresno Bee,* September 11, 1928.
   *The Fresno Bee,* July 2, 1935.
ROLINDA, ROBBERS & RAILS
   Ben Walker Collection, Fresno Historical Society Archives.
A FARM HOUSE IN THE TOWER DISTRICT
   American Association of University Women, *Heritage Fresno Homes and People,* pg. 52.
RELIGION & CIRCUIT RIDERS
   L.A. Winchell Papers, Ms. 3, Chapter 22, pp. 13, 14.
A MAN NAMED ERCLAS
   Interview with Mary Carr.
   *The Fresno Bee,* July 21, 1927.
COALINGA'S VANISHED SCHOOL
   Alvin Walker, Polk Street School, National Register Nomination, October 1, 1981.
A FAIR "SCANDAL"
   Letter from Ethel L. Smith and Clara F. Wakefield of the Women's Christian Temperance Union of Fresno County, September 8, 1920.
THE JENSEN RANCH
   Katherine J. Smith, Jensen Ranch, National Register Nomination, February 3, 1982.
A ROYAL POLICY
   Interview with B. Franklin Knapp.
FRESNO'S UNIQUE SILOS
   Interview with Tom Folsom of Zacky Farms.
   Interview with Royce Peterson, Corporate Manager of Human Resources for Zacky Farms.
   *The Fresno Bee,* January 5, 1937.
   *The Fresno Bee,* May 26, 1946.
THE EVINGER HOME
   American Association of University Women, *Heritage Fresno Homes and People,* pg. 17.
JAMES' TALE
   David Bice James, *Reminiscences of Early Days in the "Southern Mines,"* Ms. 3, pg. 9.
FRESNO'S GREENE HOUSE
   American Association of University Women, *Heritage Fresno Homes and People,* pg. 61.

*Legends & Legacies*
316

# Notes

A HONEYMOON COTTAGE IN KEARNEY PARK
Interview with Althea Wheat.
PANS, PICKS, & PERSISTENCE
David Bice James, *Reminiscences of Early Days in the "Southern Mines,"* Ms. 3, pp. 2-4.
THE GIFFEN ESTATE
American Association of University Women, *Heritage Fresno Homes and People,* pg. 78.
INDIANS & INDENTURES
Clough and Secrest, *Fresno County - The Pioneer Years*, pg. 20.
*The Fresno Bee,* August 23, 1938.
FRESNO'S JAPANESE BANK
Karen Weitze and John Edward Powell, "Short Historical Notes Descriptive of the Industrial Bank of Fresno," October 18, 1992.
THE STREETS OF LATON
J. Randall McFarland, "Streets of Yore," *The SelmaEnterprise*, February 28, 1990.
CHRISTMAS AT KEARNEY
No notes.
ELECTIONS IN EARLY CALIFORNIA
David Bice James, *Reminiscences of Early Days in the "Southern Mines,"* Ms. 3, pg. 9.
BEANS & BURROS
David Bice James, *Reminiscences of Early Days in the "Southern Mines,"* Ms. 3, pp. 6, 7.
A FRIDAY EVENING IN FOWLER
J. Randall McFarland, "An archaic club, " *The Selma Enterprise*, April 18, 1985.
Interview with J. Randall McFarland, August 12, 1997.
A VALLEY CALLED WONDER
Information provided by the Wonder Valley Ranch Resort.
THE ROBINSON HOME
American Association of University Women, *Heritage Fresno Homes and People,* pg. 64.
DUNCAN'S VISION
"Bob Duncan," biographical information provided by the Sports Information Office, California State University, Fresno.
THOSE IRREVERENT HUMBUGS
Bill Patterson, "Jim Savage & E Clampus VitUs," *Fresno Past & Present,* Vol. 27, No. 1, pg. 1.
A BEAUTY NAMED DAGMAR
American Association of University Women, *Heritage Fresno Women and Their Contributions,* pp. 36, 37.
MAYOR OF BROADWAY
American Association of University Women, *Heritage Fresno Homes and People,* pg. 12.
A TWIST OF FATE
American Association of University Women, *Heritage Fresno Women and Their Contributions,* pg. 26.
June English, *Ash Tree Echo*, Vol. 4.
*Fresno Morning Republican,* Mary Donleavy obituary, June 8, 1927.
THE HANGER HOME
*The Fresno Bee*, September 10, 1992.
SHAKESPEARE & A HOT STOVE
As told to the author by Mary Helen McKay.
PRODUCERS DAIRY
Producers Dairy, informational material.
A FISHY PRANK
*Fresno Morning Republican,* June 11, 1906.
A SHEEPMAN NAMED KENNEDY
John C. McCubbin, *The McCubbin Papers,* pp. 162-164.
Edwin M. Eaton, *Vintage Fresno,* pp. 105-108.
HORSES & HORSELESS CARRIAGES
*Fresno Morning Republican,* November 29, 1924.
THE SPENCER HOME
American Association of University Women, *Heritage Fresno Homes and People,* pg. 51.

# *Notes*

THE "PAINTED DOG"
  *Fresno Morning Republican,* July 7, 1921.
THE HOME OF MR. MAIN
  American Association of University Women, *Heritage Fresno Homes and People,* pg. 50.
THE COBB HOME
  American Association of University Women, *Heritage Fresno Homes and People,* pg. 46.
THE FORCES FOR RIGHTEOUSNESS
  *White Ribbon Reform Club Membership Booklet,* 1881.
JUSTICE IN FINE GOLD GULCH
  Clough and Secrest, *Fresno County - The Pioneer Years,* pg. 222.
STOP, GO & MOVE ON
  *Fresno Morning Republican,* January 8, 1927.
THE KNAPP CABIN
  William Tweed, Knapp Cabin, National Register Nomination, May 21, 1976.
A TALE OF TWO TREES
  Jim Drago, editor, *Going Places,* California Department of Transportation, May/June, 1991.
  Interview with Jose Ruano.
A CAVEMAN NAMED DAVID
  *Fresno Morning Republican,* June 27, 1929.
A GHOSTLY STEAMSHIP
  M.L. Coultrap, "Republican Staff Men Seek Lost Steamboat; Find?," *Fresno Morning Republican,* November 15, 1931.
CAMEL'S THORN
  *Fresno Morning Republican,* June 20, 1931.
  *Fresno Morning Republican,* September 7, 1931.
THE STONER MANSION
  Rex V. and Janet V. Campbell, The Stoner Mansion, National Register Nomination, August, 1984.
BUDGETS & CENTS
  *San Francisco Chronicle,* May 8, 1935.
THE HANSEN HOME
  Jan Ewert, The Miles Hansen Home, National Register Nomination, June 20, 1983.
THE SHARER HOME
  American Association of University Women, *Heritage Fresno Homes and People,* pg. 86.
THE OLEANDER SOCIAL SCENE
  Clough and Secrest, *Fresno County - The Pioneer Years*, pp. 185, 187.
THE "GRAPEVINE"
  John Broeske, KMJ Radio, news release, information gathered from California Highway Patrol offices in Bakersfield, Fresno, Fort Tejon, and San Bernardino; CalTrans offices in Fresno, Bakersfield, and San Bernardino; and the Fresno County Library Reference desk, June 22, 1993.
THE OWEN HOME
  American Association of University Women, *Heritage Fresno Homes and People,* pg. 79.
  Tim Tune, Owens Home, Local Official Register of Historic Resources.
THE ROOSTER CROWS AT MIDNIGHT
  *The Fresno Bee,* October 22, 1936.
CHECKERBOARDS & COURTHOUSE PARK
  *The Fresno Bee,* November 11, 1937.
  *The Fresno Bee,* November 15, 1937.
SPEEDOMETERS & RED FACES
  *The Fresno Bee,* December 11, 1936.
MR. DILLION'S WAR
  Louise Kimball, "Fresnan Recalls Civil War As Busy One, W.H. Dillion Declares It Was Hard Life," *Fresno Morning Republican,* March 31, 1929.
HAPPY BIRTHDAY, FRESNO COUNTY LIBRARY!
  No notes.

# Notes

PROBLEMS WITH NUDISTS
*The Fresno Bee,* May 10, 1938.
*The Fresno Bee,* May 11, 1938.
NINETTA SUNDERLAND HUSTON
American Association of University Women, *Heritage Fresno Women and Their Contributions,* pg. 61.
IF I WERE MAYOR…
*The Fresno Guide,* September 15, 1938.
JOSEPHINE RUTH GIBSON
American Association of University Women, *Heritage Fresno Women and Their Contributions,* pg. 41.
HENDERSON'S EXPERIMENTAL GARDENS
*Fresno Morning Republican,* January 18, 1931.
Interview with Don Kleim.
A WEIGHTY SUBJECT
Interview with Bill Ennis.
THE GREAT EMANCIPATOR
*The Fresno Bee*, April 29, 1942.
THE CORSET LADY COMETH
As told to the author by Catherine McKay Morison.
THE KUTNER HOME
American Association of University Women, *Heritage Fresno Homes and People,* pg. 23.
THE GREGORY HOME
American Association of University Women, *Heritage Fresno Homes and People,* pg. 66.
THE ALTA 2
*The Fresno Bee,* June 22, 1938.
*The Fresno Bee,* July 1, 1938.
THE STORM'S EYE
*The Fresno Bee,* March 15, 1938.
A CLUBHOUSE ON CALAVERAS
*The Fresno Bee,* May 14, 1938.
THE DANCE OF LOVE
*The Fresno Bee,* August 8, 1940.
LIFE IN JAIL IN 1888
"Fresno's Yesterdays, Fifty Years Ago," *The Fresno Bee,* July 3, 1938.
THE LADY EDITOR
"Fresno's Yesterdays Twenty Years Ago," *Fresno Morning Republican,* September 17, 1917.
PIONEER GRAVES
*The Fresno Bee,* February 11, 1940.
*The Fresno Bee,* June 9, 1940.
LONG SKIRTS & LEERING EYES
"Fifty Years Ago," *The Fresno Bee,* September 11, 1938.
THE SIERRA POET
*The Fresno Bee,* August 20, 1940.
A TRIPLE CELEBRATION
*The Fresno Bee,* April 7, 1940.
AN UNIDENTIFIED PROSPECTOR
*The Fresno Bee,* June 9, 1940.
A TRACT HOME ON WEST GRIFFITH
Benjamin V. Amirkhanian, William Saroyan Home, Local Official Register of Historic Resources.
THE MARACCI HOME
Interview with John Edward Powell.
Christopher Campbell, Maracci Home, Local Offical Register of Historic Resources
A MAN & HIS MUSEUM
*The Fresno Bee,* June 16, 1938.

# Notes

THE PUPPET LADY
*The Fresno Bee,* March 29, 1944.
A SHIP NAMED McCLATCHY
*The Fresno Bee,* March 17, 1944.
MR. BLANDINGS DREAM HOUSE
*The Fresno Bee,* December 19, 1948.
Anne Edwards, "Mr. Blandings' Dream House," *Architectural Digest,* Vol. 48, No. 6, pp. 72-78.
THE HOME OF DR. BURKS
Cheryl Thompson, Prudence Zalewski and Jan Booth, Dr. Burks Home, Historic
Inventory Resources Form, October 20, 1989.
THE CARRIAGE PAINTER
Fresno Historical Society, *Imperial Fresno,* pg. 65.
A. A. ROWELL
*Fresno Morning Republican,* November 9, 1919.
SPACE SHIPS IN JULY
*The Fresno Bee,* July 7, 1947.
THE MOST BEAUTIFUL BABY
*The Fresno Bee,* October 10, 1962.
A SOCIETY DEBUT
*Fresno Morning Republican*, May 15, 1919.
A LYON & A GOAT
*The Fresno Bee,* September 1, 1940.
BEATING THE HEAT
*Fresno Morning Republican*, July 7, 1928.
THE HIGH COST OF LIVING
"Twenty Years Ago," *The Fresno Bee,* September 20, 1939.
BUILDING SAFETY
"Fifty Years Ago," *The Fresno Bee,* July 30, 1939.
A TREE FOR A HORSE
"Fifty Years Ago," *The Fresno Bee,* July 30, 1939.
THE PROJECTOSCOPE
Clough and Secrest, *Fresno County - The Pioneer Years*, pg. 327.
COLONEL JAMES N. OLNEY
Clough and Secrest, *Fresno County - The Pioneer Years*, pp. 76, 77.
MEMORIES OF MARCHING THROUGH GEORGIA
*Fresno Morning Republican,* February 12, 1928.
COATES & TRAVER, ARCHITECTS
John Edward Powell, Biographical notes on W.D. Coates and Harrison D. Traver.
*The Fresno Morning Republican,* October 17, 1919.
AKIRA YOKOMI
George Teraoka, Interview.
Sylvia Castro Uribes, "Homage Paid to Slain Owner of Central Fish," *The Fresno Bee,* June 30, 1996.
THE PONDEROUS INKSTAND
*The Fresno Bee,* February 17, 1950.
MELONS IN AUGUST
Fresno's Yesterdays, *Fresno Morning Republican*, August 3, 1925.
OPENING NIGHT AT THE BARTON
*Fresno Morning Republican,* June 8, 1924, Fresno Memories, Ernestine Winchell
A DOG & A QUACK
*Fresno Morning Republican*, March 24, 1925, Fresno's Yesterdays.
FATHER OF RAISIN DAY
*Fresno Morning Republican*, May 2, 1925, Fresno's Yesterdays.
THE COURTHOUSE - THE INSIDE SCOOP
*Fresno Morning Republican,* Date unknown, possibly 1926, Fresno Memories, Ernestine Winchell.
THE STOREKEEPER & THE CHICKEN
*Fresno Morning Republican,* May 27, 1923, Fresno Memories, Ernestine Winchell.

# Notes

THE FABULOUS FASCINATOR
*Fresno Morning Republican,* October 1923, Fresno Memories, Ernestine Winchell.
AN OPENING NIGHT TO REMEMBER
*Fresno Morning Republican,* January 9, 1929.
STAGES & TRAINS & MAIL
*Fresno Morning Republican,* May 18, 1924, Fresno Memories, Ernestine Winchell.
Clough and Secrest, *Fresno County - The Pioneer Years,* pg. 58.
FRESNO'S FLAG
*Fresno Business Journal,* May 1996.
Ovoian, Gary, *Fresno County: A Story of Diversity and Change,* pp. 10-3 - 10-5.
RELIGION & THE MILL DITCH
*Fresno Morning Republican,* Date unknown, Fresno Memories, Ernestine Winchell.
A HIDDEN TREASURE
Interview and tour of Fresno Water Tower with Rick Ransom of Brooks, Ransom Associates.
EIGHTY FLYING FINGERS
*The Fresno Bee,* February 8, 1938.
THE COURTHOUSE ELEVATOR
*The Fresno Guide,* May 19, 1937, George Whitesell.
BIBLIOCOSMOS
*Bibliocosmos,* Fresno County Free Library Publication, Brochure.
THE CENTRAL SCHOOL
*Fresno Morning Republican,* June 10, 1899.
PICKING DAISIES
As told to the author by Eugenie Loverne Kinsley McKay.
THE FRESNO BUBBLER
Stammerjohan, George R., *Historical Sketch of Millerton Lake,* pg. D-5664C-180.
LOVE BY WIRE
Hurst, Harry, *Alta Pioneers,* Published in the *Alta Advocate,* Dinuba, pg. 35.
THE PETRIFIED WOMAN
*Fresno Morning Republican,* January 29, 1905.
*Fresno Morning Republican,* January 31, 1925, Fresno's Yesterdays.
A PHOTO FLASH
*Fresno Morning Republican,* January 15, 1905.
TO DANCE OR NOT TO DANCE
*The Fresno Bee,* November 9, 1938. "Some Sentinel District History."
THE CHICAGO STUMP
Interview with Steve Scott.
Johnston, Hank, *They Felled the Redwoods,* pp. 17-19.
THE DONNER RESCUE
Wallace W. Elliot, *History of Fresno County, California,* pp. 204, 205.
SCHOLARSHIP & SERVICE
Interview with Mary Helen McKay.
Tokalon Honor Fraternity Handbook.
*Daily Collegian,* April 29, 1974.
A VISIT FROM THE GENERAL
*Fresno Morning Republican,* October 2, 1878.
HEATON SCHOOL
Author's reminiscence
THE SKUNK IN THE CLOAKROOM
Author's reminiscence
MR. WEST COAST RELAYS
*Flint Hanner Night,* Program, June 9, 1964.
MR. SHAVER & HIS LAKE
Eaton, *Vintage Fresno,* pp. 26-29.
Paul Vandor, *History of Fresno County,* Volume II., pp. 1305, 1306.
A FERRY ACROSS THE RIVER
Paul Vandor, *History of Fresno County,* Volume I, pp. 98, 99.

# Notes

FIRE ON THE FOURTH
  Paul Vandor, *History of Fresno County,* Volume I, pp. 113, 114.
MEN & WOMEN & MARRIAGE
  Paul Vandor, *History of Fresno County,* Volume I, pp. 131.
JULY 4, 1874
  Paul Vandor, *History of Fresno County,* Volume I, pp. 328.
PAGES FROM A PIONEER'S MEMORY
  Eaton, *Vintage Fresno,* pg. 14.
  Minnie Jo Aldrich, Letter.
A LAWYER NAMED GRADY
  Max Hayden, "Lawyers, Lawsuits & Loopholes," *Fresno Past & Present,* pg. 7.
A MAN NAMED SHAW
  Clough, et al., *Fresno County in the 20th Century,* pp. 73, 323, 327.
  Threna Klohs, Shaw and Hedges Families, Manuscript.
LIVERY STABLES & DEMOCRACY
  Paul Vandor, *History of Fresno County,* Volume I, pg. 311.
CENTERVILLE & CANALS
  Clough and Secrest, *Fresno County - The Pioneer Years,* pp. 117, 285.
  Paul Vandor, *History of Fresno County,* Volume I, pg. 367.
JOHN C. HOXIE
  Clough and Secrest, *Fresno County - The Pioneer Years,* pg. 76.
  Paul Vandor, *History of Fresno County,* Volume I, pp. 609-611.
THE SAD TALE OF TRAVER
  John C. McCubbin, *The McCubbin Papers,* pp. 75-79.
  Brooks Dewitt Gist, *Empire Out of the Tules,* pp. 58-60.
THE TRAVER CALABOOSE
  John C. McCubbin, *The McCubbin Papers,* pp. 92, 93.
  Interview with Patricia Fey, Consultant to the Kings County Museum.
A PARKWAY FOR THE RIVER
  Charles Henry Cheney, *Progress of a City Plan for Fresno.*
  Coke Hallowell, Interview and tour.
  Mary Savala, Interview.
THE LEWIS S. EATON TRAIL
  John Buada, Interview and tour.
  Coke Hallowell, Interview and tour.
A HOUSE WITH A VIEW
  John Buada, Interview and tour.
  Coke Hallowell, Interview and tour.
  Gene Rose, Interview and tour.
  David Phillips, Interview.
THE HONORABLE ELISHA COTTON WINCHELL
  Paul Vandor, *History of Fresno County,* Volume I, pp. 635 - 638.
JOHN W. HUMPHREYS
  Paul Vandor, *History of Fresno County,* Volume I, pp. 1103, 1104.
  Robert M. Wash, Interview.
  Zona Humphreys, Interview.
THE MAN WHO LIVES ON MISSOURI HILL
  Robert M. Wash, Interview.
SUNNYSIDE
  Robert M. Wash, "The History of Sunnyside: A Place With Space," Chapter 1, "Origin &
  Very Early Days," *Sunnyside Up.*
  Robert M. Wash, "The History of Sunnyside: A Place With Space," Chapter 7, "How
  Sunnyside Got Her Name," *Sunnyside Up.*
LONE STAR
  Robert M. Wash, "John Wash School Named For Pioneer of Education," *The Fresno County
  Sun.*
  Robert M. Wash, Interview and assistance in preparation of manuscript.

# Notes

Paul B. Real, "Lone Star," *Fresno County Centennial Almanac,* pg. 103.
Brenda Moore, "Lone Star community Marks A Century," *The Fresno Bee.*
"YANK" HAZELTON
William B. Secrest, "Church Wars," *Fresno Past & Present*, Vol. 37, No. 4, pp. 2, 3.
"William Hazelton," History of the State of California Biographical Record, pg. 1447.
Robert M. Wash, "William Hazelton." Speech given at the dedication of the Hazelton Monument.
CAN THE CANAL BUILDER AND THE RANCHER BE FRIENDS?
William B. Secrest, "Church Wars," *Fresno Past & Present*, Vol. 37, No. 4, pp. 3-6.
Robert M. Wash, "William Hazelton." Speech given at the dedication of the Hazelton Monument.
THE DISPUTE CONTINUES
William B. Secrest, "Church Wars," *Fresno Past & Present*, Vol. 37, No. 4, pp. 5-10.
Paul Vandor, *History of Fresno County,* Volume I, pg. 183.
THE BURRIS FAMILY
Patricia Fey, Interview and tour of Kings County Museum.
A MUSEUM IN A PARK
Patricia Fey, Interview and tour of Kings County Museum.
THE BROOKS-FOSTER WAGON
Patricia Fey, Interview and tour of Kings County Museum.
CENTENNIAL FARMS
Fresno County Centennial Farms Program Application.
Fresno County Centennial Farms Inventory.
J. Randal McFarland, Interview.
JUDGE SAMUEL A. HOLMES
Paul Vandor, *History of Fresno County,* Volume I, pp. 853, 854.
Stephen R. Henry, "S. A. Holmes, Superior Court Judge," *Fresno Past & Present,* Vol. 36, No. 4, pp. 2-4.
MR. HISTORIC PRESERVATION
Patricia Fey, Interview.
James Lutz, Posthumous Presentation of California Preservation Foundation's 1996 President's Award to Russel Fey.
David Fey, Sarah Fey & Ellen Fey, "Russell Conway Fey," Memorial Brochure.
JAMES SMITH & SMITH'S FERRY
John C. McCubbin, *The McCubbin Papers,* pp. 25-36, 43.
Clough and Secrest, *Fresno County - The Pioneer Years,* pp. 55-57.
THE RABBIT DRIVE
Paul Vandor, *History of Fresno County,* Volume I, pp. 211, 212.
TIBURCIO VASQUEZ
Clough and Secrest, *Fresno County - The Pioneer Years,* pp. 228-232.
Paul Vandor, *History of Fresno County,* Volume I, pp. 172-176.
A TASTE OF NORTHERN ITALY
Olga Porasso, Interview.
Joe Porasso, Interview.
HAPPY JACK & THE HANGMAN'S KNOT
Ward Grimes, "Happy Jack Hawn Tied Knot For Fresno's Only Hanging," *The Fresno Bee.* Approximately 1952.
ROEDING PLACE
Robert M. Wash, "The History of Sunnyside: A Place With Space," Chapter 9, "Roeding Family Leaves Rich Legacy In Sunnyside," *Sunnyside Up.*
Robert M. Wash, Interview and assistance in preparation of manuscript.
FANCHER CREEK NURSERIES
Robert M. Wash, "The History of Sunnyside: A Place With Space," Chapter 9, "Roeding Family Leaves Rich Legacy In Sunnyside," *Sunnyside Up.*
Robert M. Wash, Interview and assistance in preparation of manuscript.
DEDICATION OF A COURTHOUSE
Paul Vandor, *History of Fresno County,* Volume I, pp. 155, 156.

# Notes

THE FRESNO PLAQUE
 *The Fresno Bee,* June 28, 1954.
THE ULTIMATE FRENCH DIP SANDWICH
  Woody Laughnan, "Sidney Janofsky," *The Fresno Bee,* March 23, 1987, pg. B1.
  Woody Laughnan, "Sandwich King," *The Fresno Bee,* March 24, 1987, pp. B1, B6.
  Patricia Tsai, "Long Live The 'Sandwich King,'" *Tower News,* June 27, 1990.
  Julie C. Ford, "This ol' cowpoke has a tale or two," *Northwest Neighbors,* October 12, 1991.
NORTHFIELD'S GREAT LADY
  Edwin M. Eaton, *Vintage Fresno,* pg. 27.
  American Association of University Women, *Heritage Fresno Homes and People,* pp. 68, 69.
  American Association of University Women, *Heritage Fresno Women and Their Contributions,* pp. 34, 35.

# Bibliography

Aldrich, Minnie Jo. Letter. Pioneer Families File. Fresno Historical Society Archives.

American Association of University Women. *Heritage Fresno Homes and People*. Fresno: Pioneer Publishing Company, 1975.

-----. *Heritage Fresno Women and Their Contributions*. Fresno: Pioneer Publishing Company, 1987.

Amirkhanian, Benjamin V. William Saroyan Home. Local Official Register of Historic Resources. City of Fresno. April 20, 1988.

The Ansel Adams Gallery. Yosemite National Park. Biographical information.

*Bibliocosmos*. Fresno County Free Library Publication. Brochure.

"Bob Duncan." Biographical information provided by the Sports Information Office. California State University, Fresno.

Boyett, Deborah. Boyette Advertising. *4C's Celebrates Centennial.* May 3, 1991.

-----. "Fresno Adventist Academy Centennial 1897-1997." News Release. July 28, 1997.

Broeske, John. KMJ Radio. News Release. Information gathered from California Highway Patrol Offices in Bakersfield, Fresno, Fort Tejon, and San Bernardino; CalTrans Offices in Fresno, Bakersfield, and San Bernardino; and the Fresno County Free Library Reference desk, June 22, 1993.

Buada, John. Interview and tour of San Joaquin River Parkway.

Campbell, Christopher. Maracci Home, Local Official Register of Historic Resources. City of Fresno. August 11, 1988.

Campbell, Rex V. and Janet V. The Stoner Mansion. "Summary of Statement for Historical and Architectural Significance." National Register Nomination. August, 1984. Fresno Historical Society Archives.

Carr, Mary. Interview.

Caughey, John W. *California*. 2nd Edition. Prentice-Hall, Inc., Englewood Cliffs, N.J., 1953.

Cheney, Charles Henry. *Progress of a City Plan for Fresno.* June 1, 1918. Reprinted by Fresno-Clovis area Planning Commission. Files of John Edward Powell.

Clarey, Kathey and Doug Hoagland. "Fresno laughs along with 'Fresno.'" *The Fresno Bee.* November 17, 1986.

Clough, Charles W. and William B. Secrest, Jr. *Fresno County - The Pioneer Years*. Fresno: Panorama West Books, 1984.

Clough, Charles W., et. al. *Fresno County in The 20th Century, from 1900 to the 1980s.* Fresno: Panorama West Books, 1986.

Coultrap, M.L. "Republican Staff Men Seek Lost Steamboat; Find?" *The Fresno Morning Republican.* November 15, 1931.

Drago, Jim. Editor. *Going Places.* California Department of Transportation. May/June, 1991.

Drith, Donna. Interview.

Eaton, Edwin M. *Vintage Fresno*. Fresno: The Huntington Press, 1965.

Edwards, Anne."Mr. Blandings' Dream House." *Architectural Digest.* Vol. 48, No. 6. Courtesy of John Edward Powell

Elliot, Wallace W. & Co. *History of Fresno County, California*. San Francisco: Wallace W. Elliot & Co., 1882.

English, June. *Ash Tree Echo*. Vol. 4.

Ennis, Bill. Interview.

Ewert, Jan. The Miles Hansen Home. "Summary of Statement for Historical and Architectural Significance." National Register Nomination. June 20, 1983. Fresno Historical Society Archives.

# Bibliography

Fey, David, Sarah Fey & Ellen Fey. "Russell Conway Fey." Memorial Brochure.

Fey, Patricia. Consultant to the Kings County Museum. Interview and tour.

*Flint Hanner Night*. Program. June 9, 1964. Provided by Sports Information Office, California State University, Fresno.

Folsom, Tom. Interview.

Ford, Julie C. "This ol' cowpoke has a tale or two." *Northwest Neighbors*. Vol. 4, No. 34. October 12, 1991.

Fresno County Centennial Farms Inventory. Provided by office of John Kallenberg, Secretary, Fresno County Historic Landmarks and Records Commission. Fresno County Free Library.

Fresno County Centennial Farms Program Application. Provided by office of John Kallenberg, Secretary, Fresno County Historic Landmarks and Records Commission. Fresno County Free Library.

Fresno City & County Historical Society. *Imperial Fresno*. Facsimile reproduction. Pioneer Publishing Company, Fresno, 1979.

*Fresno Past & Present*. Fresno Historical Society. Quarterly Journal. Vol. 12, No.2, pg. 3.

*Fresno Past & Present*. Fresno Historical Society. Quarterly Journal. Vol. 25, No. 3.

Gist, Brooks Dewitt. *Empire Out of the Tules*. Self-published. Tulare, 1976.

Goodman, Stephen Kent. "Fresno's Forgotten Ragtime Composers." *West Coast Rag*. Vol. 3, No. 3. February, 1991.

Greenberg, Rabbi David L. Interview.

Grimes, Ward. "Happy Jack Hawn Tied Knot For Fresno's Only Hanging." *The Fresno Bee*. Date unknown. Approximately 1952.

Grosz, Shelly. Interview. August 13, 1997.

Hallowell, Coke. Interview and tour of San Joaquin River Parkway.

Hamilton, Mrs. E.A. Donor. Photo and information. Fresno Historical Society Archives.

Hamlin, Kent. *Fresno Daily Legal Report*. April 5, 1984.

Harrison, Doug. District Manager. Fresno Metropolitan Flood Control District. Interview.

Hayden, Max. *Fresno Past & Present*. Quarterly Journal. Fresno Historical Society. Vol. 32, No. 1.

Henry, Stephen R. "S.A. Holmes, Superior Court Judge." *Fresno Past & Present*. Quarterly Journal. Fresno Historical Society. Vol. 36, No. 4.

Hohmann, Ken. Interview.

Horn, John. Interview. August 13, 1997.

Hostetter, George. "Horn Photo, Kodak adding to Fig Garden's Picture." *The Fresno Bee*. July 16, 1997.

Huber, Sharon. Interview.

Hurst, Harry. *Alta Pioneers*. Published in the *Alta Advocate*. Dinuba. 1924.

Humphreys, Zona Aldrich. Interview.

*Insight*. Journalism Department publication. California State University, Fresno. Vol. XXI, No. 23.

James, David Bice. *Reminiscences of Early Days in the "Southern Mines,"* edited, with annotations, by L. A. Winchell. Ms. 3. Fresno Historical Society Archives.

Johnston, Hank. *They Felled the Redwoods*. Los Angeles: Trans-Anglo Books, 1966.

Jones Family Papers. Fresno Historical Society Archives.

Kiester, Edwin Jr. "A Christmas That Never Was," *Modern Maturity*. Vol. 34, No. 6. December 1991-January 1992.

Kimball, Louise. "Fresnan Recalls Civil War As Busy One, W. H. Dillion Declares It Was Hard Life." *Fresno Morning Republican.* March 31, 1929. Fresno Historical Society Archives.

Kleim, Don. Interview.

Klohs, Threna. Shaw and Hedges Families. Manuscript. Pioneer Families Collection. Fresno Historical Society Archives.

Knapp, B. Franklin. Interview.

Laughnan, Woody. "Sidney Janofsky," *The Fresno Bee.* March 23, 1987, pg. B1.

-----. "Sandwich King," *The Fresno Bee.* March 24, 1987. pp. B1, B6.

Laval, Jerome D. *As 'Pop' Saw It.* Fresno: Graphic Technology Co., 1975.

Lutz, James. Posthumous Presentation of California Preservation Foundation's 1996 President's Award to Russel Fey. Presented at the annual conference in San Jose on May 31, 1996.

Martinez, Jose. Letters to the Editor. *The Collegian.* Vol. 201, No. 21. March 8, 1994. California State University, Fresno independent daily newspaper.

Mathes, Pauline. *Bit of Sweden In the Desert.* Fresno: Pioneer Publishing Co., 1991.

McCubbin, John C. *The McCubbin Papers.* Edited with introduction and notes by Kenneth Zech. Reedley: Reedley Historical Society, 1988.

McFarland, J. Randall. Interview. August 12, 1997.

-----. "An archaic club," *The Selma Enterprise.* April 18, 1985.

-----. "Streets of Yore," *Selma Enterprise.* February 28, 1990.

McKay, Mary Helen. Interview.

Moore, Brenda. "Lone Star Community Marks A Century," *The Fresno Bee.* June 20, 1982.

Morison, Catherine McKay. Interview.

Olsson, Cindy. "Kingsburg: From 'Tough Place' to 'City of Churches.'" *Fresno Past & Present.* Quarterly Journal. Fresno Historical Society. Reprinted from the *Kingsburg Recorder.* Vol. 30, No. 3.

Ovoian, Gary. *Fresno County: A Story of Diversity and Change.* Fresno County Office of Education, 1990.

Owen, Jason. "Sigma Nu Stages its Comeback," *The Collegian.* Vol. 102, No. 20. March 7, 1994. California State University, Fresno independent daily newspaper.

Patterson, Bill. "Jim Savage & E Clampus Vitus," *Fresno Past & Present.* Quarterly Journal. Fresno Historical Society. Vol. 27, No. 1.

Peterson, Royce. Corporate Manager of Human Resources for Zacky Farms. Interview.

Phillips, David. Interview.

Porasso, Joe. Interview.

Porasso, Olga. Interview.

Powell, John Edward. *Archifragment: Ode To a Fallen Bracket.* Essay accompanying a mural for the Fresno Art Museum. November, 1991.

-----. Biographical notes on W. D. Coates and Harrison D. Traver.

-----. The Fresno Bee Building. "Summary of Statement for Historical and Architectural Significance." National Register Nomination. March 29, 1982. Fresno Historical Society Archives.

-----. Interview.

Producers Dairy. Informational material.

Ransom, Rick. Brooks, Ransom Associates. Interview and tour of Fresno Water Tower.

# Bibliography

Real, Paul B. "Lone Star," *Fresno County Centennial Almanac.* Fresno County Centennial Committee. 1956.

Rehart, Schyler. "The Famous Feud: M. Theo. Kearney and Chester H. Rowell," *Fresno Past & Present.* Quarterly Journal. Fresno Historical Society. Vol. 30, No. 3.

Rose, Gene. Interview and tour.

Rotary Office Staff. Interview.

Ruano, Jose. Interview.

Savala, Mary. Interview.

Schwarz Family Papers. Fresno Historical Society Archives.

Scott, Steve. Interview

Secrest, William B., Sr. "A Man Named Ingvart." *Fresno Past & Present.* Vol. 33, No. 2. Fresno Historical Society Quarterly Journal.

-----. "Church Wars," *Fresno Past & Present.* Vol. 37, No.4. Fresno Historical Society Quarterly Journal.

Seeger, Diane. Santa Fe Depot. "Summary of Statement for Historical and Architectural Significance." National Register Nomination. May 28, 1976. Fresno Historical Society Archives.

Shipp Family Papers. Fresno Historical Society Archives.

Sitterding, Linda. Interview.

Smith, Ethel L. and Clara F. Wakefield of the Women's Christian Temperance Union of Fresno County. Letter. September 8, 1920.

Smith, Dr. Ephraim K. and William E. Patnaude. Romain Home. "Summary of Statement for Historical and Architectural Significance." National Register Nomination. October 8, 1980. Fresno Historical Society Archives.

Smith, Katherine J. Jensen Ranch. "Summary of Statement for Historical and Architectural Significance." National Register Nomination. February 3, 1982. Fresno Historical Society Archives.

Solo, Sheldon. Interview.

Stammerjohan, George R. *Historical Sketch of Millerton Lake.* Sacramento, 1980.

Steinberg, Jim. "'Fresno' saga of 'greed, lust' takes to the streets," *The Fresno Bee,* July 16, 1986.

Stiltz, Susan. Executive Director, Tree Fresno. Interview.

Sun-Maid Growers of California. *The Sun-Maid Story.* Provided by Public Information Office of Sun-Maid Growers.

-----. *History of the Sun-Maid Organization and Its Antecedents.* Provided by Public Information Office of Sun-Maid Growers.

Taylor, Roger. Interview.

Thompson, Cheryl, Prudence Zalewski and Jan Booth. Dr. Burks Home. Historic Inventory Resources Form. Fresno County Landmarks Commission. October 20, 1989.

Tokalon Honor Fraternity Handbook.

Tondel, George Healey. Interview.

Tsai, Patricia. "Long Live The 'Sandwich King,'" *Tower News.* Vol. I, Issue 7. June 27, 1990.

Tuck Family Papers. Fresno Historical Society Archives.

Tune, Tim. Owens Home. Local Official Register of Historic Resources. City of Fresno. September 30, 1980.

Tweed, William. Gamlin Cabin. "Summary of Statement for Historical and Architectural Significance." National Register Nomination. March 9, 1976. Fresno Historical Society Archives.

-----. Knapp Cabin. "Summary of Statement for Historical and Architectural Significance." National Register Nomination. May 21, 1976. Fresno Historical Society Archives.

-----. Shorty Lovelace Historic District. "Summary of Statement for Historical and Architectural Significance." National Register Nomination. August 29, 1977. Fresno Historical Society Archives.

Uribes, Sylvia Castro. "Homage Paid to Slain Owner of Central Fish," *The Fresno Bee*. June 30, 1996. pp. B1, B3.

Vandor, Paul. *History of Fresno County*. Volumes I & II. Los Angeles: Historic Record Company, 1919.

*Villager*, 30th Anniversary of Fig Garden Village Edition. Fig Garden Village 30th Anniversary Commemorative Poster. Provided by Greg Newman.

Waiczis, Michael R. and William B. Secrest Jr. *A Portrait of Fresno 1885-1985*. Fresno: Val Print, 1985.

Walker, Alvin. Polk Street School. "Summary of Statement for Historical and Architectural Significance." National Register Nomination. October 1, 1981. Fresno Historical Society Archives.

Walker, Ben Collection. Fresno Historical Society Archives.

Wash, Robert M. Interview.

-----. "John Wash School Named For Pioneer of Education," *The Fresno County Sun*. April 1, 1995.

-----. Pioneer Families Dinner Speech. Fresno City Centennial. November 14, 1985.

-----. "The History of Sunnyside: A Place With Space." Chapter 1. "Origin & Very Early Days." *Sunnyside Up*. Vol. IV, Issue 2, February, 1991.

-----. "The History of Sunnyside: A Place With Space." Chapter 7. "How Sunnyside Got Her Name." *Sunnyside Up*. Vol. IV, Issue 7. July, 1991.

-----. "The History of Sunnyside: A Place With Space." Chapter 9. "Roeding Family Leaves Rich Legacy In Sunnyside." *Sunnyside Up*. Vol. IV, Issue 9. September, 1991.

-----. "William Hazelton." Speech given at the dedication of the Hazelton Monument. Jim Savage Chapter 1852 E Clampus Vitus. September 30, 1995. Unpublished manuscript. Courtesy of Mr. Wash.

Weitze, Karen and John Edward Powell. "Short Historical Notes Descriptive of the Industrial Bank of Fresno." October 18, 1992.

Wheat, Althea. Interview.

*White Ribbon Reform Club Membership Booklet*. 1881. Fresno Historical Society Archives.

"William Hazelton." History of the State of California Biographical Record. San Joaquin Valley, CA, 1905. Courtesy of Robert M. Wash.

Winchell, L.A. Papers. Fresno Historical Society Archives.

Winton, Jim. Interview.

Wisehart, Bob. "Finally A Soap With a Sense of Humor." *The Fresno Bee*. TV Week Section.

Wonder Valley Ranch. Informational material.

Zylka, Claire Baird. Ken Greenberg, and Jessie Myers Thun. *Images of an Age, Clovis*. Fresno: Pacific Printing Press, 1984.

*Daily Collegian*. April 29, 1974.

*Fresno Morning Republican*. October 2, 1878.

-----. June 10, 1899.

-----. October 30, 1904.

-----. January 15, 1905.

-----.. January 29, 1905.

-----. April 19, 1906.

-----. June 11, 1906.

-----. May 25, 1912.

-----. May 26, 1912.

-----. May 27, 1912.

-----. September 17, 1917.

-----. May 15, 1919.

-----. October 17, 1919.

-----. November 9, 1919.

-----. July 7, 1921.

-----. Date unknown. Fresno Memories. Ernestine Winchell.

-----. May 27, 1923. Fresno Memories. Ernestine Winchell

-----.. October, 1923. Fresno Memories. Ernestine Winchell

-----. May 18, 1924, Fresno Memories, Ernestine Winchell.

-----. June 8, 1924. Fresno Memories. Ernestine Winchell

-----. November 29, 1924.

-----. January 31, 1925. Fresno's Yesterdays.

-----. March 24, 1925. Fresno's Yesterdays.

-----. May 2, 1925. Fresno's Yesterdays.

-----. August 3, 1925. Fresno's Yesterdays.

-----. Date unknown, possibly 1926. Fresno Memories. Ernestine Winchell

-----. January 8, 1927.

-----. June 8, 1927. Mary Donleavy obituary.

-----. February 12, 1928.

-----. July 7, 1928.

-----. January 9, 1929.

-----. June 27, 1929.

-----. January 18, 1931.

-----. June 20, 1931.

-----. September 7, 1931.

*The Fresno Bee*. March 26, 1926.

-----. June 15, 1926.

-----. July 21, 1927.

-----. May 21, 1928.

-----. May 24, 1928.

-----. September 11, 1928.

-----. July 2, 1935.

-----. October 27, 1935.

-----. October 22, 1936.

-----. December 11, 1936.

-----. January 5, 1937.

-----. November 11, 1937.

-----. November 15, 1937.

-----. February 8, 1938.

-----. March 15, 1938.

-----. May 10, 1938.
-----. May 11, 1938.
-----. May 14, 1938.
-----. June 16, 1938.
-----. June 22, 1938.
-----. July 1, 1938.
-----. July 3, 1938.
-----. August 23, 1938.
-----. September 11, 1938.
-----. November 9, 1938. "Some Sentinel District History."
-----. July 10, 1939.
-----. July 30, 1939.
-----. September 20, 1939.
-----. February 11, 1940.
-----. June 9, 1940.
-----. April 7, 1940.
-----. August 20, 1940.
-----. August 21, 1940.
-----. September 1, 1940.
-----. April 29, 1942.
-----. March 17, 1944.
-----. March 29, 1944.
-----. May 26, 1946.
-----. July 7, 1947.
-----. December 19, 1948.
-----. February 17, 1950.
-----. September 27, 1950. Teilman obituary.
-----. June 28, 1954.
-----. October 10, 1962.
-----. June 22, 1969.
-----. October 13, 1974.
-----. August 21, 1977.
-----. September 10, 1992.
-----. January, 1997. Fresno Metropolitan Flood Control District Supplement.
*Fresno Business Journal.* May, 1996.
*The Fresno Guide.* May 19, 1937. George Whitesell.
-----. September 15, 1938.
*San Francisco Chronicle.* May 8, 1935.

## Symbols

13th Infantry, Company H (Union Army) 96
18th Avenue (Kingsburg) 75
2nd California Volunteers 210
4C's Business College 34
76 Land and Water Company 271

## A

A Street 114
A. B. Long and Son 259
Academy 243
Adams, Ansel 52
Adams Avenue 158
Adams, Dave 204
Administration Building 64, 230
Adoline Avenue 121
Adult Literacy Council 130
Ahwahnee Hotel 57
Ainsworth, Elizabeth 212
Air Force 201
Akers, Anderson 269
Akers, Mary 287
Alabama settlement 299
Alamo House 104
Albany County, New York 286
Aldrich, Minnie Jo 265
Alexander Pantages Theatre 226
All-America 256
Allied Architects 233
*Alta 2* 179
Alta California 159
Altamont Addition 14
Alvarado, Texas 240
Amador Street 104
American Avenue 275
American Express Overlook 277
American Judicature Society 281
American Legion 58
Anchor, Oregon 243
Ancient and Honorable Order of E Clampus Vitus 124, 281, 287

Andreasson, Andrew 103
Annex Building 294

Arcadia, California 194
Architect and Engineer 193
Arctic Circle 76
Arkansas 164, 294
Arkelian, Eddy 307
Armenian community 85
Armenian National Committee 85
Armenian Town 192
Armona 296
Arte Americas 67
Arthur, Johnny 226
Ashlan Avenue 198
Ashman, Scott 221
Associated Women Students 247
Astor, Mary 44
Athens, Alabama 272
Atlanta, GA 210, 211
Audubon Drive 277
Austin, Minnie F. 174
Austin, Russ 279
Australia 134
Avenue 11 147

## B

B. F. Shepard Company 103
Babcock extinguisher 227
Bach 230
Badlam, Alexander 133
Bailey, Leroy E. 86
Bakersfield 32, 179, 188, 298
Baley, Gillum 143, 210
Baley, Rebecca 270
Bancroft, Stevens 16
Bank of Italy 112
Baptist Church 229
Barbour, George W. 105, 109
Barkle, T. J. 214
Barris, Emery 273
Barstow Avenue 65, 170
Barton, Leland 216
Barton, Mrs. Robert 216
Barton Opera House 20, 24, 31, 66, 209, 216
Barton, Robert 216

Baseball Hall of Fame 12
Bates, Tom 290
Battle of Bull Run 127
Bax 230
Bay Berry Antique Store 130
Bebora, Mr. 218
Bell, Robert 195
Bell's Station 51
Belmont Avenue 39, 82, 83, 94, 101, 120, 132, 171, 190
Bennet, James Gordon 196
Berg, Fred A. 130
Berg's Furniture Store 130
Berkeley 16, 301
Berry, Fulton G. 133
Bethel Avenue 100
Bibliocosmos 234
Big Dry Creek 36, 58, 160, 227
Big Dry Creek Dam 58
Big Fresno Flood of 1884 58
Big Hat Day 33
Big Jake 283
Big Salt Slough 149
Biltmore Bowl 182
"Biola flip" 46
Black, F. P. 130
Black Hawk Stables 143, 238
black mission figs 304
Black's Package Company 130
Blackstone Avenue 14, 45, 65, 121, 195
Blackstone, Sir William 14
Blaine, Verna 202
Blake, Barbara 230
Blasingame home 212
Blasingame, Lee 212
Blasingame, Minta 212
Blasingame Ranch 36
Blasingame, Wade 12
blastaphaga (wasp) 304
Bliss Avenue (Laton) 113
Bliss, Oliver 113
Bloomington Avenue 92
Blue Danube Waltz 230
Blue Key 247
Blue, Monte 22, 226
Boalt Hall 281

# Index

Bog Slough 149
Bond, Gladys 182
Booth, John Wilkes 127
Boy Scout Camp 43
Boy Scouts of America
   Council 43
Bozeman, Pres 241
Bracebridge Hall 57
Braddock, Pennsylvania
   1
Bradford, Dagmar Alix
   126
British Columbia 96
Broadway
   15, 20, 27, 91, 128,
   130, 261, 266, 307
Broadway (New York)
   166
Brooding, David 156
Brooks, Frances Foster
   294
Brooks, Judge
   Thornberry 294
Brooks-Foster Wagon
   294
Brown Avenue 64
Brown, Edmund 61
Bubbs Creek 146
Buena Vista Slough 179
Bullard Avenue 309
Bullard Elementary 170
Bullard, Frank 259
Bulldog Foundation 121
Bulldog Lane 38, 39
Burbank, Luther 171
Burke & Monroe's
   drugstore 15
Burks, Floyd 198
Burks Home 198
Burnett, Carol 55
Burns, Hugh 61
Burrel, CA 297
Burrell, A. W. 306
Burris, David 293
Burris, Edward Everett
   293
Burris, Franklin Marion
   293
Burris, Henry Clay 293
Burris, Joshua Sinclair
   293
Burris Park
   274, 293, 294, 296
Burris Park Museum 274
Bush, George 45
Butler, A. A. 284

Butler Avenue 108, 284
Butterfield Overland
   Mail Company 227
Butts, Archibald 265

## C

C Street 292
Cadman, Charles
   Wakefield 126
Cajon de las Uvas 159
Calaveras Street
   63, 67, 128, 181
Calcutta 182
Caldwell, Bill 290
California Associated
   Raisin Company
   76, 108
California Bridge &
   Building Company 6
California Burn
   Foundation 120
California Collegiate
   Athletic Association
   256
California Highway
   Patrol 159
California History Room
   165
California legislature 283
California Packing
   Company 123
California Packing
   Corporation 61
California Preservation
   Foundation 301
California Raisin
   Growers Association
   76
California School of Fine
   Arts 126
California State
   Legislature 61
California State Traffic
   Association 145
California State
   University, Fresno
   38, 166, 301
California Wildlife
   Conservation Board
   277
Calimyrna fig 304
Calithumpians 261
CalMat Company 279
Calship Company 196
Caltrans 81, 147

Cambridge Avenue 64
camel's thorn 150
Camp Barbour Treaty
   111
Camp Pashayan 277
Camp Pinedale 70
Campbell's Crossing 263
Canada 96, 214
Canadian Army 214
Cantua Man 241
Canyon of the Grapes
   159
Capri fig 304
Capri moth 215
Caro, Michigian 136
Carquinez Straits 179
Carroll, Billy 182
Carson Canyon 141
Carson, Kit 41
Carson River 141
Casa Blanca 283
Cashron, Dora 240
Cassidy's Ferry 105
Cassidy's Gravelly Ford
   263
Castro Avenue (Laton)
   113
Castro, Manuel 113
Cathay Hotel 182
Cedar Avenue
   12, 39, 158, 267
Cedar Grove 146
centennial farm 297
Centerville
   36, 111, 263, 269, 287,
   290
Central California
   181, 260, 270
Central California
   Colony 61
Central California
   Commercial College
   34
Central California
   Conservatory of
   Music 66
Central Californian 25
Central Fish Company
   213
Central Pacific Railroad
   6, 18, 69, 221, 261
Central Park 209
Central Park (New York)
   75
Central School 235
Central Valley

34, 46, 52, 54,
  60, 61, 67, 75, 76,
  86, 91, 94, 100, 102,
  122, 124, 132, 147, 149,
  153, 159, 163, 171, 179,
  184, 196, 200, 201,
  202, 210, 213, 215,
  227, 245, 249,
  256, 271, 274,
  297, 302, 304
Centre Plaza Holiday Inn
  56
Centrella Hotel (Pacific
  Grove) 51
Champ Camp 120
Champion Mill 28
Chan, Charlie 42
Chance Bros. Grocery
  Store 242
Chance Field 12
Chance, Frank 12
Chandler, Wilbur F. 65
Chapman College 139
Chapman, R. M. 240
Charlie Chan in Shanghai
  44
Cheney, Charles Henry
  276
Chestnut Avenue 108
Chestnutwood Business
  College 34
"Chic Sale" 194
Chicago
  89, 164, 215, 244, 307
Chicago Cubs 12
"Chicago Stump" 244
China Clipper 17
Chinatown
  5, 27, 112, 213, 271
Chinese community 24
Chinese Merchants
  Association 50
Chinese Temple 5
Chowchilla, CA 87, 91
Chowchilla River 210
Christmas 57
Christmas Tree Lane 43
Church Avenue 55, 77
Church Endeavor Society
  158
Church, Moses
  4, 28, 82, 231, 269,
  288, 290
Church, Moses J. 229
City Planning Commis-
  sion 301

Civic Center 233
Civil War
  32, 36, 50, 96,
  164, 200, 210, 211,
  287, 299
Civil War Revisited 281
Clampers 124
Clark, A. M. 221, 249
Clark, Amaziah W. 134
Clark and McKenzie 136
Clark, George W. 211
Clark, Mrs. A. M. 249
Clark Street 161
Clarke, Mae 17
Clayton, The Reverend
  50
Cleveland, E. A. 174
Clinton Avenue 138
Clovis 33, 81, 157,
  160, 166, 190,
  201, 259, 284
Clovis and North avenue
  275
Clovis Avenue 70, 284
Clovis Rodeo 33
Coalinga 92, 98
Coalinga earthquake 98
Coalinga Recreation
  District 98
Coast Guard Auxiliary
  44
Coast Range 94
Coates & Traver 212
Coates, William D., Jr.
  212
Cobb, Charles H. 139
Cobb Home 139
Cobb, Ty 12
Cody, Lew 22
Coelho, Tony 56
Cohan, George M. 166
Cold Slough 149
Cole, Clovis
  81, 157, 160
Cole, Ida 81
Cole, S. H. 81
Cole, Sally 36
Cole, Stephen 160
Cole, William T. 36
Coleman, Dabney 55
College Avenue 64
College Day 247
College Night 247
College Open House 247
Colton, Dr. 209
Colwell mansion 134

Community Chest 43
Conchita. See Gladys
  Bond. 182
Confederate Army
  249, 299
Confidence Oil Company
  92
Congregational Church
  85, 158
Converse Basin 244
Converse, C. P. 263
Converse Flat 263
Corbett (boxer) 209
Cornell Avenue 64
Cornell, R. G. 87
Cornerstone Day 305
Corrales, Pat 12
Courthouse Park
  20, 50, 162, 183,
  208, 229, 298, 311
Cowan, Thomas 69
Cowen's store 109
Coyle (policeman) 242
Crawford, Joan 226
Crawford, Lanson H.
  228
Crawford, W. T. 119
Craycroft, Harry J. 212
Craycroft, Mrs. Harry J.
  212
Creagor, Clarey 276
Crematory Field 65
Crichton, James G. 135
Crocker Hoffman Land
  and Water Co. 307
Crumley (gold miner)
  109
CSUF Foundation 121
Cumberland Presbyterian
  Church Choir 242
Cupid's Bower 237
Cy Young award 12

**D**

D Street 83
Dakota Avenue 58
Daley, Mr. 4
Daley, Mrs. 4
Dallas, TX 54, 56
Dalton brothers 41
Dalton, Grat 120
Dalton Mountain 120
Danish Missionary
  Society 158
Davidson Raid 164

Davis, Jefferson 210, 281
Davis, L. L. 53
Day, Alice 226
Deaf Dick 210
Declaration of Independence 261
deFalla 230
Del Rey 180
Del Rio Avenue (Laton) 113
Delaware River 196
DeLong, Charles W. 227
Dempsey, Jack 86, 87, 91
Detroit, MI 259
DeVaux, D. W. 91
Development Department 276
DeVoe (policeman) 242
Dewey Decimal System 234
DeWolf, F. E. 291
DeWoody Avenue (Laton) 113
DeWoody, T. J. 113
Diana's Bower 237
Diarbekir, Turkey 215
Dillard, Cruz Estrada 45
Dillion, W. H. 164
DiMaggio, Joe 12
Dinuba, CA 134
Divisadero Avenue 37
Divisadero Street 39, 177
Dockery Avenue 275
Dog Creek 58
Doggett, R. V. 241
Doherty, Angelina 104
Doig, Dale 55, 56, 202
Dole, Robert 85
Donleavy, Mary Brannan Roberts 127
Donner Party 245, 296
Dorsey, Tommy 44
Douglas, Bernaline 195
Downtown Association 228
Drake, Charles B. 297
Drake Ranch 297
Drake's Address to the Flag 261
Drama Critics Award 192
Draper, Josiah 69
Draper Street

(Kingsburg) 75
Dressel, John C. 112
Drew, A. M. 14
Driver, George 82
Droge, Peter 76
Dry Creek 229
Dublin, CA 209
Duncan, Bob 121
Duncan Ceramics 121
Dunn, Gordon 307
Dusenberry, Ernest 233
Dusy, Frank 249
Dutter, Max 241
Dynasty 54, 56

## E

E Street 63
Earp (policeman) 242
East Coast 124, 136
East Shields Avenue 121
Easterby, A. Y. 4, 171, 269, 288, 290
Easton 190, 284
Eaton, Edwin M. 228
Echo Avenue 39, 212
Edgerly Block 34
Edison, Thomas 209
Einstein, Louis 249
Eisen, Francis 171, 174
Eisen, Gustavus 190
Ellis, S. M. 162
Ellsworth, Dick 12
Elm Avenue 77
Elwood Road 120
Emancipation Proclamation 173
"Emancipator" 18
Emma Miller Study Club 42, 131
Emporium Building 119
England 209, 214
Englebright, Congressman 265
Ennis, Bill 172
Ennis Finer China & Crystal 90, 172
Ericson, Andrew 75
Esrey, Amanda 245
Essays on Nature 214
Estrada, Cruz 45
Estrada, Manuel 45
Europe 76
Evers 12
Evinger Home 104
Evinger, Simeon 104

Exeter 148
Expositor 28, 184, 258, 261

## F

F street 112
Faber, Mrs. James 143
Fabulous Fresnans 310
Fagan's store 115
Fages, Don Pedro 159
Fahler, A. 162
Fairbanks, Douglas, Jr. 226
Fallen Monarch 53
Fancher Creek 171
Fancher Creek Nurseries 190, 304
Far Western (athletic association) 256
Farley, Andrew 69
Farmer's Exchange 255
Farrar, Len 6
Fashion Fair 267
Fast, Paul 66
Father of Raisin Day 219
"Father of Reedley" 32
Faymonville, Mr. 306
Fennacy, John E. 79
Ferguson, J. W. 184, 261
Fey, Pat 302
Fey, Russell C. 301
Fifth Street (Clovis) 33
Fig Garden 58
Fig Garden District 310
Fig Garden Flood of 1938 58
Fig Garden Swim and Racquet Club 91
Fig Garden Village 78, 79, 83
Fine Gold Creek 109
Fine Gold Gulch 109
Fine Gold River 144
Firebaugh 94, 267, 274, 307
Firebaugh's Ferry 153
First Christian Church 200
First Unitarian Church 50
First World War 206
Fiske, John Dewey 15
Fiske, Mrs. John Dewey 15
Fiske Opera House 207

Fitzgerald, Cissy 209
Fleming, Russell
153, 227
Flint, O. A. 180
Florida Keys 17
Folkine, Dimitri 182
Folsom Prison 299
Ford's Theater 127
Forkner, J. C.
108, 178, 304
Forkner, Jesse Clayton
310
Forkner, Lewella Swift
309
Forkner-Giffen Tract
108, 178, 310
Forman (policeman) 242
Forquera, Louisa 45
Fort Barbour treaty of
peace 306
Fort Miller
27, 141, 205, 210, 270
Fort Tejon 159
Forthcamp, John 37
Forthcamp Street
37, 177
Foster, John Clark 294
Four Creeks 105
Fourth of July 255, 261
Fourth Street (Clovis) 33
Fowler, CA
119, 188, 190, 213
Fowler Avenue
157, 275, 284
Fowler Friday Evening
Club 119
Fowler Lake 179
France 214
Franklin and Kump 63
Franklin Street 37
Frederick, A. W. 243
Free and Accepted
Masons 306
Freeway 180 38, 139
Freeway 41 42
Fremont Expedition of
1844 124
Fremont, John C.
41, 105, 245
French's Ranch 105
Fresno (miniseries)
54, 55, 56
Fresno Academy 82
Fresno Adventist
Academy 82
Fresno Art Museum 60

Fresno Arts Center 228
*Fresno Atlanta Post* 92 96
Fresno Auto Dealers
Association 139
*Fresno Bee* 25, 63,
91, 126, 168, 186,
188, 194, 196, 205,
230, 276
Fresno Brick & Tile
Works 138
Fresno Bubbler 237
Fresno Business College
34
Fresno Canal and
Irrigation Company
26, 269
Fresno City and County
Historical Society 67,
89, 96, 105, 111, 126,
228
Fresno City Council
61, 267
Fresno City Hall 42
Fresno City Park Band 20
Fresno Colony 77
Fresno County
14, 21, 32, 36,
81, 95, 98, 99, 108,
110, 111, 136, 141,
144, 146, 150, 151,
156, 157, 160, 171,
183, 185, 205, 210,
261, 263, 267, 269,
270, 279, 281, 288,
297, 299
Fresno County Abstract
Company 136
Fresno County Board of
Supervisors 113, 155
Fresno County Chamber
of Commerce 65
Fresno County Court-
house 41, 305
Fresno County Fair 99
Fresno County Free
Library 41, 165, 234
Fresno County Historic
Landmarks and
Records Commi 297
Fresno County Historical
Landmarks and
Records Adv 281
Fresno County Historical
Society 281, 311
Fresno County Hospital
195, 255

*Fresno County in the 20th
Century* 281
*Fresno Daily Evening
Exposito*r 209
Fresno District Fair 202
Fresno Elks Club 204
Fresno Expositor 34
Fresno Flume and
Irrigation Company
259, 309
Fresno Genealogical
Society 165
Fresno Guide 2, 169
Fresno High
12, 121, 310
Fresno High School
16, 42, 166, 212, 235
Fresno Meat Company
104
Fresno Metropolitan
Flood Control District
58
Fresno Metropolitan
Museum 63, 67
Fresno Military Band
20, 48
*Fresno Morning Republican*
8, 18, 63, 126, 143,
145, 148, 149, 164,
183, 186, 203, 206,
208, 211, 221, 242,
243
Fresno Municipal Band
20
Fresno Normal School
166, 170
Fresno Opera House 15
Fresno River 124
Fresno Slough 283
Fresno Society for the
Hard of Hearing 181
Fresno State College
42, 64, 121, 126,
230, 247, 256, 267
Fresno State College
Religious Conference
197
Fresno State Normal
School 21, 64
Fresno State Teachers
College 64
Fresno Station
11, 69, 96, 143,
185, 207, 227, 229,
237, 255, 261, 311
Fresno Street

6, 8, 31, 42, 55, 83, 114, 143, 221, 229, 231, 235, 238, 265
Fresno Superior Court 299
Fresno Symphony Orchestra 50
Fresno Tigers 12
Fresno, Tree 14
Fresno Union Academy 82
Fresno Weather Bureau 205
Fresno's Centennial 265
Fresno's Official Register of Historic Resources 81
Friant 36, 189
Friant Dam 185, 189, 237, 278
Friant Road 277, 279
Friends of Lewis Eaton 277
Frisselle, Samuel Parker 126
Froelich, Mrs. Otto 249
Froelich, Otto 223, 227, 249
Fruit Avenue 82, 138
Fruit Vale Estate 29, 107
Fulton Mall 28, 90, 132, 267
Fulton Street 15, 28, 31, 34, 37, 38, 39, 80, 104, 139, 172, 177, 226, 308
Fun With Nudists 168
Funch, Alan L. Sr. 78
Funch, Ellen (Sherman) 78

**G**

G Street 213
G.A.R. 200
"Galloping Goose" 16
Gamlin Cabin 53
Gamlin, Israel 53
Gamlin, Thomas 53
Garden of the Sun Corral of Westerners Internation 281
Garrison, Samuel J. 3
Gates, Robert 86
Gearhart, Baldwin &

Price 48
Gearhart, James W. 48
Geary Street 307
Gehrig, Lou 12
Geis, S. W. 306
General Grant National Park 53
George Greiersen & Co. 223
George Photography Studio 112
Georgia 294
German Syndicate 190, 284
Germany 66
Gerner, Sophia Hazelton 291
Giant Sequoias 53
Gibbs, M. K. 168
Gibson, Hoot 120
Gibson, Ruth 170
Giffen, Wylie M. 108
Glen Agnes Elderly Housing 138
Glenn, Bill 290
Gluck 230
Gold Rush 95, 109, 115, 124, 141, 144, 286, 293, 294
Golden Bears 16
Golden Dawn Ranch 190
Golden Dawn Subdivision 190
Golden Gate Bridge 125
Golden Gate Park 75
"Golden Raisins" 56
Good Templars Lodge 158
Goodman, Bernard 104
Goodman, Sol 128
Goshen 69
Grady Opera House 266
Grady, Walker Drane 266
Grady's Opera House 66
Grand Army of the Republic 50, 96
Grand Central Hotel 10, 15
Grand Rapids, MI 259
Grant Avenue 201
Grant, Cary 197
Grant, General 53
Grant Grove 53
Grant, U. S. 211

Grant, Ulysses S. 205, 249
"Grapevine" 159
Great Camp Pinedale Offensive 70
Great Depression 233
Great Rolinda Train Robbery 94
Greeley, Horace 196
Green Building 242
Greene and Greene 106
Greene, Charles 106
Greene, Henry 106
Greensboro, North Carolina 256
Gregory and Company 178
Gregory, Fred W. 178
Gregory Home 178
Griffen and Skelly 123
Griffith Way 192
Griffith-Skelly Company 61
Griffiths, Frank 296
Grodin, Charles 55
Grosz, Shelly 83
Grosz, Stan 83
Grove, Pacific 17
Gunner, Voss 307

**H**

H Street 6, 27, 298
Half Dome 52
Hall, Jon 42, 44
Hall, Vesta 253
Hall, Zack 221
Hallowell, Coke 276
Hamburg, Germany 190
Hamilton, Charles K. 19
Hammat, Hattie May 251
Hammatt, Rhoda 230
Hammer Field 70
Hampden, Walter 166
Hanford, CA 274
Hanford Auditorium 296
Hanford Exchange Club 296
Hanford High School 212
Hanger Home 130
Hanger, William H. 130
Hanner, J. Flint 256
Hanner, Miss 203
Hansen Construction

Company 81
Hansen Home 156
Hargrave, Douglas 173
Hargrave, Elizabeth 173
Harkleroad, Dudley 42
Harlan, Elisha 297
Harlan Ranch 297
Harrington, J. B. 199
Harris, M. K. 221
Harris, Richard 179
Harrison, M. A. 86, 87
Harsburgh, James 22
Harsburgh, James, Jr.
  219
Hart, T. C. 270
Hartman,
  Clarice Roberts 230
Harvard Avenue 64
Hatch, Lucy H. 174
Hawn, Jack Allen 298
Hawthorne School 235
Hayes, Rutherford B.
  297
Hazelton, Douglas 287
Hazelton Ranch 287
Hazelton, William
  286, 288, 290
Hazelton, Yank 4
Heald, Anthony 55, 56
Heald Business College
  34
Heaton Elementary
  School 251, 253
Heaton, T. L. 251
Hedge-Row 174
Hedges Avenue 267
Hedges, H. P. 267
Helm Building 90, 172
Hemingway, Ernest 17
Henderson's Experimen-
  tal Gardens 171
Henry, S. W. 255
Hensley, John M. 144
Her Majesty's Army 137
Heritage Fresno: Homes
  and People 301
Herndon Avenue 43, 70,
  264
Herndon Bridge 86
Herndon Canal 58
Herndon School 298
Highway 152 159
Highway 180 269
Highway 99 43, 65,
  86, 147, 159, 264,
  277

Hill, Pete 71
Hill, W. W. 263
Hiram College 301
Historic Preservation
  Commission 301
History of Fresno
  County 142
Hobbs-Parsons Produce
  Company 265, 298
Hodge, Karney 228
Hodgins, Eric 197
Hog Camp Ranch 307
Holland, Charles 214
Holland, Elizabeth 214
Holland, John 214
Holland, Joseph S. 214
Holland, Mrs. Joseph S.
  214
Holland, Richard 214
Hollister, CA 153
Hollywood, CA 22, 42,
  44, 54, 55, 192
Holmes, Samuel Ash
  299
Homan and Company
  178
Homan, Frank 178, 311
Home Avenue 251
Honorary Citizen of the
  City of Fresno 202
Hoot Owl Club 158
Hoover, Herbert 126
Horn, Bradley 83
Horn, John 83
Horn, Peter 83
Horn Photo 83
Horn Photo/Kodak Image
  Center 83
Horn, Rueben 83
Hornitos, CA 307
Horton, Edward Everett
  226
Hotel Barbara 91
Hotel Californian 226
Hotel Fresno 43, 91
Hottentot, The 226
Hovsepian, J. N. 215
Hoxie, John 306
Hoxie, John C. 270
Hoxie, Mary J. McKenzie
  270
Hughes, Mellie 275
Hughes, Thomas 89
Hughes, William M. 89
Humboldt Valley 141
Humphreys, James 272

Humphreys, John W.
  272
Humphreys Station 272
Huntington Boulevard
  106, 212
Huntington Hall 309
Huntzicker, Ernest 181
Huntzicker, Mary 181
Hurricane 44
Huston, Walter 166
Huston-Sunderland
  Scholarship 166
Hyde, Floyd 228
Hyde, Spyars Singleton
  269

**I**

I Street
  15, 27, 261, 266
I. Magnin & Company
  67
Illinois 141, 200
Illinois Volunteer
  Infantry 211
Ina Gregg Thomas
  Memorial Scholarship
  247
Independent Order of
  Odd Fellows 306
India 137
Indian Geyser 237
Indianapolis Avenue 58
Industrial Bank of Fresno
  112
Ingalls, Ernest 179
Interstate Highway 5
  267
Invalid's Delight 237
Inyo Street 45
Irving, Washington 57
Irwin, May 209
Ishpeming, Michigan 75
Isthmus 36
Isthmus of Panama 270

**J**

J Street 15, 28, 34, 229,
  242
J. B. Hill Feed Company
  101
J. C. Forkner Fig Garden
  Incorporated 178
Jack (Indian boy) 111

Jack's Wild West Riders 298
Jacob & Einstein 153
Jacob and Silverman's store 290
James, David Bice 105, 109, 115
Jamison (gold miner) 109
Janofsky, Shirley 308
Janofsky, Sidney 307
*Japanese American Newspaper* 112
Japanese Association of Fresno 112
Jean's 42
Jensen, Christian 100
Jewish community 85
Jim Savage Chapter (E Clampus Vitus) 124
Jim Savage Chapter E Clampus Vitus 281, 287
Johnson, Rafer 256
Jones, Calvin 28
Jones Ferry 36, 153
Jones Hotel 28
Jones, Lefty 12
Jones, Mrs. Calvin 132
Jones Store 263

### K

Kaiser Wilhelm 30
Kalamazoo, Michigan 96
Kallecheta 182
Kazato, Helen 230
Kearney Boulevard 26, 54, 55, 56, 265
Kearney estate 126
Kearney, M. Theo 29, 54, 76, 107, 114, 126, 265
Kearney Mansion 54, 107, 114, 126, 265
Kearney Park 107, 114, 124, 265, 281
Kearney Vineyards 107
Kemp, Barry 54, 55
Kennedy, Robert 134
Kerckhoff Avenue 81
Kerman 94
Kern County 150, 187
Kern County Chamber of Commerce 179
Kern Street 139, 213

Kinema Theater 8, 104
Kingriver 269
Kings Canyon 190, 284
Kings Canyon National Park 53, 73, 146
Kings County 104, 150, 170, 274, 293, 296
Kings County Museum 293, 294, 296
Kings River 26, 32, 69, 73, 105, 113, 123, 146, 151, 179,227, 241, 263, 269, 271, 283, 287, 288, 293, 294, 296
Kings River Switch 69
Kings River Thermal Tract 151
Kingsburg, CA 69, 75, 113, 296
Kingsbury 69
Kingston 113, 153
Kingston Avenue (Laton) 113
Kingston Ferry 296
Kipling, Rudyard 137
Kirk (state superintendent of public instruction) 235
Kitt, Ah 27
Kitt, Becky 27
Kitt, Jefferson Shannon 27
Kleim, Don 171
Klondike Street 136
KMJ radio 63
Knapp Cabin 146
Knapp, George Owen 146
Knights of the Golden Circle 210
"Know Nothing" party 115
Knowles, Harvey 173
Korea 164
Kruger, Otto 166
Kump, Ernest, Sr. 193
Kutner & Goldstein 24
Kutner, Louis 24
Kutner, ouis 177
Kutner-Goldstein 176
Kutner-Goldstein Company 177
Kutner-Vucovich Home 177

### L

L Street 6, 104, 143, 207, 221, 238, 270
La Paloma Vineyard 76
La-Ache 111
Ladies' Aid Society 158
Laguna De Tache 26
Laguna de Tache Grant 113
Laguna de Tache land grant 294
Lake Okanogan 96
Lambert, William 306
Lamour, Dorothy 44
Lane, Andrew 105
Langford, Frances 42, 44
Lansing Way 58
Laplanders 76
Lathrop 69, 305
Laton 113
Latta, Don 179
Latta, Frank 179
Lauder, Harry 8
Laval, Claude C., Jr. 2
Laval, Claude C. "Pop" 1
Laval, Jerome D. 2
Le Grand, CA 187
Leach, Lewis 255, 306
Lehman, Solomon 243
Lemoore, CA 245
Lemoore Naval Air Station 113
Leon Peters Valley Business Center 121
Leonard, Dutch 12
Levis Ranch 297
Lewis Bros. troupe 261
Lewis, Joshua 240
Lewis S. Eaton Trail 277
Liberty Cemetery 128
Liberty Farms 179
Liberty, Louisiana 164
Liberty ship 196
Liberty Theatre 212
Lincoln, Abraham 173
Lincoln, Mrs. Abraham 127
Lincoln, Nebraska 301
Lincoln, President Abraham 127
Lindenmuth, Margaret 195
Lindsay 148

Lisenby Memorial
  Bandstand 20
List of Historic Resources
  177
Liverpool, England 134
Local List of Historic
  Resources 104, 192
Local Register of Historic
  Resources
  92, 106, 160, 192
Lochead, Robert 137
Locher, Charles 42, 44
Locher, Felix 42
London 214
Lone Star, CA 281
Lone Star Hall 275
Lone Star School District
  275
Lone Star Village 275
Lord, Mrs. 261
Los Angeles, CA 36, 65,
  66, 69, 75, 86, 91,
  105, 154, 159, 182,
  188, 213, 226, 283,
  307, 309
Los Banos 94, 159, 307
Louie, Dago 307
Louisiana 164
Love, Erclas Herbert 96
Lovelace, James Walter
  (Shorty) 73
Lowell Elementary
  School 309
Lowell/Jefferson
  Redevelopment
  Project 160
Loy, Myrna 197, 226
Lyon, Parker 10
Lyon, W. Parker
  194, 204

**M**

M Street 15, 103, 311
Madary, M. R. 267
Maddox Airport 65
Madera 86, 147,
  205, 249, 292, 299
Madera County
  86, 87, 91
Madera Irrigation
  District 145
Magnolia Hall 261, 306
Magnolia Saloon 6
Maharajah of Kucia 182
Maharanee of Kucia 182

Main, Eugene 138
Main Home 138
Mainstreet Program 301
Malaga grapes 100
Malin, Oregon 294
Maloney, Jim 12
Manassa Mauler 91
Maracci Home 193
Mariner's Point 185
Marion, Brian 40
Mariposa, CA 272
Mariposa Battalion 306
Mariposa County
  281, 287
Mariposa Indian War
  210
Mariposa Mall 90
Mariposa Street 6, 42,
  66, 82, 128, 134,
  178, 221, 227, 229,
  231, 307
Markarian, Melcon 304
Marks, Bernard 249
Marks, Mrs. Bernard
  249
Maroa Avenue 64
Marshall, James W. 194
Maryland 170
Mason Building 10,
  28, 132
Masonic fraternities 306
Mathewson, Eugene 10
Mathias, Bob 256
Mathson, Arch 202
Mattei Building 10
Maupin, W. T. 15, 25
Maximilian, Emperor
  164
Maxwell & Mudge 242
Maxwell, Mr. 242
Mayflower 214
"Mayor of Broadway"
  128
"Mayor of Chinatown"
  27
McCall Avenue 171
McCarthy, D. B. 255
McClatchy, Eleanor 196
McClatchy family 63
McClatchy Publishing
  Company 63
McCray, Ira
  111, 255, 263
McCray's Stable 27
McDonald, Belle 243
McKay, Belle Ellen 77

McKay, Wilbur 131
McKenzie, W. H. 270
McKinley Avenue 251
McKinley, Major 209
McLaughlin, Frances 230
McLaughlin, Victor 120
McMurty, P. H. 155
McWhorter, Margaret
  247
Medal of Freedom 52
Memorial Auditorium 55
Mendota, CA 94, 149
Mennonite Brethern
  Biblical Seminary 108
Merced, CA 305
Merced River 57
Merced Street 27, 229
Mercury 89
Methodist Episcopal
  Church South 200
Metropolitan Museum
  56
Meux Home Museum 39
Mexican War 286
Mexico 164
Meyers, Joseph 261
"Michael" Kearney 29
Michigan
  32, 96, 259, 309
Midwest 136
Milburn Unit 277
Millbrook Avenue 38
Miller & Lux Canal Farm
  307
Miller, Beulah 131
Miller, Big-Foot 115
Miller, Emma 42, 131
Miller, Mrs. S. A. 143
Miller, Mrs. W. P. 42
Miller, Patsy Ruth 226
Miller Road 267
Miller, Ron 202
Miller, S. A. 143
Miller, W. P. 42
Millerton, CA
  4, 27, 28, 36, 95,
  111, 134, 141, 153,
  183, 185, 205, 207,
  210, 223, 227, 237,
  255, 258, 263, 270
Millerton Lake
  109, 144, 185, 201, 237
Milton, Barbara J. 297
Milton Farm 297
Milton, Richard W. 297
Minassian, Roger 85

Mississippi 36, 164
Missouri 141, 282, 293
Missouri Hill 281
Missouri Hill Ranch 297
Mitchell, Jan 276
Mix, Tom 22, 87, 120
Moad, Mallory 60
Modesto, CA 34,
    301, 305
Modesto Bee 196
Mojave Desert 194
Monmouth, Illinois 164
Mono Street 83, 103
Montana, Bull 226
Monterey, CA 214
Monterey Peninsula 51
Montgomery, Maude
    274
Moore, Victor 166
Morgan (police chief)
    242
Morgan, Lucretia 243
Morison, Catherine
    McKay 230
Mount Pleasant Baptist
    Church 173
Mountain View
    Cemetery 96
Mr. Blandings Builds His
    Dream House 197
Mud Spring Mine 270
Mullins Field 65
Mundorff Home 106
Murphy Avenue 113
Murphy's Slough 113,
    149
Murrieta, Joaquin 41,
    153
Myers, M. 218

**N**

N Street 25, 84, 128, 229
Napa Avenue 82
Napa County 293
National Collegiate
    Athletic Association
    256
National Guard Band 20
National Jewish
    Congress 85
National Park Service
    146
National Register of
    Historic Places
    53, 62, 63, 74, 98,

100, 146, 151, 156,
    232
nation's official Christ-
    mas Tree 53
Nelson, Thomas 36
Nevada 194
Nevada Falls 187
New Orleans, LA
    164, 294
New Palm Garden 31
New York
    36, 52, 215, 244, 286
New York City, NY 1
New York Yankees 12
Newton, Francis 42
Nolan, W. N. 240
North Avenue 275
North Carolina 173, 299
North, J. W. 158
North, May 158
North Park 37,
    80, 130, 139, 177
Northfield 309

**O**

O Street 6, 45,
    66, 82, 186, 221,
    229, 235
Oakdale, CA 307
Oakland, CA 6, 43, 192
Odd Fellows 306
Ohio 96, 283, 301
Oken family 120
Okonogi, Buntaro 112
Old Administration
    Building 64, 247
Old Black Swamp 96
Old Fig Garden
    58, 108, 178, 198,
    284, 310
Old Friant Road
    279, 280
Old Maid's Club 158
Old West 124
Oleander 158
Oleander Athletic
    Association 158
Oleander Dramatic
    Society 158
Olive Avenue
    82, 292, 307
Olney, James N. 210
Omar Khayyam's
    Restaurant 307
Oothout home 284

Oothout, William N.
    284
Open Range Law 288
Orange, CA 188
Oregon 147
Oroville, CA 307
Osborn residence 60
Oscar 192
Otis Elevator Company
    172
Otis, Harrison Gray 196
Overhulser, Charlie 221
Owen, Carrie (Cole) 160
Owen, Charles 160
Owen Home 160
Owen, J. J. 184
Owen, Mrs. J. J. 184
Owens Mountain 160
Oxford Avenue 267

**P**

P Street 42, 44, 131
Pacheco Pass 51, 159
Pacific Gas & Electric
    Company 195
Pacific Grove 16, 51
Painted Dog 137
Palm Avenue
    58, 70, 101, 197
Pan American Airlines 17
Panama 36, 294
Panama Pacific Interna-
    tional Exposition 270
Paris 192
Parlier 188
Pashayan, Chip 45
Patigian, Haig 50
Patterson, Darryl 12
Peach Avenue 275
Pearson, Monte 12
Pegasus 234
Pennsylvania 283
Pennsylvania Avenue
    (Washington, D.C.)
    211
Pentagon 244
People's Railroad 18
Persian melon 215
Peters, Leon 43
Peterson Mill 157
Peterson, Miss 203
Petit Courier 184
Petkovich, Nick 218
Philippine Islands 301
Phillips, John Pressley,

Sr. 279
Phillips, Martha 279
Phillips, Mrs. W. W. 306
Phillips, Ruth 279
Phillips, William Walker 279
Phillips-Carter, Mrs. V. 145
Pianoforte Club 230
Pico, Don Pio 113
Piedmont 125
Piemonte's Italian Delicatessen 292
Pierce Lumber Company 101
Pierson Dude Ranch 120
Pierson, George S. 120
Pilgrim Armenian Congregation Church 85
Pine Flat Dam 26
Pine Ridge 187, 272
Pine Ridge Railway 92
Pio Pico Avenue (Laton) 113
Pioneer Families Committee 265
Placerville, CA 294
Playland 43
Poison Meadows 187
Polk Avenue 55
Polk Street (Coalinga) 98
Polk Street School 98
Pollasky Avenue 33
pomegranate melon 215
Pony Express Museum 194
Pool, Woodson 275
Porasso, Gino 292
Porasso, Joe 292
Porasso, Larry 292
Porasso, Olga 292
Porterville High School 212
Powell, John Edward 60
Prescott, F. Dean 134
Prescott, F. K. 10
Prescott, Jessie Kennedy 134
Preservation Committee of the Fresno Historical So 301
Princeton Avenue 64, 138
Producers' Bar 20 Dairy Farms 132

Producers Dairy 132
Proffitt Home 38, 39
Proffitt, Ida 37
Proffitt, John William 37
Progress of a City Plan For Fresno 276
Prohibition 31
Prohibition party 200
Projectoscope 209
Pryce, Thomas 261
Pryor, Charles A. 48
Pub, The 307
Pulitzer, Joseph 196
Pulitzer Prize 192, 196

## Q

Q Street 134
Quinnby, E. E. 155
Quist Dairy 55

## R

R Street 39
rabbit drive 116
Rachmaninoff 230
Radin & Kamp 65
Rainbow Ballroom 20
Raisin City Band 20
Raisin Day 219
Raisin Day Classic 22
Raisin Day Committee 219
Raisin Day Festival 22, 219
Raisin Day King 22
Raisin Queen 22, 166
Raisin Week 256
Raisina Vineyard 61
Ramsey, W. C. 34
Rank Island 278
Ratcliffe Stadium 71, 247
Ratliff, Harriett 230
Raymond, California 173
Red Bank Creek 58
Red Bank Fancher Creek Flood Control Project 58
Red Cross 58
Red Lion Inn 214
Red's Beanery 16
Reed, Thomas Law 32

Reedley 283, 297
Reese Davis Ranch 297
Reimers, Johannes 304
Republican 29
Rex Theater 168
Rhoads, Daniel 245
Rice, John 209
"Ridge Route" 159
Riggs, R. W. 258
Rio de los Santos Reyes 113
River Committee 276
River of the Holy Kings 113
Riverdale 297
Riverside, California 61
Riverside County 150
Riverview Ranch 279
Roberts, Joseph W. 127
Robertson, William 219
Robinson, C. H. 188
Robinson, Kevin 177
Robinson, Mrs. C. H. 188
Robinson, Mrs. Raymond 123
Robinson, Raymond 123
Robinson, Virginia 177
Rockies 141
Rocky Mountains 73
Roeding family 303
Roeding, Frederick 171, 284
Roeding, Frederick C. 190, 303
Roeding, George 190, 284
Roeding, George C. 265
Roeding, George Christian 303
Roeding, Mrs. George 203
Roeding Nursery 123
Roeding Park 20, 43, 303
Roeding Place 303
Rolinda 94
Rolph, James 87
Romain, Frank 61, 284
Romain Home 62
Rosendahl, E. G. 75
Rosendahl, Frank D. 75
Ross, Henry 134
Rotary 43, 67
Rowell, Albert Abbott 200

Rowell Building 200
Rowell, Chester
  49, 200, 229, 249
Rowell, Chester Harvey
  29, 203
Rowell, Cora 203
Rowell, Dr. 2
Rowell family 85
Rowell, Jonathan 200
Rowell, Milo 200, 265
Rowell, Mrs. Chester
  Harvey 203
Rowland, W. R. 154
Royal Insurance
  Company 103
Rubinstein 230
Rushford farm wagon
  294
Russell, William 22
Russell, William E. 273
Russian Ballet 182
Ruth, Babe 12
Ruth Gibson School 170
Ryce, Andrew 134
Ryce, Marion 134

**S**

S Street 134
S.S. C. K. McClatchy
  196
Sacramento
  63, 141, 194, 196,
  246, 299
Sacramento Bee 196
Sage, John E. 188
Sage, John Epler 187
Sage, Mrs. John E. 188
Saint Louis 164
Salt Lake City 241
Salvation Army 43, 158
Sample, David Cowan
  36, 80
Sample Sanitarium 80
Sample, Thomas 80
San Diego 234, 286
San Francisco
  18, 24, 26, 31, 36, 52,
  65, 66, 69, 75, 126,
  133, 160, 174, 178,
  179, 184, 190, 192,
  212, 227, 244, 249,
  270, 284, 294, 303,
  307
San Francisco and San
  Joaquin Valley

Railway 18
San Francisco Chamber
  of Commerce 179
San Francisco Chronicle
  155, 307
San Francisco Committee
  of Vigilance 190
San Joaquin River
  27, 36, 70, 105, 109,
  115, 118, 123, 179,
  227, 263, 267, 276,
  280, 298
San Joaquin River
  Parkway 277
San Joaquin River
  Parkway and
  Conservation Trust
  276, 279
San Joaquin Street
  61, 130
San Joaquin Valley
  18, 22, 34, 36, 46, 99,
  105, 109
San Joaquin Valley
  Aeronautical
  Association 65
San Joaquin Valley Civil
  War Round Table 281
San Joaquin Valley Land
  Association 190
San Jose High School
  256
*San Jose Mercury* 184
San Juan 188
San Luis Obispo 188
San Pablo Avenue
  92, 136, 251
San Pedro 182
Sandwich, Massachusetts
  270
Sanger 37
Santa Barbara 146
Santa Fe 58, 209
Santa Fe Avenue 18
Santa Fe Railroad
  19, 134, 275
Santa Fe Railway 18
Santa Rosa 171
Saroyan, Aram 307
Saroyan Theater 56
Saroyan, William
  192, 307
Saroyan's Nook 307
Sassoon, Victor 182
Savage, James D. 306
Savage, Jim 105, 124

Savala, Mary 276
Sayle, Claudius G. 306
Sayle, Judge 143
Sayles, James, Jr. 111
Schaeffer, Maude 247
Schorling, Helen 230
Schultz Ranch, Inc. 297
Schuttler Wagon Works
  294
Schwarz, Edward 31
Scott, William Y. 269
Scottsburg
  263, 269, 287
Seals 12
Seaver, Tom 12
Second Baptist Church
  173
Segel, Kenneth 85
Seligman, Emil 273
Selland Arena 103
Selland, Arthur L. 228
Selma 100, 156,
  164, 188, 200, 241,
  297
Selma, Dick 12
Semorile Hotel 271
Sentinel School District
  243
Sequoia Gigantea 89
Sequoia Hotel 134
Seven Ages of Man 216
Seventh Street (Traver)
  271
Seventh-day Adventist
  Church 229
Severance School of
  Dance 181
Seymour 3
Shanghai 182
Shanklin, Clara 143
Shanklin, J. W. 143
Shanklin, John 249
Shanklin, Mrs. John 249
Shannon & Hughes Store
  and Saloon 6
Shannon, Jefferson 27
Sharer, John William 157
Shaver, Charles B. 259
Shaver Lake
  43, 259, 272
Shaw Avenue
  39, 78, 157, 267
Shaw, Threna Hedges
  267
Shaw, William 267

Shehadey, Larry 132
Shepard-Knapp-Appleton 103
Sherman, George 78
Sherman, William T. 211
Shields Avenue 70, 78, 138
Shiloh 32
Shipp, William Walter 36
Shorb-Neads 212
Short family 67
Short, Frank Hamilton 24, 67
Short, Julia B. 174
Short, Nellie Curtis 67
Shorty Lovelace Historic District 74
Sierra 53, 95, 115, 1 24, 141, 151, 187, 228, 278, 279, 281, 283
Sierra Avenue (Kingsburg) 75
Sierra Club 52
Sierra Nevada 73, 109, 120
Sigma Nu 38, 39, 212
Simpson, T. W. 221
"Six Hundred" 29
Skelton, H. 115
Slater's Furniture 197
Smith, A. A. 75
Smith, Amantha Ann 32
Smith, C. Aubrey 44
Smith, D. C. 20
Smith, George 290
Smith, Harry 173
Smith, James 32, 263, 283
Smith, Jedediah Strong 41
Smith, Maggie 253
Smith, Mrs J. L. 261
Smith, Peg 276
Smith's Ferry 32, 283
Smith's Mountain 283
Smyrna figs 215, 304
Solano County 36
Soldier's Three 137
Solo, Sheldon 38
Sonoma, CA 293
Sonoma, Mexico 45
South Fork Canyon 146

Southern California 147
Southern Pacific 19
Southern Pacific Depot 11
Southern Pacific Railroad 208, 271
Spanish-American War 120
Spears, Cisero 273
Spectrum Gallery 301
Spencer, Wright H. 136
Spokane, WA 96
Spreckels, Claus 18
Spreckles, J. D. 10
Squaw Valley 297
St. Agnes Hospital 138
St. John's Cathedral 128
Stammer, Mrs. Walter 212
Stammer, Walter 212
Stanford, Leland 69
Stanford, Mrs. Leland 69
Stanford University 256
Stanislaus Street 14, 270
Starks, Leonard F. 63
State Highway Commission 61
Steffens, Lincoln 196
Steinbeck, John 212
Steuben County, New York 259
Stevens, A. T. 96, 143, 238
Stevens, Clara 17
Stevens, Clark 16, 143, 238, 249
Stevenson Creek 259
Stevenson House 214
Stevenson Meadow 259
Stevenson, Robert Louis 214
Stillman, Joseph 15
Stingley (policeman) 242
Stockholm 75
Stockton, CA 18, 69, 134, 179, 227, 255, 283, 305
Stockton Chamber of Commerce 179
Stoner, Bertrand 151
Stoner, Kitty 151
Stover, Paul 291
Stratford Weirs 179
Strathmore 274
Strauss 230
Sullivan (hunter and

trapper) 96
Sullivan, Burns and Blair Funeral Home 61
Summit Lake 149
Sun Maid Raisin Growers Association 108
Sun-Maid Raisin Company 76
Sunderland, Al E. 67
Sunderland, Ninetta Eugenia 166
Sunnyside 190, 275, 284
Sunnyside Country Club 203
Sunnyside Golf and Country Club 284
Sunnyside Vineyard 284
Suratt, Mary 127
Sutter's Fort 141, 194, 245
Swanson, C. R. 296
Swartz, A. C. 37
Swedish colony 75
Swedish Festival 75
Sweem, J. B. 269
Sweem's ditch 269
Sweet, S. 153
Swift, Harvey 259
Swift, Lewis P. 259, 260, 309
Sycamore 264
Sydney, Australia 134

## T

T Street 60, 128
T. K. Tomita-General Business Agency 112
Tache Avenue (Laton) 113
Tachi Indians 113
Taft, William Howard 265
Tatarian, Roger 276
Taylor, Estelle 86, 91
Taylor, Robert 44
Taylor-Wheeler 197
Taylor-Wheeler Builders 198
Teague, C. C. 284
Tehachapi Mountains 105, 159
Tehipite Valley 142
Teilman, Ingvart 26, 113
Tejon 105

Temperance Avenue 281
Temperance avenue 190
Temple Beth Israel
  85, 128
Tennessee 37, 128
Teraoka, George 213
Terminal Island 182
Terrace Avenue 197
Texas 37, 164, 286
"The Grove" 51
Thesta Street 161
This Is My Valley 281
Thomas Flyer 265
Thomas, Frank W. 247
Thomas, Ina Gregg 247
Thomas mill 283
Thompson grapes
  100, 108
Thorn Birds, The 54
Three Rivers 73
Three-fingered Jack 41
Tiburcio Avenue (Laton)
  113
Tilton, J. Wesley 48
Tilton's Band 48
Titanic 265
Titus, Issac S. 306
Tivy Valley 151
Tokalon 247
Tokalon Alumnae 247
Toll House 157
Tollhouse 272
Tollhouse grade 157, 272
Tollhouse Road 36, 272
Toomey, William F. 177
Toronto, Canada 61
Tower District
  48, 64, 92, 212,
  230, 284, 292, 308
Traffic Association of
  California 18
Training School 310
Traver 240, 271, 273
Traver, Charles 271
Traver, Harrison B. 212
Treadwell, John 134
Treasure Island 179
Tres Pinos 153
Trevelyan, Colonel 29
Trimmer Springs Road
  120
Truax, Police Chief 163
Tuck, Frank 27
Tuck, John 27
Tucker, Len 12
Tulare Avenue 275

Tulare County
  91, 134, 273, 293
Tulare Lake
  149, 179, 188, 296
Tulare Street
  18, 25, 28, 34,
  39, 42, 71, 112, 200
Tule River 105
Tuolumne County
  270, 272
Turkestan 150
Tuttle's Drugstore
  (Pacific Grove) 51
Tuttletown 270
Twain, Mark 133

**U**

U Street 81, 201
U. S. Army Corps of
  Engineers 58
U. S. Mail Telegraph
  Stage Line 227
Under The Trail 187
Union Army
  50, 96, 127, 211
Union League 210
Unitarian Church 85
United Presbyterian
  Church 10, 188
United States Army
  Signal Corps 70
United States Bureau of
  Reclamation
  185, 189
United States Depart-
  ment of the Interior
  244
United States Post Office
  227
United States Postal
  Service 172
United States Supreme
  Court 281
United States Weather
  Bureau 205
University Avenue 64
University of California
  50, 107, 126
University of California
  at Berkeley 16, 301
University of California
  at Santa Cruz 281
University of Pennsylva-
  nia 212
University-Sequoia

Club 284
University-Sequoia-
  Sunnyside Country
  Club 284
Utah 194

**V**

Vacaville 36
Valley Children's
  Hospital 43
Valley Railroad 158
Van Ness Avenue
  42, 45, 48, 61, 63,
  64, 67, 104, 130,
  193, 200
Van Ness Boulevard
  58, 59, 178, 198
Van Ness Extension 309
Vasquez, Tiburcio 153
Vassar Avenue 64
Velguth building 261
Ventura Avenue 12
Ventura Street 103
Vermont 200
Veterans Memorial
  Auditorium 235
Vicksburg 210, 211
Vietnam 164
Vietnam War 11
Villalon & Kump 198
Villalon, Henry 198
Vincent, Frank 298
Vincent, J. P. 14
Vincent, Joseph P. 92
Visalia, CA 45, 48,
  148, 227, 305
Visalia stage 153
Vista Pharmacy 71
Vucovich, Milan 177

**W**

Wade, David H. 148
Wagons West Interna-
  tional 294
Wainwright, Charlie 221
War Between the States
  249
Warner Brothers 226
Warner's Theatre 226
Warnor's Theatre 226
Wasemiller, Paul G. 228
Wash, John S. 275
Wash, Robert M.
  113, 311

Wash, Robert Martin 282
"Washboard" 159
Washington Avenue 160
Washington Colony 158, 200
Washington, D.C. 56, 85, 127, 211, 244
Water Tower 55, 231
Wawona Grove 89
Webb, Becky 120
Webb, Paul 120
Weber, Jesse 275
Webster's Drug Store 42
Weiland, John 31
Weiland's brewery 31
Wells Fargo Express Company 215, 233
Wendover, England 214
West Coast 8, 52, 270
West Coast Relays 256
West Fresno 112, 213, 292
West, Joseph 243
West Springfield, Massachusetts 141
Westerners International 281
Weston, Edward 52
Wheat, Althea 107
"Wheat King of the Nation" 81
Wheatville 69
Wheeler, Benjamin Ide 50
Whiskey (burro) 118
white Adriatic figs 304
White Avenue 161
White, Ellen G. 82
White Friant Lumber Company 259
White House 209
White, Jim 249, 283
White Ribbon Reform Club 143
White, Tadema 42
Whitehurst, Daniel 61
Whitehurst, William 61
White's Bridge 249
Whites Bridge Road 94, 132

Whitmore's ferry 113
Whitney and Stinchfield 259
Wienerwurst Band 20
Wilburn, Julia 293
Wilkerson, H. E. 43
Willard, Charles F. 19
Williams, W. M. 279
Williams/Phillips Home 279
Willow Unit 277
Wills, Ted, Jr. 12
Wilmington, Delaware 196
Winchell, Anna Cora 141
Winchell, Elisha Cotton 141, 306
Winchell, Ernestine 142
Winchell, Iva Mary 141
Winchell, Laura C. Alsip 141
Winchell, Ledyard Frink 141
Winchell, Lilbourne Alsip 141
Winchell, Lillibourne 205
Winds of War, The 54
Winnes, Harry F. 273
Winton, J. Martin 71
Winton, James Michael 72
Winton, Jim 71
Wishon home 212
Withrow, Miriam Fox 230
Wolf, Katie 202
Wolfe, Thomas 192
Women's Christian Temperance Union 99
Women's Club 33
Women's Week 247
Wonder Valley 120
Wonder Valley Dude Ranch 120
Woodman's brass band 306
Woodville 105
Woodward, O. J. 10
Woodward Park 20, 277
Woodward, Roy 65
Woolley, Ellamarie 234
Woolley, Jackson 234

Works Progress Administration 233
World Series 12
World War I 98, 146, 237
World War II 44, 45, 70, 78, 101, 121, 164, 213, 301
World's Columbian Exposition 89, 244
Worth, Miss 203
Wright, Frances McGill 188
Wright, Franklin 43
Wright House 188
Wright Irrigation Law 92
Wright, J. H. 188
Wright, Lewis 188
Wright, Mrs. J. H. 188

# X

*no entries*

# Y

Yale Avenue 64
YMCA 43, 92
Yokomi, Akira 213
Yokomi, Fanpachi 213
Yokomi, Sunayo 213
Yokuts Indians 120
Yolo County 32
Yosemite 187, 205, 238
Yosemite Avenue 139
Yosemite Hotel 249
Yosemite National Park 52, 89
Yosemite Valley 57, 249
Young, Loretta 226
YWCA 43, 310

# Z

Zacky, Al 101
Zacky, Bob 101
Zante currants 76
Zapp's Park 267
Zerlang, MS 80

# About the Author

Cathy Rehart's mother's family arrived in Fresno Station in 1873, the year after the town was founded. She was born in the Sample Sanitarium on Fulton Street, is a third generation graduate of Fresno High School and a second generation graduate of Fresno State College with a BA in English and history. She is the mother of three grown children.

During the years her children were in school, her involvement in their activities resulted in service on several PTA boards, the Fresno High School Site Council and the Cub Scouts. Later she served as first Vice-Chairwoman for the Historic Preservation Commission for the City of Fresno; as a member of the Board of Directors of the Fresno City and County Historical Society; as chair of the Preservation Committee of the FCCHS; and a President of the La Paloma Guild, the FCCH's auxiliary.

From 1986 to 1994, she held the position of Education/Information Director for the FCCHS.

Her work as a freelance writer includes writing the KMJ Radio scripts for "The Valley's Legends and Legacies" —from which this book is derived—and other writing projects on local history.